Other Books by Amy Asbury

VALLEY GIRL: CHILDHOOD IN THE 80'S

CONFETTI COVERED QUICKSAND

SMELLS LIKE:
MUSIC, DRUGS AND LIFE IN THE 90'S

THE
SUNSET
STRIP
DIARIES

AMY ASBURY

Distributed by Ingram Content Group

ISBN-10 061543987X

ISBN-13 978-0-615-43987-7

Printed in the United States of America

10 9 8 7 6 5 4 3 2

ESTEP & FITZGERALD BOOKS

DEDICATED TO A.J.M.
REST IN PEACE.
I MISS YOU.

THIS IS THE STORY OF MY YOUNGER
YEARS AS I REMEMBER THEM. SOME
NAMES AND MINOR CHARACTERISTICS
HAVE BEEN PURPOSELY CHANGED.

THE SUNSET STRIP DIARIES

Table of Contents

CHAPTER ONE

This Can't Be Happening

My childhood ended the day I woke up with my underwear missing.

I was eleven years old, almost twelve. I got up to go to the bathroom and as I started walking, I realized I was not wearing underwear and my girl parts felt smooshy and puffy. I knew I wore underwear to bed; I never slept without underwear. I looked down and realized that not only was I not wearing underwear, and not only was I all weird down there, but I was wearing some sweats that were way too small and also way too hot for summer. I had no memory of changing myself or being changed. I didn't tell anyone.

I turned twelve in September 1985. I went on with my life and tried to ignore the incident as I entered the seventh grade that fall. I was nervous because I knew I wouldn't know anyone at the school I was going to attend. My friends were all going to the local public junior high schools, and I was enrolled at a private school called Middleton, because my mother had heard horror stories about the other schools. I decided to wear my floral cotton pants (tapered and rolled at the ankle) and a white tank top with a pink fishnet shirt over it for the all-important first day of school. I wore pink karate shoes with white fishnet bobby socks and my hair was a little below my ears. I thought I looked like Madonna, but I am sure I just looked like a hot sack of crazy.

Middleton Christian School was very different from any school I had ever attended. It was still in Los Angeles' San Fernando Valley, as my grade school had been, but it was a private school-something to which I wasn't accustomed. It looked like an office building inside; I was expecting to see some cubicles and insurance salesmen with files in their hands. The whole place was air-conditioned (what?!), properly insulated and professionally painted. That really threw me off. It didn't have that familiar school smell of dusty books, musty classrooms that smelled of mildew, or cheap cafeteria food; all of which would have comforted me in some way. Instead, I smelled new, sour paint and that chemical smell of newly cleaned carpet. There was even fluorescent lighting overhead; no natural sunlight against faded, mint green walls. The place was *beige*. There was a fish-eyed receptionist in the lobby with some potted palm plants next to her desk and, for visitors, a few couches that were nicer than the ones in my parent's living room. There was an elevator that was supposed to be for wheelchairs, but it ended up taking lazy teachers to the second floor. As I passed them waiting for the doors to open, drinking their coffee and avoiding eye contact, I often noted that I made it to the second floor via the stairs before the elevators doors even opened for them.

There were bright yellow bathrooms that had a little foyer separating the sinks from the stalls. The stalls had working locks and there was no graffiti to read while I was peeing. There was green grass and climbing trees out front and even a little marquee that stated it was the new fall semester.

There was a shrew of a woman named Mrs. Baxman who was

the bell. By that, I mean she used a big old bullhorn to call everyone back in from recess and lunch. She was fucking *loud*. She always looked disastrous in a denim shirt, jeans, beat-up tennis shoes and some do-it-yourself orange peroxided hair. The kids looked nicer than she did, but no one ever made fun of her or crossed her. There is an instinct in kids that tells them who they can pick on and who would beat them upside the head with a shoe- and she fell into the latter category.

I don't remember much of what happened on my first day of school, with the exception of that entirely ridiculous outfit, for which I should have been issued twenty-five fashion police citations. I just remember that most of the kids knew each other from the previous year. I was one of the outsiders, along with a big-mouthed girl named Jennifer Bettina, who took to me and stuck by me. I thought she cramped my style even worse than it already was, and I tried to get away from her. She finally dropped me, and before I could even smile with relief, I was quickly irritated: she started hanging with one of the popular girls and the whole class started calling her "Bitsy." I was shocked that they accepted her. I was like, *Wait! She is a total dork!* But her confidence made her surpass me in the social scene, despite her buckteeth and Sun-in'd hair. I couldn't bring myself to talk to anyone and had my head down all of the time, so I was ignored. I knew I was no beauty, but I was convinced I was better than *that* ho.

Bitsy was always talking about guys and sex and things that embarrassed me. I was always terrified that she would ask me if I had ever kissed a boy or had a boyfriend. I didn't want to be put on the spot and that type of girl was always the first one to call me out. I ended up hanging out with another shy girl by default. She had no one else to hang with and didn't even like me; there were just no other choices. We barely spoke to each other. Her name was Marcia Alvarado and she was very small and Latin, with very big bangs and a moustache that would have made Tom Selleck jealous.

The majority of the girls at Middleton were white, pretty and rich. They were mostly German and Scandinavian blonds, with the exception of Kelly Fiorella, who was brunette, Italian, and channeling Annette Funicello. They grouped up while walking to the P.E. field to play softball, singing the Pet Shop Boys' "West End Girls." I would trail behind them, wondering how I could learn the words, too. They must have had the tape and could really listen to the songs. I didn't have any tapes. I would wait until a song came on the radio or on MTV and record it with my tape recorder, hoping to get it from the beginning, without the DJ talking over it. The girls also grouped up and sang Wham! and Madonna songs. There was nothing worse than crunching on the little rocks behind them, all the way to the field, looking at their cool rolled-up sweats, and perfectly worn T-shirts. I always had dorky socks and stiff, new-looking (read: cheap) sweats.

The band A-ha was the biggest deal that school year. It was all about their song "Take on Me" and the accompanying music video, which was, like, the craziest thing any of us had seen in the way of special effects. Robert Palmer's "Addicted to Love" was the other big video, along with Peter Gabriel's "Sledgehammer." The Middleton girls were all into New Wave or mainstream pop. There was no love of rap like there was at my grade school, Tadley, where the black kids breakdanced to Run DMC and sang LL Cool J's "Rock the Bells." There were no rocker kids: no one who wore Ozzy or Def Leppard concert T-shirts, or brought Motley Crue records to school or sang Van Halen and Quiet Riot songs. I missed the mixture of different cultures and ethnicities of kids.

Middleton had a strict dress code. You couldn't wear T-shirts or any of the stuff people wore at Tadley. I wondered what the hell kind of choices that left for me. I remember looking around at the clothes the girls wore; they looked really fancy. It took money to acquire the things they had. They all had elaborately styled hair and polished accessories (well, if huge geometric shapes could be considered polished). I never saw so many fashionable and brand name items of clothing at once. They wore the pants that were rolled at the ankle, little ankle boot type shoes, big colorful shirts, hanging belts and big earrings. Their hair was usually worn short (just past the ears). They wore Swatch watches, sometimes two or three at a time. Even their sweatshirts (which had to be worn with a collar) were expensive: Ton Sur Ton, Guess?, Esprit or Benetton. My stuff normally came from Marshall's, so I was very uncomfortable. I thought it was why I didn't fit in with the other kids.

I didn't know how I wanted to look. I still kind of wanted to hide my body. A boy in class named Chris Shivas made a comment about me having big boobs, and I felt very uncomfortable. I took to wearing my dad's big shapeless sweaters and shirts. I felt disgusted with my body, ashamed of it.

We had to visit an "old folks' home" to do some charity work that year. We were to bring either a) a hairbrush/comb set; b) slippers; or c) some other shit that I don't remember. My mom wrapped a pair of slippers and off I went. Each of us was to find a random old person and give them our gift. I felt shy and nervous looking around the room at the elderly men and women, many with canes, walkers, or wheelchairs. I decided someone in a wheelchair was the worst off. I approached a woman with a pink blanket over her lap and gave her the slippers. She looked at me as if I were the biggest asshole she had met in her 105 years. She yanked up the blanket to show me she had no legs, let alone feet. Some of the kids around me snickered. I wanted to dissolve into the linoleum. I went off to hide behind a group of eighth graders who were in a semi-circle, singing the theme song to *Gilligan's Island* as if it were an award-winning Broadway melody. The elderly people just stared at them. A few old men yelled and cursed at them, which is what I would have done.

I was scared of the older kids in the eighth and ninth grades; they looked like 35-year-olds to me. All of the ninth grade guys had popped collars, feathered hair, and Ray Ban sunglasses. They had names like *Cliff* and *Blake,* names that sounded like the preppy kids who picked on the Karate Kid or some other 1980's underdog. The boys in my grade were not like the ones I had known in the public school system. It was a different dynamic. The Middleton kids were all sheltered and had very similar tastes. It was clear none of them were "bussed in" from downtown Los Angeles, like many of the boys I used to know. It was clear they had never *been* on a bus, period.

I got more into the groove of the place throughout the year and made the best of it, and even had some laughs somewhere in there, I am sure. There were boys I daydreamed and fantasized about, just like any other twelve-year-old.

One in particular was an Italian boy named Mark Poletti. He was cute, social, and the class clown. His personality reminded me of Mike Seaver on the TV show *Growing Pains*. There was a popular song at the time called "How Will I Know?" by Whitney Houston, and I thought of him every time I heard it. I secretly pined after this boy all through the school year, not seeing any zits or braces or ridiculous eighties clothes. I imagined us making out for hours.

The Middleton teachers seemed strange to me. Switching classes and teachers every hour was no fun. I could never bond with the people sitting next to me, because it would be different each hour. There was a very pious woman named Ms. Cavovsky who wore not a stitch of makeup and had perfectly feathered hair. It would have looked fabulous had it still been 1981. But it was the mid-eighties and it was all about high, hair-sprayed stiff bangs. Ms. Cavovsky had big thighs and often rocked a camel toe (I couldn't help but stare at the private parts of every one of those teachers, for some reason). She was very, very serious. She didn't joke around; she didn't smile. She was all about business and was strict. She would have made an excellent nun, now that I think about it.

The person who I most checked out was Mr. Sterling, who was the principal but taught seventh grade Bible class for shits and giggles. He loved to talk about masturbation and how terrible it was. He always smirked and looked around the room when he talked of having lascivious thoughts. I used to hold my breath and think, *Can he read my mind?! Oh no! He looks like he knows what I have been thinking!* Truth be told, he *did* know what we were all thinking. We were teenagers! I always looked right at his crotch and I am telling you, there was no way to avoid it. His package was smashed up in his tight slacks, causing a huge bulge that was eye level to everyone sitting at a desk. Because he was sitting and slouching over that ancient old podium, the tip of his tie was like an arrow pointing to his package. How could I not stare? It was madness. Anyway, Sterling looked and acted a bit like Richard Gere. He was cocky and confident and cool.

There was a Japanese English teacher named Mr. Isumi. He was always dragging his words and acting as if he were the coolest thing to hit the planet. He was King Shit on Turd Island. He wanted validation from the boys and tried to flirt with the girls. He was sort of a dick and never smiled. He drew weird things on the marker boards and tried to crack teenage jokes. He was most known for saying "Hey, ah, *guys*?" when we were not paying attention. I seem to remember him wearing a lot of light blue. His class was when I did most of my daydreaming about Mark Poletti.

There was a serious history and science teacher named Mr. Westchester, whom I always pictured as one of Jesus' disciples, dressed in a beige hooded robe, because he had that dark curly hair and a beard. He was very on point and had little tolerance for teenagers. He was always let down by our performance and irritated at our stupidity. It is crazy to think he was only twenty-six at the time, but he was, as per my diary. Mr. Westchester hated it if you closed your book before the bell rang and made anyone who did so stay one minute after class. I hated that, because I needed that minute to put on *more* makeup over the three pounds of makeup already on my face.

My makeup application was frightful. First of all, I wore tinted Clearasil pimple cream as foundation. Yes, you read correctly. It was meant to cover one or two zits, but I rubbed it all over my face- and I didn't even *have* zits at the time. It was so thick! It crusted right over my eyebrows, which were big and sparse at the same time. I then used navy blue eyeliner on the inner rims of my eyes, which always seemed to then smear down under my eyes. I applied some chalky lavender eye shadow to top things off. And then to really get the party started, I doused myself in this cheap drugstore body spray that was a knockoff of some other reputable brand. I thought, *This is perfume and I am a girl. I had better drown myself in it.* Needless to say, I am sure I smelled like an old lady's crotch.

So not only did my scent, social skills, clothes and makeup application suck, but my hair sucked. I was determined to use mousse, as Tiffany Nixon had in the sixth grade. I couldn't figure out how to use the stuff, so I just put a big puffy glob of it in my hair and let it dry. I had crusty, oily, wavy bangs and an all-around assholey hairstyle. I had to invent that word just for my hair.

Okay, so I was down because of the whole pre-pubescent hormones thing and the not-fitting-in thing. That was probably normal. It made me moody. But some other things started to seep into the family that poisoned me further. I will tell the story just how it looked and felt to me, because I only know it from my angle.

My mother had been very involved in my life when I was a young child. Not only had she always worked at the schools I attended, but she had always told me how 'smart' I was and was very supportive of me. I hadn't needed to be pretty or athletic. I was 'smart.' I was really fulfilled with that identity, whether or not it was even true. My mother always seemed so impressed with me and so proud of me. But in that seventh grade year, not only did she no longer work at the school I attended, but she stopped telling me how great I was. I was surely moody and bitchy so that couldn't have helped. Maybe she had other things on her mind and didn't have the inclination to continue with her encouragement; understandable in hindsight, but hurtful to a twelve-year-old with already low self-esteem.

Then it got worse. She stopped communicating with me almost altogether. I was confused. It didn't make sense that someone who had been so loving toward me in the past would suddenly stop liking me. But it appeared to be true. I thought something was really, really wrong with me. I didn't know what I did. The few times I did catch her eyes, they were dead and flat and black. I didn't talk about it and tried not to think about it. I even thought, *Good, who wants their mom all over them in junior high?* I went on and tried to live my life as a regular preteen. She still had talks with me about puberty and from time to time tried to take me somewhere nice- she wasn't beating me with a hanger. But something was wrong.

Our family took our last trip with our family friends, the Ashfords, that winter. We rented a cabin at Pine Mountain and one of the things I remember most was that I had an uneasy feeling during the entire trip. Something happened to me just before that trip or during that trip. It didn't involve the Ashfords. It was within my family. I asked my younger sister, Becky, about it.

My sister says:
"Yeah. That was the year I started staying away from home a lot. I don't know what it was, but I do remember feeling weird at Pine Mountain too! I remember I was really embarrassed for some reason and the dog they brought wouldn't stop sniffing my crotch. I wet my pants… and I NEVER wet my pants. I felt uncomfortable during that trip. I kept walking out in the leaves by myself. Mom came looking for me a few times."

As much as my mother hurt me with her dead eyes and cut off communication, my bad feeling started to gravitate toward my father. I started to feel uncomfortable when he kissed me. It wasn't the little dry pecks he gave me as a child. It was different. When he kissed me, I felt his moustache and a bunch of blubber in my lips and mouth. It was slobbery. I had to tighten my mouth and shut my eyes very hard. I would wipe off my mouth afterward, making sure he saw me do it. I felt disgusted and angry. It built up like a volcano inside me.

One day he held his eyes on mine from across the living room and fumbled with his crotch. I felt furious. I winced and twisted up my face in disgust. I couldn't talk though. That's the weird thing. My mouth wouldn't say *stop*. My arms could never push. My legs couldn't run. He was my dad. I kept thinking...*No...I must be taking this wrong...this can't really be occurring. This is too bizarre.*

He started to wear these Capezio dance shoes and was always tapping his feet and shifting around anxiously. I thought he was going to break out in a tap dance like Gregory Hines or something. His moods became erratic. He started acting extremely haughty, arrogant, and full of himself. He seemed to think he was very wise and started quoting Bible verses that my sister and I didn't understand, as if the verse were some sort of code that we best figure out soon. We would be like "*Huh*?" His logic was usually lost on us.

Sometimes he had a lot of anger and couldn't express it, but his eyes showed it. He tilted his head very far back and got a very serious look on his face and had his eyebrows up. His words wouldn't come to him at those moments, but something was streaming through him that was thick and electric and angry. It looked to me as if he wanted to say something to really, really hurt me. Other days, it seemed he had an overwhelming urge to *physically* hurt me. I didn't understand. He had always loved me so much. He was always so much fun and so sweet to me when I was little. I couldn't understand what had changed between us.

My dad was angry one time and took my lavender chair and smashed it in a million pieces over the desk in my room. It was my special desk, where I wrote my plays and commercials. I shrank back, covered my face, and curled inside myself. He felt terrible afterwards and kept bringing it up. He said he would make it up to me. I winced. I just wanted him to stay away.

On another day, he said he was taking me somewhere special and it was a surprise. I felt totally uncomfortable at the thought of being alone with him but there was nothing I could do. My mother wouldn't make eye contact with me and I couldn't even identify my thoughts if she had. I couldn't let myself have the thought that kept tapping at my mind. *NO! No. No. That is too weird.* I felt trapped and miserable. I can barely remember the night. I was so full of disgust and anger and fear, I couldn't speak. I don't think I said two words. We were driving in the dark for a really long time when I finally realized we were arriving at Disneyland. It was my very favorite place. But I didn't want to be there with him. I was thinking, *Why the heck are we arriving here in the dark? It is nighttime. This place is about to close down.* I thought it odd, because we wouldn't be able to go on many rides at such a late time in the evening.

He took me to dinner at my favorite spot in New Orleans Square and got me my favorite dish, a French dip. After dinner, he wanted to walk around holding my hand and I felt very uncomfortable. Everything was so serious and quiet. I felt like his date. I wanted to just…*run.* I wanted someone to save me. There was no one to protect me. I can remember none of what we talked about, only that I was squirming inside and couldn't wait to be home. I looked at my makeup in the mirror in the car on the way home and my eyeliner had slid down my face, making two black eyes. I was mad that he let me walk around like that the whole night. He said something about not caring, that he loved me no matter what. Part of me thought, *What if he really was just trying to bond with me?* and I felt bad. But my gut instinct told me I was in danger.

Not too long after that, my dad pulled me aside at my grandmother's house, knelt down to me, and told me he loved me more than he loved my sister. I felt disturbed and confused. Why couldn't he just be normal?!

Okay, so there I was, twelve years old. Something went down about six months prior that required someone removing my underwear and changing my clothes and now my parents were acting really, really weird. If I were to acknowledge what was going on, I would not survive. What was I to do, run away? Go out and get a job at twelve years old? I had to go on. I depended on my father for a roof over my head, for food, for clothing. My mother was completely shut off from me and even if she weren't, I doubt I would have confided in her because my trust level was at an all-time low. The boundaries in my life were being smeared all over the place, like paint on a canvas. It was as if suddenly everything that meant security and protection had crumbled. My perception of reality was whirling, twirling into a hurricane, piercing the blue sky and ripping it open to show a dark place. It made me feel crazy.

I started to fall into a depression. I didn't feel safe in my house. In order to avoid running into my father, I decided that staying in my room was the safest thing to do. That room was no safer than the rest of the house, but I didn't have many options. I completely took myself out of reality when I was in my room. I read books at a feverish pace, escaping into the stories. I pretended I was the characters I read about and made up games by myself. Sometimes I was a scullery maid on creaky floorboards talking to mice. Other times I was a child living in a manor on the English countryside. I wanted to be anywhere but in my own life.

I regressed to playing like a child again. I set up my stuffed animals as a little family and talked to them and had tea parties with them. I pretended they loved me and could hear me and listened to me. I know that sounds all "Oh, poor me," but that is what I did. I also talked to my doll Holly as if she could really hear me- normal for a five-year-old maybe, but not for someone in junior high school. I hung with my sister if she was home and

I spent time with my childhood friend Karen, but I didn't make any friends at school because I rarely spoke. I no longer went outside. I wouldn't join my family when they went out to dinner. I did have my days where I was okay and most days I was a normal preteen, thinking about boys and movie stars. But inside I felt...*off*. I didn't want anyone *looking* at me. I felt like everyone could see *inside* me. I didn't want anyone to see I was damaged and bad in my core.

I wrote in a journal:

I keep ruining everyone's time. That isn't something I would normally do. I am not doing it on purpose. It's just that I keep doing it, no matter how bad I don't want to. I don't want to swim or eat or play video games. I just can't have fun anymore. I feel like everywhere I go I am holding my breath. I don't like Disneyland anymore or Knott's Berry Farm. I don't like going to eat or joining anything. I hate going outside in the front yard or any public places, even walking to the store. I even hate the beach. I hate everywhere, except for the homes of people I know very well.

One thing drew me out of my room that year. My family went to the drive-in movie theater to see *Ferris Bueller's Day Off*. I was excited to see the movie because I could be cool at school by knowing some of the lines. I thought that maybe I could impress Mark Poletti. There was tension between my parents on the drive over, but I ignored it. I just wanted to see cute Matthew Broderick and his crooked grin.

We parked, and the next thing I knew, my dad was punching me with a closed fist. It was quick and swift and without warning and he wouldn't let up. He was punching, punching, punching. The look on his face was terrifying, like a killer must look. I saw hate, disgust, and anger. My mother sat there looking straight ahead. My sister was crying. My father finally gave me an idea as to why I was being hit. It seemed like he just came up with it on the spot: it was for not eating what my mother cooked for

24

dinner.

Shit, it was technically true. I hated her vegetables. I had a gag reflex for canned French string beans. But she hadn't cooked in ages. Several months, at least. I thought, *Wait...this couldn't be why he is punching me. He couldn't have that much anger toward me for not eating some shitty string beans.*

Finally, my mom said, "Well, I don't exactly cook these days..." and he stopped pounding me for a second. I thought, *Oh thank God...my mother is coming to my defense!* But then she said, "Even if I did, she wouldn't eat it anyway." He started punching me again, as if I were a man.

I tried to cover my face with the pillow I had brought from home. I thought...*Wow...this person has a very serious anger toward me. Both of them do.* I had done something *really, really* wrong to make them not like me anymore. I felt like I was being blamed for something really big. I remember feeling so confused that my mother just sat there and did nothing while he beat me. I hated both of them. When I look back, I think that my mother might have been angry with my father for not sticking by her when she tried to discipline us, and he was trying to make an effort at that time.

My sister says:
"It just turned you inside out and you became the official family 'problem.' I was your playmate everyday though and I remember you as a kid. Up until then you were great – you were smart and involved and creative and fun. You were always cool and nice. I don't see how all of a sudden you were the devil. All of a sudden, I started seeing hostility when it never existed before. It was a little shocking."

One day I was really sick in my room and couldn't move out of bed. I needed my mom for something and she couldn't hear me because she was *screaming* in the living room at the top of her lungs, singing "Too Low for Zero" by Elton John. I kept calling for her, but she couldn't hear me. She was having a nervous breakdown. There was a definite problem in the family that no one was talking about. It was just eating everybody and nobody would do anything about it. It just festered, right there in our house. Right there in suburbia. Right there in a family that had gone to church and ate popsicles and had camping trips.

I didn't think about my weight at all until one particular overcast day. My dad was in one of his unpredictable moods and I was lagging on getting laundry out of the dryer. He angrily told to get off my *fat ass* and get the laundry. Then he smacked me in an angry, puppy-kicking way. I looked at his eyes and they were full of anger. *Fat.* He said…fat ass. Was I… fat? Is that why they were mad at me? I wished I could just be a kid again. I was hurt by my dad's comment and immediately started to cry. Then I got angry.

I didn't know if I was mad about the fat thing or him smacking me. It wasn't some big fiasco where I was being beat to a pulp, by any means. But regardless, I gathered myself by my T-shirt and went up to him and looked him straight in the eyes. I said in a thick, sobbing voice, "If you *ever* touch me again, I am calling the *police.*"

He backed off a little and looked at me. We locked eyes. My eyes said I meant business.

He got the picture. I saw it click in his head that I wasn't just talking about being smacked on the butt for not getting the laundry. I was talking about him crossing a line with me. I was so scared that I started to shake uncontrollably. I thought my legs would give out. I sat down in a dirty, faded brown director's chair on our patio and sobbed really hard. He tried to console me and I snatched my arm away from him.

I would love to say I felt much better after standing up to him and defending myself, but I didn't. I felt very alone. I really just wanted to end my life. I wanted to die more than anything. I went into the bathroom, took out a bottle of Windex, and thought...*I should just drink this. Then I would be dead.* But of course I couldn't bring myself to do it. I tried to find other ways to hurt myself instead, like carving in my skin with a knife or a pin. I cut into my arms and cried and cried and cried. When I felt that horrible, I would repeat to myself over and over, *You are not really a part of this family, you are completely separate from them and you are not even from here. You are here for future reasons that have nothing to do with today. Your reason for existence has nothing to do with this family or these times.* I know, that sounds crazy. But that is the message I somehow got in the back of my brain. I used it to comfort myself when I thought I couldn't go on. I remember not being clear on where I was supposed to be 'from,' so I made up that I was from Jupiter, so I could at least have a visual. But being from Jupiter was the least of my worries.

When I look back on it, I sometimes think, *Was this just puberty? Was this what normal teens did when going through puberty? Was I getting a lot of hormones, maybe?* But then I realize that it was a combination of that and something else. I couldn't admit it or even think about it for years because it was so gross. My father had been behaving sexually toward me, before all of the anger and terror started. That was the main problem, and it was too late to take it back. Then there was the secondary problem: the lack of protection from my mother. Why wasn't she there when I needed her? I wouldn't let my mind think about that either, until several years later, when I told her about my suspicions in a long letter.

The letter was five pages, listing all of the things that I remembered about my dad's inappropriate behavior. I pictured her reading the letter. I thought she would first have a heart attack and then wake up and become hysterical. She would climb to the top of a mountain with a rifle in her hand and vow to kill the man who dared touch her child. I pictured her in a prairie dress, cocking a rifle and wiping back tears. I pictured her putting the rifle to my father's crotch with a fierce, unwavering look in her eye and telling him: "Nobody touches my child and gets away with it. Now you have me to deal with," and pulling the trigger.

But that's not what happened.

What did happen was this:

I received a letter in return, containing exactly one paragraph. In the paragraph, she wrote that she believed me. *Oh…Okay, good. That is good,* I thought. Then I read on. It said that she had suspected it. That took a minute to absorb.

Wait…wait…she…suspected it? She…was aware? What the fuck?

I picked up the phone and called her, pressing her for more details. She admitted that once, before they had us kids, he looked at an album cover of a shirtless child and said it was "hot." Then she told me about another time when she caught him in the nude while my sister and I were in the next room playing, and he purposely didn't cover himself. There was another time when he called out one of our names during a romantic moment with her. There was the time that he watched a bunch of older boys have their way with a ten-year-old girl on his street. I didn't know how old he was when it happened- was he the same age as the girl? Was he older? My mom then mentioned that there was a time that he bragged to his friends about having sex with a twelve-year-old (cue the sound of tires screeching to a halt) WHAT?! I was taken aback with the information my mother gave me. Who was that twelve-year-old? Was it me? Did it happen when *he* was twelve? When he was younger? Did my father still crave twelve-year-olds? Is that why I woke up the way I did just before my twelfth birthday? Is that why I felt danger around him? It was so disturbing, I couldn't process it. But there was something that I *could* process. My mother thought something horrible could have happened to me, her child, and she never once asked me if I were in danger, if I needed help or if I were okay. Not one peep. She would have taken it to the grave had I not brought it up myself.

I sat down. I was furious; dizzy with rage. I didn't know who I was more angry with, my perverted father or my negligent mother. Not only did she turn a blind eye to her child being in danger, but she purposely avoided me! How could she have turned on me? Why was I not worth helping, saving, rescuing? Was she told that I had some part in it? That it was my idea? I will never know. And she will never tell.

So if that right there didn't drive me to become completely nuts, I don't know what could have done it. Needless to say, I hated both of my parents with fervor. But that was later. At this point in my story, I hadn't put it all together in my head yet. I felt confused, disgusted, scared, and angry. I didn't say much. I came off as moody and pissed off at home and shy and isolated at school. As much as I hated Middleton at first, I was beginning to prefer being it to being at home.

Okay, let's get off this deep dark subject because I am getting depressed just writing it. (Sighs.) So while that all sucked majorly, something even worse happened that June. Something that made me think the world was ending. (Takes deep breath...)

Wham! broke up.

Yes, Wham. I literally wept at the thought of losing two bronzed, highlighted ass-shakers from my TV screen. How could they do that to me? To the *world*? It was probably more important to me at the time than my lame parents.

In all seriousness though, I somehow trudged through the school year, making the best of my situation. I had fun with my friend Karen on the weekends. I loved watching MTV and making up dances. I still read a lot of books. I accepted that I was not popular at school and I was okay with it. I would never be one of the girls that the boys liked.

29

But then one day, one sweet day…my luck changed. Let me start by saying that spending so much time in my room had allowed me to figure out how to do my hair (Aqua Net sprayed into my bangs and the sides of my hair to make them stick out like puppy ears.) It also gave me a lot of time to practice my eighties makeup and change things around a little (pale metallic pink lipstick and peach cream blush.) I got some better fitting clothes in light pinks and light blues. I laid off the body spray. I got a little bit of a tan. I didn't look as much like a *Dance Party USA* cast off.

The next thing I knew….(*drum roll*)….my crush… Mark Poletti…. (*screams*) appeared to be interested in me! ME! I thought…*No…this can't be! I like a guy and he…likes me BACK? This sort of thing doesn't happen to me! No way!* One of the popular girls, Christy Schmidt, tried making conversation with me. She said, "What do you think of Mark?"

I don't remember what I said- I probably said something safe, like, "He is nice." I thought I must have misunderstood, that she couldn't really be talking to me.

Mark and I had lockers on the bottom row. His was only a few down from mine. I remember getting my books out of my locker and smelling something like cinnamon. I sniffed harder. Was that…*aftershave* I smelled? I looked over at Mark and he appeared all shy suddenly. He was no longer acting like the class clown, or the social guy cracking jokes. He looked at me and said, in a deepened voice, "Hi." It dawned on me at that point that he did like me. My first thought was *Cool!* And my second thought was *Shit. What do I do!*? I was mortified at the thought of dating him. What if he wanted to kiss me? I didn't know how to kiss! How would we see each other? I would have to tell my parents in order to go anywhere with him.

I pictured myself in the backseat of our brown car, driving to his nice house over by the Country Club. My dad would act weird and embarrass me and my mom would get awkward. Screw *that*!

It would be *so* embarrassing! I didn't see any way it could work. I knew I would be too frightened to kiss him because I couldn't even *talk* to him without stuttering. I also decided that it was too embarrassing to let my parents know I liked a boy in my class. I shut down out of fear and decided to ignore him completely. I was so glad summer vacation was only weeks away, because I wouldn't have to see him all summer, and the whole thing could blow over by fall. So I tried waiting it out and pretended I didn't get the signals.

On the last day of school, Mark came up to me, kind of defeated, and was like, "See you next year," in his forced, low 'man' voice. He was looking me in the eyes. I *wished* I were not so chicken. I wished I would have gone for it. But I lost him, and moved on into the summer even more boy crazy. I daydreamed of him saying that line, over and over. It was like fuel, keeping me going, giving me something else to concentrate on besides my parents and the house of crazy. "Live to Tell" by Madonna was on MTV a lot around that time. I listened to it as if it was the deepest thing I had ever heard, like it was written by the Dalai Lama or something, while fantasizing about making out with Mark.

My sister Becky was two years younger than I was and did not talk about boys, so I was often drifting off into my own world. It saddened me that boys were taking over my brain, but it was not controllable. I pictured doing it with Mark, but I didn't know what that really entailed. I just knew white stuff came out and I pictured it like the white chocolate pouring out of the pan in the Nestle commercial, in slow motion. I thought it would be at least a half-gallon of liquid.

That summer, Karen and I watched either a) *The Roller Derby* b) *The Big Spin* or c) this movie called *Desert Bloom* with Annabeth Gish. We watched and rewatched that damn movie over and over again, quoting the lines. I think I memorized that entire script. We ate Doritos, drank Diet Pepsi, and sometimes her dad got us Value Packs at McDonald's. I always got Chicken

McNuggets with barbecue sauce and she got a Filet-O-Fish. We then spied on the boys in her condo complex; all of whom were skaters.

At that time, skaters were guys who not only rode a skateboard, but wore very specific T-shirts featuring different surfboard companies, such as *Town & Country, Local Motion* and *Maui and Sons*. Skaters liked New Wave/Pop type of music; they were not into any sort of rock. They were more on the conservative side, with short hair and long bangs usually over one eye. They were tan, fit, and usually smoking hot. You never saw a fat skater.

Karen and I perked up if we heard skateboard wheels. We were such nerds though, that we couldn't just say hi to boys. We would do something like throw rocks at them or start a fight with them somehow. We were really immature because we were deathly shy. She was even worse than I was. I wanted to see one guy in particular named Jim. He was drop dead gorgeous with bright blue eyes and dark hair. He was so good looking, it *hurt*. I thought my underwear would burst into flames. I remember watching a girl flirting with him. I was in awe of her for having the confidence to talk to him, unlike me who hid and sounded like Igor in a cave.

In any case, I had a little boost of confidence from Mark Poletti and his aftershave. I ventured out of my room and even out of the house a little bit. I tried flirting with boys on my own street. They didn't shoot me down. I got a few smiles and some romantic tension with a boy named Chad. It was enough for me to feel happy. In between water balloon fights and crank calls, Karen, Becky and I watched video after video on MTV. Karen and I fell in love with a group called Bananarama and their remake of "Venus." It was the first tape I bought. My sister got into Bon Jovi and David Lee Roth. We lived for music. It was the backdrop of everything exciting we felt inside: all of the possibilities with boys, all of the butterflies.

CHAPTER TWO

The Choice

Eighth grade was no joy, but it was better than seventh grade. I was *full* of angst. Just *thinking* about it makes me want to take some Valium. I was back to staying in my room with the door closed, and all I did was write in my diary and daydream about boys. I guess that is pretty typical. I read *Wuthering Heights* for a book report and got totally obsessed with it. I was suddenly writing in my diary as if I was on the moors with Heathcliff. I wanted romance; I wanted to be in love. I was writing things like, *"If all else perished and he remained, I should continue to be!"* I was completely boy crazy. The difference between my boy craziness and other girls my age was that they were boy crazy while talking to *actual boys* at The Galleria or Skateland. I was boy crazy behind the closed doors of my room, and I wanted to shout from rooftops and wear flowing gowns on mountainsides while being boy crazy.

For the first half of the school year, I was still pretty innocent as far as my thoughts and interests were concerned. I became really interested in old film stars, like Rita Hayworth, Barbara

Stanwyck, Marilyn Monroe and Natalie Wood. I hung up their black and white pictures and wished I could do my hair and makeup like theirs. They were so glamorous in sparkling gowns, with shiny hair styled in waves and long eyelashes.

My mom got me a big fat Warner Brothers Studios coffee table book for Valentine's Day that year. She saw me fawning over it at a bookstore and decided to get it for me, along with a jar of peppermint candies. I loved the book and what it held in it. It was pictures of a different time. I felt homesick for it. I had recently watched *Meet Me in St. Louis* and *Little Women* and they made me long to be in another decade. I felt pain in my heart at the voices of the actors and actresses, their attire, the sets and the songs. Things like love and family seemed sweetly simple yet things like décor and manners were more formal. While watching those 1940's movies, I felt more at home than I did in my own family. When times were bad, I used those old films and pictures to bring me security.

I really started piling on the makeup even more that year. I felt relief each time I applied another layer to my face. It was a literal mask I hid behind. I felt braver with it. When I took it off at home, I felt vulnerable. I started wearing tons of foundation in the wrong shade; tons of dark, loose powder from a pink plastic container (both hand-me-downs from my aunt Billie), along with loads of blue eyeliner that winged out at the sides. I reapplied it all after each class and sometimes during class. One of the more outspoken ninth graders looked at me one day and said, "Dude, you are going to *drown* yourself in foundation!" I always had tons of makeup on the collars of my shirts and jackets. I looked like a broken-down, teenage Joan Collins.

Like most teenagers, I was curious about sex and was too frightened to ask my parents how it worked. I wasn't sure how my mother would react, but I knew I didn't want to ask her. My dad wasn't as pervy toward me that year, maybe it was because I was no longer twelve. Nevertheless, I didn't want to rehash his feelings by asking him about the facts of life. That would be a stupid move. I didn't have any friends to ask- Karen was still hanging up posters of kittens. So I took my cues from music and TV.

I liked a new group called the Beastie Boys; I thought Ad-Rock was cute. I didn't know then that *anyone* looks cute next to Mike D. and MCA, but that is neither here nor there. I listened to my *Licensed to Ill* tape, rewinding it repeatedly to try to decipher the lyrics to get some sort of clue as to what people did behind closed doors. They were risqué and talked about having sex with girls, although I could barely decode what they were talking about between their thick Brooklyn accents and their slang. It didn't make much sense to me. A wiffle ball bat? Forty Deuce? Turn tables? White Castle? I could not have picked worse teachers.

I started actively searching for meaning in other songs on the radio by groups like Def Leppard, Ratt, and, of course, Madonna. Most of the music I was listening to was from the viewpoint of a man, and what I learned from it all was that men desired women and wanted to do stuff with them. I just couldn't figure out exact directions. I remember many Genesis songs, songs from Janet Jackson's *Control* album and songs from Bon Jovi's *Slippery When Wet* album. Despite the racy album name, Bon Jovi wasn't too bad. They were kind of like long-haired Bruce Springsteens. They were from New Jersey and they sung about the prom, waitresses and steel workers being broke; blue collared, anthem-type of songs. I liked hearing the songs through the wall when my sister played them. She always found hip music before I did.

There was a new Glam Rock band out at that time called Poison, and they really caught my eye. They had a catchy song called "Talk Dirty to Me." They always appeared to be in the dead center of a huge party. Their videos were a mess of electric green, hot pink, red, baby blue and leopard skin. They wore lipstick and had long hair, sprayed with what looked like tons of Aqua Net. They were always checking out chicks walking by, humping the microphone stand, gyrating, and flicking a tongue between two fingers. They were still *guys*. It was confusing, yet exciting: the beauty of women, yet the sexuality of men. A perfect combination if I ever saw one. I was intrigued.

I lost interest in Mark Poletti that year because I saw that there was some fresh meat in the grade below me. There was one boy in particular who I found super cute, named Zack. He was in my English class and kept turning around in his chair and checking me out. I didn't know what to do. I panicked and pretended it wasn't happening. He was a tall kid with dark blond hair that looked wet with gel; big wide-set blue eyes and some freckles. He tried getting my attention for a few weeks, and I just couldn't bring myself to look back at him or show any interest even though I found him totally cute.

I fantasized about Zack and was flattered he liked me. I never dreamed another girl would swoop in and take him away. I became friends with popular Kelly Fiorella that year. She was a talkative, social girl who dated all of the boys and somehow remained a good girl. She found Zack attractive and she wanted to date him. It took all of two days for them to become a couple. She had another girl go up to him and ask what he thought of her (which apparently was the way to get someone to go out with you in junior high), and the word was out that she was interested. The next thing I knew, they were boyfriend/girlfriend. I was crushed. I wanted to cry tears of navy blue eyeliner. I couldn't believe he went for it! He was no dummy; he was like, *Where do I sign up?*

I fantasized that he would tell her in a very dramatic *Days of Our Lives* tone, *"No...my heart is with someone else,"* but he never did. I was mean to Kelly and didn't want to hear her lispy, lovesick ramblings. She asked me to sit with them at lunch. Both Zack and I were uncomfortable. I wondered though…what did they *talk* about? How did it go? How did one have a boyfriend at thirteen? We couldn't drive…How was it *done*? Did you have to do more than kiss? I felt really behind. What if something embarrassing happened between the boy and me? It was such a small school. I would have to see the boy every day. What if he laughed in my face because I didn't know what to do with him? Everyone would know about it. I just couldn't do it.

I set my sights on another boy named Eric. He was a troublemaker who was always in the principal's office. Now that I look back, he was not cute. He was sort of scrawny and had squinty eyes. Anyway, we were supposed to do some performance for the school and he chose me as a partner. We were supposed to represent the 1960's and do the Twist. I made sure I was absent that day, because there was no way I was getting on the Middleton *stage* and doing some lame dance. But that was all insignificant as far as I was concerned because a real live boy had requested *me* as his partner!

Suddenly, I was in love. I wrote about Eric in my diary, filling it up with flowery prose. I think I filled two or three diaries with nothing but Eric, Eric, Eric (*cuckoo clock noise*). Then I started to become seriously psycho. I started crying over him in my room, listening to love songs and lighting candles. The Jets' "You Got it All" would make me sprout tears and Bon Jovi's "Never Say Goodbye" would make me do the ugly cry face and want to stab myself in the heart. I thought of nothing but squinty-eyed Eric. Every day I would put on my makeup and do my hair thinking of him, hoping to run into him. He never even *spoke* to me! I never even had a conver*sation* with this boy! I just stared at him, trying to lock eyes with him. At first he looked back. Then he started to realize I was crazy and he wouldn't meet my gaze. He was probably thinking, *I will never request a dance partner again for the rest of my life!* My sister tried to comment on my obsession and I yelled, "You don't know what love is!" through tears and snot as she looked at me with a raised eyebrow. I was a giant, heaving bowl of crazy with sprinkles on top.

I still liked the blond boy, Zack, and to my dismay, he became best friends with Eric. Once that happened, they both avoided me completely. They even started to make fun of me. I remember one day hearing them snicker after I walked by in my one-inch Payless pumps with socks, wearing my mom's ill-fitting black and white checked shirt, a long white skirt, and my clown makeup. Another time I was walking up the stairs in front of them and the sole of my shoe fell off. I had to pick the sole up and put it in my book bag. I was so embarrassed.

**

There was a hole punched in the wall by my bedroom around that time. We found out that my mother had done it, but we weren't allowed to talk about it. My parents were acting odd and secretive. A few days later, I was told I was to move out of my bedroom. It was the first room before a long hallway, separated from the rest of the bedrooms in our house. I was being moved to a room down by my parents' room and sister's room. While my room was in transition, a big cockroach fell from the ceiling and hit a book on my bed. I wondered if there was some sort of evil marking that room.

Things felt out of control in my home life, so I started to discipline myself very strictly in private. I studied French in my room. I tried to memorize Bible verses and lines of Shakespeare. I decided I needed to sing the National Anthem each day while doing a backbend. I don't know what the hell I was thinking, but it was part of a ritual. In hindsight, I guess it made me feel like I could control something.

In addition to all of the other secretive weird bullshit going on in my family, there was another development taking place. I was breaking away and developing an identity of my own. Yes folks, I was a teenager and that is what teenagers do. My father had a hard time accepting it. As soon I started to develop interests and tastes that were completely different from his, he became insulted. He saw he was no longer my hero. I didn't look up to him. I didn't value what he valued. It hurt his feelings. Maybe that is what he used as justification to hurt me the way he did. I don't know.

My father did not value typical American commercial success. He had more of an alternative view of things. He was a former hippie, first off. My mother and he had run off to live in the hippie communes in the early seventies, before I was born. They literally lived in a cave, naked. And it is worth noting for the sheer sensationalism of it that they ran into Charles Manson and company while they were hitchhiking around L.A.

So, as you can imagine, my dad thought corporate America was the devil. He didn't own a suit. He didn't see a need for higher education. It was not something he told us was of any importance. He didn't trust the government, he didn't like rules. And just like my mother, he avoided anyone with money. It made him very uncomfortable, and it was made clear to me that rich people were the bad guys. My dad loved the desert, the sand, and being outdoors around nature. He loved playing the guitar and singing, having long philosophical talks with people around a fire, or playing chess. None of that was bad, it just wasn't what his teenage daughter liked. I was not impressed with him, like so many others were.

I *did* value commercial success. I wanted refinement, glamour, and culture. I was interested in advertising, journalism, literature, filmmaking and all of the performing arts. I loved learning. I craved discipline. I was interested in traveling to other countries. I wanted to run a real business one day. I always had files, briefcases, business cards and drawn-up plans of my future houses and business ventures. The more my father saw who I wanted to be, the more he didn't like what he saw. I wanted to live in a Victorian mansion with damask wallpaper and go to the ballet and shit. I wanted to run an empire by day and recline on an antique settee in the evenings, reading stacks of books from my library. I wanted to become something grand, which is the very type of person who threatened my parents. My dad made snide comments about my likes and taste quite often. He looked at my framed pictures of Natalie Wood and told me she was dead and full of worms. He taunted me about my wanting to live in London, saying that I wouldn't make it there because they didn't have my favorite breakfast cereal. I would have to eat what they had. Just little jabs like that. He picked on me.

One day I was watching some great 80's programming; a fine, highly acclaimed, culture-rich show that rivaled the Masterpiece Theatre: *Diff'rent Strokes*. Kimberly Drummond, the rich, wasp-y daughter, had this fabulous bikini figure and everyone was praising her. Then it was revealed that she had something called bulimia. She binged on food at night (I will never forget her scooping peanut butter from the jar with her fingers) and then proceeded to force herself to vomit in the toilet (as per the sound effects and the closed bathroom door). It made her look great, she got to eat like a pig and she had an official problem. She eventually got tons of attention and an intervention by her loving family, who were cursing themselves for not seeing the signs. That was it! I would get a "problem"! I would become bulimic. You are thinking, "Who is that stupid?" Well, me. I was *that* lame.

I started throwing up my food at home. Fingers down the throat, touching the little punching bag. Everything came up. I tasted it all over again. If I didn't drink enough water with my meal, the barf got stuck in my throat and I thought I would choke to death. My eyes watered, my nose ran. I never did it at school, because I only did it near my parents. At first, it was kind of a novelty. I thought, *Can I do this?* Then I started doing it all of the time, hoping my parents would catch on. They didn't.

I became dangerously bulimic at the end of eighth grade. My sister was upset by it and begged me to stop. I puked up everything, most of all fried bologna sandwiches with jack cheese and mustard, if you must know. I started to throw up without even using my finger. I just leaned over and heaved. My parents didn't notice my extreme weight loss. They didn't pick up on my immediately leaving after eating, going to the bathroom and retching and then coming back wiping my mouth. They didn't notice the sour smell of vomit anywhere. I got worse and worse. I thought, *Help! Somebody come to my rescue! I want attention here!*

I lost a lot of weight that summer. Weight loss wasn't the reason I started throwing up my food, but I was happy with my new figure nonetheless. I thought, *Whoa...this shit **works**.* Not just boys, but men started *really* checking me out. I started to like the attention. I fantasized about dressing sexier, but I was scared. I spent time in my room in large, white, men-sized T-shirts, pulling them tight around my figure to see what I would look like in a tight dress. I twisted them up and tied them in a knot under my boobs. I started cutting my long skirts into short ones. Skirts that I got for Christmas -once all the way to my ankles- were now just past my ass. Things slowly became shorter and shorter. I started doing bust exercises and sit-ups every night, like a maniac. I did calf lifts and laid in the sun a lot.

Now that I was starting to look more attractive, I wanted to do exciting and daring things. I couldn't waste my looks on sitting around watching *Charles in Charge* and picking my ass. I needed to break up people's relationships, steal boyfriends, have evil plans, and gaze up at people through smoky eye shadow. I also dreamed of being able to say gutsy lines and flip my hair back in slow motion.

I watched nighttime soap shows like *Dynasty* and *The Colbys*. Initially, it was just so I could go back to school and join the conversation with Mark Poletti. He watched *Dynasty*, and always turned around and discussed it with the people behind him in class. I initially sat and listened as they talked about the show. Then I secretly began watching it so I could interject with something interesting. I think when I finally did, it backfired on me because I tried too hard. I brought up *Dynasty* so much, that Mark started getting irritated and stopped talking about it. Eventually he made some comment about not even *liking* the show any more. It was most definitely so I would shut up. At any rate, I watched the shows and took note of two things. One: the glamour. The wardrobes consisted of jewels, gowns, furs, and large hats. There was overly-styled hair and an ocean of makeup (the more evil the woman, the more makeup she wore). Two: the balls. No, not a ball like the one Cinderella attended, but balls as in testicles. The women had *balls*. They said vicious things to each other and managed to look cool while doing so. They told someone off or slapped someone in the face, and then had a great exit where they turned and walked away effortlessly. No tripping on a pebble. No feeling nervous or regretting anything. And of course, they had a *very* glossy lip and beautifully blended eye shadow in shades of peacock. I cared not for the designer gowns, because I knew nothing of designers (and if I did, I would sure as hell not be into Nolan Miller, best believe). I did not know anything about jewels (I thought rhinestones were the shit). It was the *confidence* of these women that I wanted to emulate. I was a damned fool for taking nighttime soaps so literally, but I wanted to be like these women. I wanted to be brave, daring, and beautiful. They were my role models.

If the women on *Dynasty* were interested in a man, they seduced him. I paid close attention to that move, because it was ultra-ballsy and it looked so scary to do in real life. I mean, could I seduce one of the Middleton boys? I started to think about who would be my ideal boy to seduce. It wasn't anyone at Middleton. It was Jeff Hunter, the super cute Heavy Metal boy in my fifth and sixth grade classes at Tadley, who let Tiffany Nixon sit in his lap. I daydreamed of walking up to his door with my new look and improved figure. He lived only a few houses down and around the corner. I imagined his rocker eyeballs popping out of his head, and then him grabbing me and making out with me. I wished I could make myself go over there, but I knew I would be too scared to even try. I kept it as a daydream.

In the back of my mind, Heavy Metal was where it was at. The Middleton kids were goody-goodies, wearing collared shirts with Reeboks and watching *Moonlighting*. Ninth grade was coming up. It was my last chance to be cool at Middleton; my last chance to avoid going down in history as a loser wearing my dad's sweaters from Gemco. There would be no one in the grade above me to scare me or make fun of me if I wanted to try a new look. Even Eric and Zack were going to change schools and wouldn't be there in the fall.

I started to get really into a Heavy Metal band called Ratt after seeing the music video to their song "Dance." I thought the singer, Stephen Pearcy, was hot. He wore all white and had a black headband around his head like he was going to work out with Olivia Newton John. He had a scratchy voice that hooked me. I saved my allowance and bought their record, *Dancing Undercover*. I played it over and over and over until I memorized the entire thing. Then I saw another Heavy Metal video that inspired me: Whitesnake's "Here I Go Again." There was a flashy redhead in the video, who flipped her long, messy hair back without fear. She was lifting herself out of a car window while her old decrepit boyfriend drove through a tunnel, looking like he was thinking about his mortgage or what he should eat later. She was rolling around on Jaguars in white flowing clothes, appearing super confident. Wow! I wanted to be like *that*! I was starved for attention. My main goal in life suddenly became doing a forward walkover on a Jaguar XJ without making dents in the hood.

I was figuring out what kind of person I wanted to be, what kind of image I wanted to portray. As a kid, I thought for sure I would at least be the CEO of something. I thought I would be walking around with a briefcase or sitting in a huge office, running the world. Or at least Paramount.

But as soon as I hit puberty, I found myself lacking the confidence to make any of my dreams happen. I almost felt like a fool. Looking around, I saw that women did not run businesses (some did, of course, but I didn't know that).They were supposed to be sexy, pretty, thin and more or less subservient. They were supposed to be in the background unless they were a sex object, in which case they were openly ogled.

The women who were really sexy were the only ones who had any power over anybody. Guys fell down to their feet drooling and hitting themselves on the head with a cartoon hammer. The nice, un-sexy women were secretaries, teachers, and housewives. *Wallflowers.* I look back and I realize that part of the sadness and depression I felt as a teenager was the mourning of my old self. I knew I gave up on everything I ever wanted to do, and I was *so* disappointed in myself. I knew I lost my spark and my drive. I quietly buried it all and just drowned myself in makeup and turned up my records. It was a waste if I ever saw one.

Where did I get the message that I couldn't be something other than pretty, sexy and thin? There is the obvious: music videos, movies, TV- every piece of popular media to which I had access. It was 1987. The images and messages I grew up with were at an all-time high in sexism. I think back, and the only chance I would have had is if the movie *Working Girl* would have come out a year earlier. I wasn't exposed to any other message for girls other than you had to be sexy or you would be ignored, considered boring and be doomed to a life in the background. Screw *that*. I wasn't going out like that.

I also picked up on how my father talked about women and the things he saw as important in a woman. He was probably no different from other men during those years, but this is what I noticed: women had to be thin. That was most important. Whenever my father described a woman, he first mentioned whether she was heavy or not. It was never if she was a good person or not, or any other value she had- it was always her weight. It also didn't help that he had tried to talk me down from my ambitions, sometimes resorting to mockery. The other, stronger, message my father gave me was that I was desired sexually. I honestly remember thinking more or less, *Okay, this is my value. This what I bring to the table. This is my angle.*

I was intelligent enough to know it wasn't fair and it wasn't right, but that seemed beside the point. I remember thinking that it didn't *matter* whether or not I agreed. Things were going to go on as they were and I needed to work with it. I had to adapt. I wasn't confident enough or mature enough to take a stand and try to change things; I was determined to play the game. And believe me, I wasn't in tears thinking of having to play the friggin' game. I was excited. I was like, *Yay! I'm gonna do something bad!*

My parents were paying very little attention to me, so it was the perfect time to try something risky. I decided that my new look would be a Heavy Metal chick. It was not nerdy. It was cool. I would make myself into Jeff Hunter's dream girl. I figured I could probably pull off the look, because it didn't require a bunch of expensive clothing. The rock look was just black concert T-shirts, short skirts and high heels. I had most of that in my closet already.

The problem with me was that I saw everything in black and white. I was very extreme. When I set my mind to be cool, I was going to be cool no matter what it took. If something didn't feel right to me, I wouldn't stop and re-evaluate. I would barrel right past the feeling and push myself to follow through with the plan. I didn't consider that there were many subcultures of cool and uncool. I just knew there was good (boring, nerdy, wallflower), and there was bad (sexy, pretty, cool).

I chose bad.

CHAPTER THREE

Balls of Steel

Cue AC/DC's Back in Black

I busted through the glass doors of Middleton in slow motion, with my hair flowi- (*needle scratches record*)…wait…it was too stiff with hair spray to flow. Anyway, I strutted into the school and unveiled my new look: lots of leopard skin, short skirt, tight shirt, high heels and of course, my usual ton of makeup. My mother bought me all of the clothes. I don't know if she realized what she was buying, but I know she regretted it. I felt powerful and sexy with my new slim figure and newly bigger boobs (my dedication to bust exercises propped my C cup boobs up into the air). My nightly sit-ups made my stomach flat and my waist small. I was wearing more form fitting clothing instead of big, baggy sweaters. Upper middle class jaws dropped all through the school. I wasn't interested in any of the guys in my class, so I enjoyed the fact that they were suddenly turning into blubbering jackasses around me. I wanted to stamp out a cigarette in front of them like Sandy in *Grease*. I felt powerful, intoxicated by the attention. I was no longer a wallflower, the girl in the corner being ignored. The other girls in my class looked like children suddenly; they didn't intimidate me anymore. They could go ahead, group up, and sing some Pet Shop Boys on the way to P.E. I could steal any of their boyfriends now. *Bring it,* I thought.

My mom let me go through my metamorphosis, although she flat out told me that I looked like a 'street walker' in certain outfits. My dad angrily told me I looked like a whore. I was hurt; I thought I looked cool and fashionable, like a girl from a Motley Crue video. My mom tried to warn me a few times about dressing so promiscuously, but I ignored it. Pro*mis*cuously? What did that even mean? *Please.* What did *she* know? She wore glasses, had frizzy hair, and was not sexy. I started getting dress code violation citations at school for too much makeup and too short of skirts. My mom started to get pissed at me, but I told her the woman who wrote my citations wore ten times more makeup than me and she was out to get me.

Things got very low for my mother at the end of 1987. My grandfather was diagnosed with bone cancer and had only months to live. It was very sudden. It put her into a tailspin to see her father in such a state. She was the only person he would let take care of him. He passed away that winter, right around Christmas. My mother was absolutely *destroyed;* she could not function. She loved her father more than anything. The sad thing is, she never snapped out of it. I don't know if I ever saw her truly happy again.

As soon as her father passed away, she had even less tolerance for my father. She seemed tired; she seemed to have given up the fight. I was selfish about the whole thing- I was just happy I could do more of what I wanted. I dressed even skimpier, and started to tape pictures to my wall. Madonna? No. Puppies in a basket? No. Duran Duran? No. I taped pictures of Stephen Pearcy grinding his microphone stand and pictures of Nikki Sixx with pin-pricked pupils and an extended tongue. I took the pictures from my new favorite magazines: *Circus* and *Hit*

Parader. They were certainly not the same as *Seventeen* or *Teen-*instead of quizzes and skin care tips, I was reading about wild tours, drug abuse issues, and sexy women. Even worse than my reading about those things at fourteen was my sister reading about them at twelve. Her wall became so packed with pictures of Poison, Bon Jovi, and Cinderella, it was a collage all the way to the ceiling (she filled in hard-to-reach spaces with pictures of rockers she didn't even like all that much, like Billy Idol).

Because of my mother's creeping depression, my sister and I were sent to my newly widowed grandmother's house in Canoga Park each weekend. We didn't know why we were being sent there, but we didn't care. Instead of spending time with our grandmother, we went off on our own and became hooligans, shoplifting important items like makeup and more magazines. I remember feeling completely thrilled. I felt so free walking around in my acid washed jean jacket with Becky and Karen in tow. Men honked at us as they drove by, and my ego ballooned even further. It didn't matter that they had leaf blowers and lawn mowers in the back of their trucks and no green cards, I was getting attention. My sister and I went to Karen's on the weekends that we weren't at our grandmother's house and we watched her video tape of *The Lost Boys* (starring Jason Patric and Keifer Sutherland), about three thousand times.

We rented a video camera that winter. I was overjoyed because I *loved* filming things. I had always filmed in my head, meaning as I lived my life, I tried to see everything through a camera lens. I really loved the idea of capturing our life on film for the first time. I had **so** many things I wanted to film. One of the first things I wanted to capture was my favorite place in the world: My childhood friends Christopher and David Ashford's house. I begged my mom to take us there. I forgot if Karen's dad took us, or my mom took us- I don't remember how it was set up, but we did go over, and I ran around trying to capture all of my memories with the camera. I filmed every part of Christopher and David's house. I had grown up there and I wanted be able to always look back on it. Carol, their mother, was not home that day.

I can't remember exactly how it went down, but Carol heard that we were there filming and blew up. She was *really* upset that I was filming her house when she thought it was messy. I didn't see mess- I just saw the house I loved my whole life. It looked as it always did. I don't know what words were spoken between my mother and Carol; I just knew that Carol and my mother's friendship ended that day. We were told that we were not allowed back at the house, and that our families were no longer friends. We could see Christopher and David again when we were grown-ups, on our own time. I was absolutely floored. I didn't understand. Not see Christopher and David again until we were...*adults*? Wait...*what*? I couldn't accept it. It was as if someone had just broken the news of a death. We had been friends since we were babies. Our families were so close! I was devastated.

One day while I was looking for money to steal out of my mom's room, I found a letter in her jewelry box. It was from Carol Ashford, who wrote that I had a big mouth and some other mean things. I already thought I was a piece of shit so it didn't surprise me that someone else thought so too, but it wounded me to my core. I was deeply, deeply hurt to hear what she thought of me. Had my mother defended me? Was that why they were no longer speaking? I didn't know.

Later that year, Carol started to do some troubling and strange things and was admitted into a mental institution as a result. My sister and I went to Christopher and David's and sat out in the backyard with them. It was painful to see them hanging their heads. All four of us felt broken and weak. It shattered me. They were our dear friends and such a huge part of the happiness in my childhood. I thought, once again, *This can't really be happening*.

Carol came back a few months later. She was back to normal as long as she stayed on her medication. But she was never friends with my mother again.

My grandfather's death, my mother's depression, and the loss of my closest childhood friends hit me hard. I didn't know how to deal with my feelings. I closed myself in my room alone with Ratt, L.A. Guns and Motley Crue records blasting. Their songs were almost exclusively about drugs/strip clubs (Motley) or about girls and sex (Ratt and L.A. Guns). The subject matter was the total nightmare of most parents. I listened to the music and stared at the guys on the album covers, or looked at their pictures in magazines, for hours at a time. I fantasized about Stephen Pearcy, Robbin Crosby and Warren DeMartini of Ratt and Nikki Sixx of Motley Crue. They all had long hair and tattoos, wore eyeliner, and rocked leather pants. The thought of screwing any of them scared the shit out of me. I was certain the Ratt guys would probably give me some crazy, horrible VD and Nikki Sixx would surely sacrifice me to the devil after doing lines off my corpse.

There was other music out in 1988, but I was not interested in Joan Jett's "I Hate Myself for Loving You" or George Harrison's "I Got My Mind Set on You." Nor was I into "Don't Worry, Be Happy" from the hit movie of the year, *Beetlejuice*. Uh, *yeah*, as if it's *that* easy. I wanted to break a banjo over that guy's head.

Music and TV had been my role models for a few years by then, but this time, instead of trying to squeeze meaning out of a Beastie Boys song, I was actually getting some answers. Ratt had a song about a fifteen-year-old girl. Fifteen? Well I would be fifteen in one year! That meant I could start being a *real* rock chick!

A band called Guns N' Roses started to get really big, and I considered their *Appetite for Destruction* album a jackpot of information. I took it as my guide to life. Not having my parents' guidance is really no excuse, because I could have chosen God. I could have opened the Bible and taken my cues from it. My family was still technically Christian and I attended a Christian school. But more than that, I always had a personal relationship with God. I had been privately praying every day since I was eight years old. I had always felt close with God in the past.

This is going to sound incredibly kooky and superstitious, but I am going to tell you anyways. Though I had other Motley Crue albums, I promised God I would never buy their *Theatre of Pain* album (an album I desperately wanted, because I loved the song "Home Sweet Home"). The album cover featured an inverted pentagram, which was used in Satanism. Being Christian, I felt that it would be disrespectful to God and to my religion if I bought that particular album. I know it sounds corny but I didn't want to break the promise, so I thought I would be slick. I asked for it for my birthday and Karen bought it for me. I thought, *Hey, I didn't buy it, so it's not like I broke the promise.* Well, God doesn't play that shit.

I had a rabbit named Taffy. She was with me through all of my formative years and was as special to me as a childhood dog would be to someone else. It was she who I went to when I was sad and wanted to cry. I got a lot of comfort out of petting the little baby-soft spot between her ears. One time I was crying to her and a little tear dropped from her eye. Maybe it was just watering, but I thought, *Wow...she is sad for me!* Anyway, I walked outside to visit her that *very day* I got the Motley Crue record. When I got to her hutch and looked down into it, I shrieked and jumped back. She was lying on the side of the cage, the other rabbits still hopping around her quietly. Her eyes were white. She was dead. My heart broke in a billion, trillion pieces. She was so special to me. She was the best pet I ever had or have had since. I couldn't stop crying. I thought, *It just has to be a coincidence.* I was too scared to think it might be a sign or a warning. I shook off the feeling.

A few months later, I went to the rabbit hutch to see the remaining rabbits and there was a random crucifix that I had never seen in my life, laying underneath a pile of fur in that same corner of the cage. I thought...*This is just another weird coincidence ...right?* I know, I know, I sound like a nut. But it really happened and it scared me! I found a random crucifix! I thought I would be struck by some lightning right there in the backyard.

So anyway folks, I completely strayed from all of the things that made me special and unique. Despite all of the hard work I put into creating my sexy image, there was something about it that made me sad. It was not fulfilling like I thought it would be. It didn't make me magically happy. I dressed like a twenty-five-year old stripper. I wore more makeup than a Folies Bergère showgirl and I was still bulimic, just to top things off with a regurgitated cherry. Any time I was under stress, I left to throw up.

The staff at Middleton was concerned over my appearance and demeanor. There were special church sermons based on the bad influence of rock music, with Motley Crue lyrics quoted. I didn't flinch. I was amused at hearing my nerdy teachers talk about The Seventh Veil on Sunset Boulevard.

We had a class picnic at a park, where I took it upon myself to boldly approach a twenty-something guy with long hair and talk to him. I think I was just trying to show off in front of my classmates. One of my teachers took me aside and desperately tried to get me to slow down. I just remember hearing the eloquent words, "If you don't watch out, you are going to end up being raped in the back of a van." It was harsh, but no one was getting through to me any other way. In hindsight, that teacher was trying harder than my parents were to scare me away from the wrong path, so I have to respect that.

My sister and I wanted to see a new film about the Sunset Strip music scene in Hollywood called *The Decline of Western Civilization, Part II: The Metal Years.* I knew two things about the Sunset Strip. One, long-haired guys in bands were there. Heavy Metal type bands. Two, my mother's younger sister, my beautiful and hip Aunt Billie, used to hang on Sunset when I was a kid. She wore sophisticated and fashionable clothes; had long, dark, feathered hair, and wore tons of perfectly applied makeup. She was into bands like KISS and was dating a musician, whom she later married. I had idolized her my entire life. She was the coolest person I knew. It was always in the back of my head that her scene was where it was at. She *epitomized* cool. Aside from that, I had chosen the image of a Rock Chick. The movie was a chance for me to gather information on what I was trying to represent. I knew I needed to see it to have any credibility as a bad girl.

My mother took one of her last stands and was adamant that we not see the movie. She insisted that at fourteen and twelve, we were too young. My father, trying to be our "pal" and on our level, let us go.

I was both scared and intrigued by *The Metal Years*. The Hollywood music scene looked so wild. The girls were half-naked hoochies and the guys were…*men*. They were not boys my age. They were men who expected to *have sex*. That part scared me, but the rest of the scene looked incredibly fascinating. I was introduced to a new band in the movie called Faster Pussycat. I bought their tape right away. I was also introduced to a club called the Cathouse, which appeared to be the Mothership of the whole scene. It was run by some guy named Riki Rachtman, who appeared very confident, despite not being rock star skinny. He was a Steve Rubell type, a scene maker, the person who chose the beautiful and cool people to assemble at his club. He seemed like one of those guys who would have no problem not letting you in if you weren't pretty.

I knew I didn't live too far from the Sunset Strip. I decided I *had* to go see what it was all about. I would be a fool to not check it out! It wasn't like I lived in Wisconsin. I lived twenty minutes from Hollywood. It was too intriguing, too intoxicating, too exciting. While I sat in that theatre, I thought…*Okay…I am fourteen. I live with my parents. I don't know anyone who hangs*

*in Hollywood. I go to a Christian school. I don't drive and I
don't know anyone who drives. How am I going to do this?*

I never thought, *No way, there is no way I could pull that off,
little old me.* I was like, *I will find out what kind of person gets
into that exclusive crowd and I will make it my **mission.*** I wasn't
the type of person to do something half-assed. I was far too
manic. I had extreme enthusiasm for any subject in which I was
interested. It would have been great if I had found something
else interesting, say…tennis. But no, it was Sunset Boulevard in
Hollywood. If I was to be a *true* bad girl, I would need to put
myself in with the cool people. It might take a minute, but I was
convinced I would get there. I kept it in the back of my mind for
when the right opportunity arose.

I spent all of ninth grade flirting with the boys in the younger
grades, soaking up all of their admiration. They worshipped me
and bowed down to my hotness. I was cruising along in my life,
listening to Def Leppard's "Pour Some Sugar on Me" and
pouring beer in my hair for highlights, when it hit me. The
school year was ending. I panicked. I was going to start high
school in only a few months and *I still hadn't kissed a boy.* I had
avoided all requests for dates. I had done nothing but tease,
tease, tease. I was all talk. I preferred being admired from afar. I
didn't want to actually *do* anything with a boy. I just wanted
attention. And now I would be the dork in high school who came
from a nerdy private school and who hadn't even *kissed*
someone! I would be laughed right off the campus! I was sure
that everyone in high school was surely already having crazy
orgies. I had to get over my fear and kiss someone. And I had
exactly three months to do it. Did I find some nerd to practice
on? No. Did I pick a stranger, so in case I was a horrible kisser, I
would never see him again? No. I thought to myself, *Who do I
really want to kiss?* There was only one boy who I truly wanted
to kiss.

One summer evening, I expertly applied way too much makeup,
put on a tight, turquoise blue tank top and a white mini skirt (that

had "skorts" underneath, but we won't talk about that because it will ruin the coolness of my story). I then walked across the street and around the corner and knocked on Jeff Hunter's door. I had huge balls. They were like bowling balls, coming out of my skorts. There was also quite a big dash of crazy in the mix.

When I first met Jeff in the fifth grade, my hair was in two braids like Laura Ingalls from *Little House on the Prairie* and I wore a thick pair of glasses. It would be safe to say that this guy would *never* have considered me. It was also safe to say I no longer looked like that. I couldn't believe I was on his doorstep. I was knocking on the door of my *dream boy*. I was scared, but determined- I was pretty confident he would be attracted to me based on the reaction of most of the free world, but there was a chance he would laugh in my face or say he had a girlfriend.

He answered the door. The first thing I thought was that he looked so much smaller than I had imagined. He hadn't grown! His shoulders were bigger though, and he had some facial stubble, as well as a bit of acne. He was definitely a teenage boy. My heart started thumping hard in my chest when I realized I was looking into those eyes again after three years. He wasn't wearing a shirt, and he was chewing. His hair wasn't as long as I would have preferred; it was only a little past his ears. It was thin, wispy, and strawberry blond. I introduced myself and told him I was in his grade school classes and that I used to wear glasses. It took him a minute, but he remembered me (or at least he said he did). I think his family was having fish for dinner and the house smelled like fish, because I remember he apologized for the smell. I was thinking, *That's coming from my underwear*. Kidding, kidding. Anyway, if I remember correctly, we talked for a few minutes and all went well. He was responsive and polite. I had a feeling he was definitely going to overlook the fact that I had showed up on his doorstep unannounced. He said he was going to finish eating dinner, and asked me to come back in an hour or so. Maybe he was going to wait for his parents to go to bed, I'm not sure. I remember being both shocked and pleased with myself for going after him. I was also happy that he was interested and wanted me to come back.

I came back later that night and he led me straight to his room. I don't remember his living room at all. His room was off to the left of the front door, which was lucky for him because it was perfect for sneaking in a girl. When I got to his room, it was really dark and there were glowing posters of Ozzy and Megadeth and other really hard groups that scared me. I guess those posters were his mood lighting. I thought of how many times I had been warned about the evils of that music at my Christian school. It was kind of thrilling. We sat on his teenage boy bed in the dark and he put on some music that completely threw me off: **Eazy E and NWA!** *Rap!* I was thinking, *Wait a minute…I didn't spend years studying how to be a rocker chick to finally make it to your room and then hear some rap!* Then I think he put on some Randy Rhoads crap. He loved Randy Rhoads, Ozzy's late guitarist, whom I distinctly remembered my Aunt Billie partying with (she said he put out a cigarette on a really expensive piano at someone's house). Jeff finally turned on the TV- some bad movie. That is when we started kissing.

You know, when I think about my first kiss, I am happy it was with the boy who I had a crush on and all that. But I wish I could tell a story that involves my hair in ribbons and a boy stealing a kiss by the old oak tree. I guess it is because I waited until the summer before high school that my first kiss was nothing like that. Jeff, already fifteen at that time, started grinding on me. Dry humping. We were lying in his bed and I had no idea what to do, I just went with it. My tongue was all over the place-I was the worst kisser. At one point, I felt my tongue go into a little hole on his face. It was his nostril! (laughs) Someone actually told me months later- *Hey, you really suck; you have to get it together.*

So there I was, in this kid's bed, laying down in the dark. He started to gently push my head toward his crotch. I had no idea how to do that kind of stuff. I didn't know what it even entailed. I had to get out of there; I was in over my head. I left hours later on that summer night, with my face raw with stubble-burn. I was scared but also absolutely thrilled: I had my first kiss. And it was with my dream boy. I made it happen. I marched right up to this boy and he was interested. He was interested enough to kiss me. I made out with Jeff Hunter!

I felt on top of the world. I couldn't believe it. The next day, I called one of the boys from school that used to worship me, Todd Lewis. We had actually become friends because he was into Heavy Metal. He also wore thick glasses and had an afro, so I didn't find him cute, but he was good to bounce ideas off. I needed to get the scoop on how to do the dirty stuff. I had to figure it out- and fast. Todd explained to me what was to be done, and he only knew from watching porn and looking at dirty pictures. He told me exactly what to do. I lay on my bed and looked out the window while listening to him. I could see the tree in Jeff's back yard, where he used to have a tree house when we were younger.

With the exception of going to see the hit movie *Who Framed Roger Rabbit?* with my parents, I spent that summer hanging out with Jeff. I went further and further with him, stopping short of intercourse. I felt uncomfortable with myself. I didn't like the things I was doing. It didn't feel right inside, but I told myself I didn't want to be the one nerd in high school who hadn't hooked up with a guy. I wanted the experience and was determined to continue with it.

The thrill of landing Jeff wore off pretty quickly. I felt unhappy inside. I had no interest in being myself. I wanted to be what I thought *he* would like: someone really sexy. I dressed very skimpily, wore lots of makeup and tried to talk real "adult." I was crushed when he told me he didn't want me to be his girlfriend. I thought I was doing everything right. I looked and acted like I walked straight out of a Van Halen video; I thought it was every guy's dream. I didn't realize that my overly sexual behavior kept him from ever respecting me or really getting to know me. He treated me as I portrayed myself: some hoochie. I was *this* close to putting out my arms and shimmying at him like Pat Benetar, in my short, cut-off Guns N' Roses T-shirts, tiny miniskirts, and my light grey Vans.

My mother did her best to stop me from moving too fast. She kicked my bedroom door open on more than one occasion. I was caught in many compromising situations. Some days we weren't allowed to see each other, so Jeff hid in my closet. Other times I snuck out my window. I left my lights on and kept the music blasting before sneaking out. One time I turned on my hairdryer before I snuck out and my sister had to climb out of *her* window, and in through my window, to go and shut the hair dryer off, to make it look like I was in there doing my hair.

Jeff introduced my newly thirteen-year-old sister to his fifteen or sixteen-year-old buddy Mike Ferris. He had a mullet, buckteeth and a job at a dildo factory (yes). Mike fell instantly in love with my sister and showered her with roses and love songs on his guitar. He was goofy and clumsy, but had a good heart. My sister secretly called him "The Clums" once she got sick of him. They used to make out in her room for three hours straight. One time I got a tape recorder and put it under her bed. After a half an hour, my voice came on and said, "You're too younnnnng ...you're too younnnnng," like a man in a haunted house. I was kind of hurt that Mike liked *her* so much and Jeff was only interested in me for some action. But that is the way I behaved and what I put out there. My sister was relatively innocent and was acting like herself. I should have taken notes from her.

After a while, my mom started to bond with Jeff. She said he was climbing over the fence in the back yard to go to his friend Stephen's house one day, when he slipped and slammed his nuts onto the fence. He couldn't even move he was in so much pain. She helped him down and gave him ice and all that. After that they became BFFs, to my dismay.

My dad invited fifteen-year-old Jeff in for a beer a few times, trying to be cool with him. I thought I would like that, but I didn't. I didn't want my dad to stop me from seeing him, but I was also confused that he wasn't trying to protect me more. Jeff revealed to me that my dad went over for a talk with his dad and they smoked a joint together. My dad told his dad to make sure his son didn't get me pregnant. Get me *pregnant*? He didn't even tell him to try to prevent his son from having sex with me? It was as if my dad gave his blessing for this kid to plow me. Luckily, I never gave into actual intercourse, but hell, if I had, it would have been okay with my dad. Thanks, Dad.

CHAPTER FOUR

Down the Rabbit Hole

September rolled around and I turned fifteen on the first day of school. I went to the local public high school, which was only three houses down from where I lived. Middleton had been a very small school that had a ninth grade class of about twenty people, most of whom continued on to a private high school. My new school was HUGE, and full of people I had never before seen.

I was completely alone; I had no one to talk to whatsoever. I was walking around this *enormous* school, with all of these lockers and different buildings and I was so scared, I was shaking. I couldn't believe I had only five minutes between classes to find the next class. I couldn't even find my locker, as a matter of fact. The entire three grades of Middleton Junior High had taken place solely on the second floor of one office building! My whole junior high experience consisted of only three classrooms! I couldn't believe I had been set loose in this colossal institution with no one to tell me where to go and what to do. I wanted to run back to my house and cry for ten days straight.Not only was

I scared, alone, and ignorant of where anything was, but I had gone completely overboard on my "look." I thought, *Okay, this is high school. I need to walk through the doors looking like a hot babe!* So I put on something really skimpy, because I thought that is what high school kids looked like. I had never been so wrong.

I barreled through the doors in an off-the-shoulders black shirt, a really short skirt and very high heels. The entire place looked at me as if I was insane. I was floored. I thought, *Isn't this what I'm supposed to look like, who I'm supposed to be?* I was wayyyyy overdressed for a student and way overdressed for a teenager in general. People started laughing at me. Guys talked shit under their breath; girls giggled. I could hear people whispering that I was a hooker. I wanted to die. I teetered around in my high heels, trying to walk on cracked cement with my new books in hand and a cigarette hanging off my lips. I could barely make it up the stairs without falling. I looked around at the other girls and they were dressed in regular clothes, like the girls at Middleton. Almost all of them looked completely innocent. I looked like I was about to hit the stage at The Spearmint Rhino. I couldn't believe I was so off the mark with my look. What an idiot! No one wanted to be my friend. I would only embarrass the shit out of anyone who stood next to me. I was so humiliated that I stared at the ground all day- I couldn't look anyone in the eye.

I ran into Jeff Hunter a few times at school and he wouldn't give me the time of day. He had distanced himself from me and it was clear I was not to try to hang around him. He had quickly started dating a senior named Shannon, and she was already his girlfriend. He told her he had hooked up with me over the summer and she was not very happy about that. She took to yelling "SLUT!" at me in the halls, in front of everyone. This was only in September and I had three more years of high school to go. My reputation was completely ruined by the first month of school and, even though that girl would graduate in June, that rep stuck by me and ruined me for the rest of high school. I was still a virgin and I was already being called a whore.

But back to this scraggly, hesher bitch, Shannon. She was pretty ballsy, now that I think about it, because she was about half the size of me. I should've kicked her ass, but I didn't know that I could at that point.

I remember being pissed that I spent all of that time becoming the Ultimate Rock Chick and then looking at who Jeff Hunter chose over me. She wore flannel shirts and those knee-high, suede moccasin boots with fringe. She had huge bags under her eyes, wore no makeup, and had thin, short, feathered hair with a roach clip fastened into it. She had no tits, no hips, and no lips. *Come on!* I thought.

But I was too much of everything and I was displaying it all at the same time; I was too embarrassing for any boy to get near. I remember wondering why all of the girls in the locker room were staring at me when I changed for P.E. Must have been the fact that I was in a red lace Fredrick's of Hollywood matching bra and panty set while they were wearing Sears cotton undies. I wore full-on lingerie under my clothes! I mean, how did I even *get* that stuff?

So anyway, after a month or so, I did the only thing someone in my situation could do. I found the misfit crowd who hung out in the smoking section. They were the rejects of all of the cliques. Anyone who didn't fit in to the popular crowds went there. There were a lot of heshers (also known as rockers or Heavy Metal kids) in black Iron Maiden concert T-shirts and Vans; guys and girls in tie-dye Grateful Dead shirts; some alternative /goth /ska /skinhead /punk types in black (with a bit of purple or red); and the occasional chick who looked too old to be in school, and who looked like a stripper (that was the group I was put into and there were only two of us at most).

The group of misfit kids was pretty cool. Most of them had problems with which I could identify. I smoked Marlboro Reds with them at lunch and hoped I would make a friend. To my relief, a tough girl named Abby started talking to me. She had wide set eyes and large features; light brown, messy hair parted to the side, and lots of eyeliner. The bottom half of her hair was dyed black and the top part was light brown- it looked like it grew out and she gave up on doing her roots. She never smiled. When she talked to me, I couldn't tell if she was deciding to kick my ass or she didn't mind me. I shared a lighter with her.

I looked around my school to see if there were any guys who were into the Sunset Strip scene. They would be considered "glam" guys and would most likely be into Poison and other bands that wore makeup and looked like women. All I saw was the usual white trash heshers with thin hair and black T-shirts. I was more interested in the type of people I saw in *The Metal Years* movie: guys with dyed black hair and style. I sighed. *Nope. Not at this school.*

Or so I thought. One day while I was smoking a cigarette with Abby by the bungalows, I saw a glam guy walk by. My head turned as he passed and I nearly choked on my cigarette: he was 6' 1" or 6' 2", had long, dyed black hair, pink Converse All Stars and tight black pants. He wore a colorful t-shirt and a fedora with a leopard print band around it. I knew straight away he was the type of guy with whom I would need to align myself if I was going to get into the Hollywood music scene.

I needed info. I did some recon by asking around the smoking area, teetering around in my black velvet high heels and leopard-print tube skirt. In between games of Hacky Sack, a few hippies told me some dirt. The guy's name was Jamie. He was in eleventh grade, and he was the drummer in a band that played on the Sunset Strip. They called him a "Glam Fag." *Perfect!*

I was thrilled, rubbing my hands together. Now I would just have to get him to notice me! He appeared to be the only person who *hadn't*. Whenever he passed the smoking section, he never socialized with the big group of mostly guys. I never saw him smile, only smoke cigarettes, hit on girls, and make sarcastic remarks. He walked around with an air of conceit, aloofness, and all around dickery. I saw that he wrote "I am God" on the side of his Converse. I thought that maybe I saw wrong. Certainly no one would write such a thing...would they?

It was a Friday in mid-October when he got around to noticing me. He walked up to me and asked me what kind of bands I liked and I stuttered some sort of answer designed to impress him. While looking around at other chicks, he kind of *told* me we were going to go on a date. I was a virgin, but he couldn't tell that by my revealing clothes that I found so cool and grown up. All they did was advertise to this guy that I would sleep with him. Not what I had intended.

I awkwardly agreed to go out with him. I went home and announced to my parents that I was going to go on my first date that very night. They were like, *WHAT?* They were bumping into each other trying to figure out what to do. They hadn't thought of the rules yet, I could tell. They were probably trying to come up with something right then and there. They were used to me hanging out with Jeff at our house, but this was different: I was going to get into a *car* with a boy they had never met and drive away with him.

I was uncomfortable as I got ready that evening. Jamie had been almost *mean* to me when he asked me out. He didn't smile at me or look me in the eye when he talked to me. He seemed almost bored even asking me out. I could have sworn I saw him roll his eyes when I was answering his questions! It didn't feel right. But I had nothing to compare it to. It fit right along with my impression of men. They wanted you to be sexy and they wanted you for only one thing. I felt a red flag go up in my head, but I quickly pushed it away. I told myself I needed to do this. I needed to go. I didn't want to be the only girl who hadn't gone on a real date. The guy was a Hollywood guy in a band and he hung on Sunset. He reminded me of Tommy Lee. He wasn't some little wimp like Jeff. *I have to go on this date.* This was my chance to get into the Hollywood crowd, the one I read about in *L.A. Weekly* and *Music Connection*. This guy had a car, he had the look, and he appeared to have had the connections to where I wanted to be. I had to go.

It was freezing that fall and winter in California. I remember being very cold. I wore black tights, a black skirt, and a leather jacket over my top. I distinctly remember wearing a cross earring in one ear and a silver spider web or shark's tooth in the other. Jamie called me to get directions to my house and I was very meek over the phone. He shouted at me a few times and sounded very bored, like he was going through the motions just to screw me. He didn't even try to hide it. It was like he had done it hundreds of times and he was sure he was about to do it once again. He told me to wear something that was easy to take off, and that I had better not be on my period. Yes, you read correctly. Those were his exact words.

I was scared shitless. If I flaked, what would happen at school? This was my chance to be cool and date someone older. Maybe I could get out of doing what he was implying…maybe I was hearing him wrong. Was this what the Hollywood crowd was like? How would I ever handle it, if I couldn't even go on one date with a Hollywood guy? *I have to toughen up and deal with it.* I made myself go against my danger instinct, something I would do countless more times as a teenager. I told myself to bear whatever happened, to resist my urge to flee. That is how I dealt with my father and that is how I would soon deal with a lot more men. I would mentally shut down and bear it.

Jamie pulled up in front of my house in a white Mustang and honked the horn with the motor still running. His license plate frames said, "It's hard to be humble when you're as great as I am." My mother told me I had to bring him in to meet her and my dad. She at least knew what to do there. I ran out to the car and said that my parents wanted to meet him. He ignored me and said that we were late or something, and to just get in the car. I blindly obeyed. We sped off. I think he even burned rubber! I weakly mentioned the curfew my parents gave me and he ignored me. I looked down on the dashboard and the first thing I saw was a picture of a blond girl. I asked him who it was and he sarcastically said, "My fucking pen pal. Who do you *think*? It's my girlfriend." He had a picture of his GIRLFRIEND on his dashboard! While taking me on a *DATE*! I am not making this shit up.

I was stunned. This guy was ten kinds of rude. In two years' time, I would eat his kind for breakfast, but that night I was not there yet. I did not know my value. I was terribly scared, but strangely excited. He asked me if I had a cigarette. I said I only had one left, and he said, "That'll do." I gave him my last Marlboro Red and he popped it in his mouth while turning up the radio. He had a dark five o' clock shadow and very pale skin- I thought he was hot. He wore leather pants that I found to be a little much at the moment, but whatever. It was very L.A. Guns, a band who I liked very much. He asked me where a liquor store was, and I guess I directed him to the nearest one. I just remember him coming back with a bottle of Southern Comfort. I had never even heard of it. I had never tasted alcohol. He opened the bottle in the car as we drove and told me to have a sip.

Southern Comfort was disgusting; it lasted like licorice and cough syrup. It was warm going down my throat and I felt buzzed after one sip. *One sip.* I suddenly felt wonderful, euphoric even. I *loved* the feeling; I felt bold and happy, rolling down the window and feeling cold wind on my face. I smiled into the night air. Hearing Poison on the radio, being with a guy with long black hair and a white Mustang…This is what I wanted. This is what I was waiting for. This was the Hollywood scene and I was ready. *Let me at 'em,* I thought.

After a few sips of Southern Comfort, I became drunk. I tried to look at all of the street names on the way because I was sure I was going to end up stranded and need to call my dad. I remember seeing the street name Coldwater Canyon and thinking, *Damn... I have never been this far from home without my parents!* Jamie told me we were going to his buddy Teddy St. John's house and not to embarrass him.

I stumbled into Teddy's place completely inebriated. I somehow noticed that there were bullet holes in the wall as I was told that two other girls were going to join us. The first one came over a few minutes later and we went to pick up the second one. Once everyone was in the car, Teddy got in the passenger seat with Jamie and I got in the back with the two other girls. We drove to Santa Monica beach. They laid down a woven blanket, and starting passing the bottle around in the darkness. Jamie sighed and said to me in a bored manner, "Let's go take a walk and look at the lights of the pier." He didn't even sound like he was trying to be con*vin*cing. I was too much of an easy target.

We walked toward the ocean and he said, "Let's stop here." He laid down my leather jacket in the sand and told me to lie down. I did. He started kissing me and the only thing I could think was that it was different from Jeff Hunter. He tasted like cigarettes and I could smell his leather pants- they must have been real leather, not pleather, because they were very fragrant. He kissed me for a few more seconds and then started pulling off my clothes. The phrase "Oh shit" slid through my rubbery mind. I didn't know how to get out of it. My mind was slow; my body was limp and lifeless. I felt paralyzed. He pulled out a condom and started to put it on and lay on top of me. *Think of something!* I tried to tell myself as I heard the waves crashing near us.

Then I got an idea. I would pretend to pass out. I let my head drop backwards and shut my eyes. He yelled "Shit!" and started calling my name in a loud tone. He kind of smacked my head a little to wake me up. I pretended not to wake up and hoped he would just leave me alone and get dressed. Not a chance. He began to have sex with me, thinking I was passed out. It hurt so badly when he tore my hymen that I couldn't pretend that I was passed out anymore. I grimaced with pain. I didn't want him to do it and yet I couldn't speak. I couldn't say no. I couldn't move my body, I just laid there in the sand. It didn't even slightly cross my mind to push the person off of me and kick him the balls and yell *No!* It didn't cross my mind to push his hands away, or resist in any way at all. I truly thought it was all I was worth.

After a few thrusts he stopped, pissed off. He told me to get up and get dressed. He must have either seen that it was hurting me, or thought I was too much of a dead fish, but either way he stopped. It was too late for me though, because I had lost my virginity. I had only had my first kiss a few months prior, and I was on my very first date and had just had my very first sip of alcohol.

Later that night, as they were taking me home so they could continue to party with the other two girls (Jamie screwed another of the girls that night as well), I had them pull over so I could throw up on the side of the freeway. I was spinning and miserable. They dumped me off at my house at two or three in the morning and sped off. I don't remember which of my parents yelled at me, but I was miserable and humiliated and I knew I was in over my head.

Once I was in my room, I started crying and peeled off my zebra-striped underwear. I looked down in them and saw blood, which sobered me up enough to realize that I had lost my virginity to someone I had just met. Someone who talked down to me... someone who had intercourse with me while he thought I was passed out. I glanced down closer at the blood in my underwear and saw something shining- it was my cross earring. I am not kidding, this really happened. My heart stopped. I was staring at this cross and thinking ...*Oh shit. Is this another sign? Is the ground going to break open and suck me down into the fiery pits of hell?* I was certain God was going to plum fuck me up for being so awful and for going against all of His wishes. I was sure of it. I pulled the earring out of my underwear, put it on my dressing table, and passed out.

The next day I was told I was grounded. My parents no longer

72

trusted me and I was embarrassed and ashamed. I was torn between feeling bold and brazen that I had had such a crazy night and feeling guilty and regretful. I went from crying in my pillow to getting a rush thinking about being in the car with long-haired guys and drinking and being a grown up. All and all, I don't think I understood how special and chaste virginity was. I do remember feeling that it was very final- I couldn't turn back and be a kid again. It bothered me, but I brushed it off. My first reaction was to get out my Barbie dolls and play with them. I think I washed all of their hair. I also made sure to hang out with Karen and try to be my old self by playing around, crank calling, spying on neighbors, all the things we did as preteens.

Jamie never called me again. He completely avoided me at school. I thought, *Wow. Okay. So this is how it works?* I had this...this...certain body part. And...guys wanted to get at it. They wanted to have sex. And that was it. I ruled out that it was some pleasurable thing. It certainly was not that. It was...it was...I didn't know *what* it was to me. I suddenly had questions. I didn't know who to talk to, who to confide in. I was irked that I couldn't find out more information on sex. As much as it was flaunted all over the place on MTV, the actual details of it seemed so guarded, so hushed. I just didn't understand the whole thing. In my mind, it was definitely not something regarded as emotional, loving or in any way special- why did parents, schools, and churches try to tell you it was?

Two weeks later I met another long-haired boy at school named Matt. I don't remember if I liked him or he liked me or how it happened, but I think he just came up and asked me out. He asked me if I wanted to go to a party on Halloween weekend. It was exactly two weeks after my first date. My parents didn't stick to their "you're grounded" rule, because they let me go with him.

This boy was a senior. He was not a Hollywood guy, but what the hell. He had long, brown hair and blue eyes and looked like he could have been a bad rocker kid but he was actually somewhat of a nerd. He drove his vintage Mustang up to my house and came to the door as my mother wanted. It was all shot to hell though, when my father told him, "Don't do anything I wouldn't do," in a joking manner, with a wink-wink 'between the guys' tone. He more or less gave his blessing for the boy to screw me. I was so confused. Is this *okay* with him? My *father*?

I wore an all-white dress and really high white stilettos, trying to look like Tawny Kitaen in the Whitesnake "Is This Love?" video. I didn't realize that fifteen-year-olds, shit, even twenty-*five*- year-olds were not dressing like that. I may have been dressed appropriately for a Hollywood party, where 'over the top' was a necessity to stand out over all the other girls, but at a high school *kegger*? I was the only girl there dressed as if I was working the ho stroll. I immediately started drinking antiseptic-tasting Bacardi 151, which is apparently all they had. It took me precisely five minutes to be incredibly drunk.

I remember when it hit me I could barely stand. I felt embarrassed because I knew I had to throw up. I crept away and locked myself in the bathroom. As I was throwing up, everything started spinning. I think I passed out shortly thereafter. I don't know how long I was in there, but a girl finally broke in. I remember people helping me down the stairs so my date could take me home. I was like rubber- I couldn't even hold myself up. I heard one person saying that they should put me in a shopping cart. I remember thinking …*Wow…people are making fun of me, I am a fool.* I blacked out shortly thereafter. I don't remember getting into his car, I don't remember us driving. I just remember waking up in the backseat. It was dark and I was looking up at a streetlight. There was someone on top of me and my dress was up around my waist. The guy was having sex with me. I was being date raped.

Losing my virginity had not been my idea but I was too afraid to say no. This time I literally woke up to find this person on top of me. I was asleep! The guy stopped when he realized I was awake. He seemed to feel guilty. He tried talking with me until I sobered up. He was not arrogant like Jamie, but he had just raped me while I was passed out. He certainly didn't think my father would hunt him down and shoot him, that's for sure.

I didn't get home that night until four in the morning and I was in huge trouble. I couldn't tell my parents what had happened. I could only cry. It was a crying like no crying I had ever experienced. It was a deep, thick, hard sort of crying, coming from way inside my guts.

The next few weeks were suicidal for me. I wanted to kill myself. It hit me what I had done. I had purposely created this sexy image and I now had a reputation of being a person that was not *me*. I looked like a girl who wanted to have sex! And I didn't *want* to have sex! I had a closet full of sexy clothes and high heels and bins full of makeup. I wanted out. I wanted to say "Cut!" to the director and walk off the set. I had just started the tenth grade only a month and a half prior and I still had *three* more *years* of this? I couldn't do it. I didn't want to do it. I truly wanted to die. I couldn't talk to anyone. I couldn't look anyone in the eye. I smoked cigarettes and hid in the bathroom stalls, crying in my leather jacket. I started ditching all of my classes and failing everything. I walked around in a daze, my hair a mess, tears at the edges of my eyes.

A few weeks passed and I didn't get a period. I thought, *No way. I can't be pregnant by this Matt guy... I am fifteen. What have I done?* I waited another week. I still didn't get my period. When I was two weeks late on my period, I started to look for Matt to tell him. He tried to dodge me; I couldn't get him to talk to me. He had avoided me, just as Jamie had quickly done. He probably heard from Jamie that I was easy, for all I know. Anyway, when I finally got him to talk to me, the first thing I noticed was that he looked hideous. He had short, feathered bangs; yellowed skin, and super hesher brown hair. After getting a good look at him I thought, *Why did I go out with this ugly bastard?* He was very short with me and said he had to be somewhere. I felt like I was starring in an After School Special. I told him that I was late on my period. I can't remember what he said- I think he said he would pay for half of an abortion or something. I went home and cried my eyes out. Things were not going as planned. I was supposed to be flipping my hair in slow motion somewhere.

I was reeling into a deep depression. I knew I couldn't turn back time and take my virginity back. I did a lot of walking around by myself during that time- I walked around my neighborhood, crying and smoking. I was usually barefoot- I couldn't tell you why. I think it was the beginning of a mental illness. My mind was splitting open and I just stopped caring.

I remember pouring a big mug of orange soda and walking down the hallway to my room. In the middle of walking, I threw the mug against the wall and kept walking. The soda splattered all over the wall and the mug and ice cubes fell to the carpet. I didn't even look back or miss a beat. It was that feeling of just truly not caring. Nothing mattered- why was I even alive? I went in my room, shut the door, and started writing. My dad opened the door not too much later and asked me if the mug was mine. I lifelessly said yes. He threw each ice cube at me with force. It hurt, and I knew I shouldn't have dropped my drink on purpose, but I didn't *care*. I didn't care about *anything*. I just sat there, letting him pelt me with ice cubes, watching the look of anger on his face.

I ended up getting my period. I wasn't pregnant. God gave me a pass. Did I learn my lesson? No. I put on a Guns N' Roses shirt that Todd Lewis had given me (because he was now into Public Enemy), and went out to find more trouble. I did do one smart thing though: I put myself on birth control pills. If I was going to have sex or even just be too drunk to know what was going on, then I needed a safety net. I didn't want to add an unwanted pregnancy to the mix.

In mid-November, I was walking down the street yet again. A big red truck rolled by with a *Sunset Strip Tattoo* bumper sticker on the back. It was a sign of Hollywood, where I wanted to be. I thought, *This is my chance. I won't mess up this time.* A cute guy and his friend leaned out the window to talk to me and I felt adrenaline. I didn't think, *Walk away. Now. You are in enough trouble.* I thought, *This will be exciting. Older guys! From Hollywood!* I chatted with them for a few minutes, asking about the bumper sticker and trying to feel out if they actually hung on the Sunset Strip. They did. I gave them my number. Soon thereafter, the main guy, Casey, was picking me up from school and from my house more times than I cared for.

It was cool the first day. I went to one of his friend's houses and it was amusing. We drove to a hip record store in Sherman Oaks called Moby Disc, and Casey shoved a cassette tape down my pants and made me steal it. I had stolen plenty before, so I wasn't scared. I was excited to hang out with him and his friends, who were nineteen, twenty. One the guys had been in the *Metal Years* movie. I felt like I was getting somewhere.

After hanging out a few times, I started to realize two things: One was that Casey was not planning on bringing me to hang on the Sunset Strip with him. He wanted to scam on girls. Two, I didn't much *like* Casey. He was rude, he was disgusting, and he was fatter than I had remembered. He had a gut, a double chin, and frightful hair extensions. His head must've looked okay out of his truck window, because the rest of him looked like he had fallen from the ugly tree and hit every branch on the way down. To make matters worse, he didn't seem to have a conscience. I knew I needed to end the relationship or whatever it was, but I didn't know how to do it.

I was so intensely nervous around Casey and his friends that I never spoke. I decided I needed alcohol to calm my nerves. I meekly asked him for Southern Comfort, remembering the initial buzz I felt when riding in the car with Jamie. Casey all too gladly provided my fifteen-year-old ass with hard liquor. As soon as that occurred, things started sliding downhill faster than a fucking bobsled. I drank enough to pass out and Casey often locked me in a room full of bottles of his piss (he was too lazy to go to the bathroom), and went about his business. I recall his room having trails of ants in it as well. Sometimes he brought me to other people's houses and left me there. Once he brought over a young bisexual girl and tried to get me to have sex with her. Another time his father was chasing his friends around the house with an ax, trying to kill them. Then there was the day he took me to the house of some old, rich guy who had a teeth fetish, and offered me up like a sacrificial lamb. The guy examined my teeth and said he wanted Casey to bring me back to 'party.' I was like, *What is this all about?* Casey said that he and his friends often came to the guy's house for parties and they bit his hand and he paid them. *Good Lord,* I thought. When things like that happened, I drank up.

I often feared I wouldn't get home at night and I was scared of missing school the next day. But I was so full of self-hatred and misery, that I wanted to be anywhere but where my parents were. I just remember wanting to be away from them. Casey scared me, but I was determined to deal with it. I told myself to toughen up and handle it.

One evening, we were at some guy's house and I saw Casey go into a bathroom. He was so antsy and excited, he didn't close the door all of the way. I saw him first tearing a piece of a cotton ball...then fumbling with a spoon, and something else...what was it? A lighter? I squinted my eyes in my alcohol-induced haze and saw him tie some sort of rubber tubing around his arm and inject something into one of his tattoos, like a shot...I don't remember how long he was in there, but when he came out, he immediately laid down next to me, wrapped his limbs around me in a grip and fell straight asleep. He didn't wake up for a few hours.

I was not prepared to deal with any man, let alone a heroin addict. I was a kid. A kid from the suburbs, at that. It appeared to me that heroin was the 'in' thing to do because of Guns N' Roses, who were well-known addicts. Casey bragged of seeing Guns guitarist Izzy Stradlin buying drugs at the "shooting gallery" where he bought his heroin. He probably deliberately bought heroin just to run into him, as he loved Guns N' Roses.

Casey also bragged about being bisexual. I guess it was another 'in' thing to do. He told me some of the guys in Ratt were bi and so was this person and that person- it was like he was trying to be cool. It was the same thing I was doing, but on a higher level. It was as if he was identifying the "cool" variables in these rock stars, and trying to emulate the ones he could.

One night he said we were going to a party. *Party?* I had never been to a party, besides the one where I got so drunk I locked myself in the bathroom and woke up when the party was over. I was ready to try again. I got all dressed up in a tiny outfit that even Kelly Bundy would have thought was too skimpy. I put on some four-inch high, purple snakeskin pumps; a tiny, tight tube skirt, and a shirt that barely covered my bra on all sides. I had a huge silver heart charm resting in my visible cleavage. My midriff was on display to show that I had a six-pack from doing so many v-sits in my room throughout the past two years. I thought the party would be like something I had seen on MTV or in the movies: People would be dancing on tables. The trees out front would have toilet paper in them. Long Duck Dong would be on an exercise bike and Jake Ryan would be clearing beer cans stacked into pyramids. The Beastie Boys would be there, throwing pies at each other. A couple of the guys from Motley Crue would be arm wrestling at the coffee table and there would be a game of strip poker going on. Once again, I had this fantasy that I would walk into the party in slow motion and all heads would turn. Guys would turn to mush and similarly dressed women with less fortunate of bods would sneer with jealousy...

(small voice) But that didn't happen.

I got out of the car and realized that we were at a house party in Studio City. It was still light out. The sun was almost down and people were standing around outside ...*in jeans*. Lots of jeans. Jeans on guys, jeans on girls. The girls were wearing shirts that covered their whole bodies and they wore barely any makeup. Edie Brickell and the New Bohemians were playing on a stereo, singing "What I Am." People turned and stared all right, but they started laughing right afterward. Not what I was going for, once again. I really just did not get it. I honestly thought Kelly Bundy looked cool and I always tried as hard as I could to look just like her. Anyway, once I saw the crowd I didn't want to walk up to the party, but I had no choice. I could barely walk in my spiked heels down the driveway. I was wobbling like an old woman with Parkinson's. Twenty people were outside squinting at me and whispering to each other. I heard someone ask if I were the entertainment. Just then, I reached the end of the driveway. I had one foot on the gravel and another in the grass when my heel sank. The grass was soft, so my heel poked through to the dirt underneath. My other foot caught on the gravel. The next thing I knew, I was going down. That is where the real slow motion started- Down, down, down, down …into the splits. I had one leg out in front of me and one behind me. I couldn't get up. My skirt had ridden up around my waist. Casey grabbed my hand, yanked me up, and pretended it didn't happen, which was my preferred method of handling embarrassment.

Despite that debacle, Casey continued to drag me around with him on his errands. I thought if I waited long enough, he would take me to The Strip, but it never happened. It seemed we were always driving around. He drove really fast around canyons at night, drunk and high. I was sure we would drive straight off a cliff. Other times, he brought friends with him in the cab of his truck and made me sit in the back. Not the back seat, the back of the *truck*, like, where you would carry a dirt bike or something. I remember he and his friends stole a big hard plastic Santa Claus from someone's lawn and threw it in the back with me. I was freezing back there, rolling around with the Santa Claus while he whipped through traffic on the freeway. They were laughing at me, treating me like an animal.

I didn't care. I didn't care *what* happened to me. *Just kill me, let me die here, who gives a shit*. I didn't even care if I was alive, why I would give a shit about *that?* I was kind of just waiting to die. I tried to stand up to Casey once by slapping him in the face, but he slapped me back even harder. He said, "You think you're hot? You aren't *shit*."

Shortly thereafter, he thought it would be funny to hold a gun to my head to scare me. This was the worst possible person I could have chosen as company.

One night when I had passed out, Casey and his friend took off all of my clothes and did horrible, humiliating things to me. I would have not even known this happened, but they decided to videotape it and show everyone they knew. This event is what brought me from depressed to truly suicidal. When I think back to the way that night was going before I passed out, I remember being flirtatious with them while I was drinking. I was wearing high heels, tight pants and a tiny shirt. I know that it is a total debate among people- *is* there such thing as 'asking for it'? I can tell you what was going through my mind: I wasn't wearing skimpy clothing because I wanted sex. It was because I thought I looked cool, pretty, and sexy. I thought it gave me some power. I was also flirting. But when I was flirting, I wasn't thinking that I wanted sex. I just felt attractive and liked the attention I was receiving in return. I don't think these guys raped me, I think that they thought I was initially consenting. The fact that I passed out straight away and they went on doing who knows what- I can't come up with anything to play devil's advocate for that. They were totally vile and corrupted and I was the perfect target.

Casey tried to show me the tape one day. I was so incredibly disturbed, I couldn't even speak. There were close ups of my private parts, which were still unmanicured, due to my being so young and not knowing how to groom. It was humiliating, embarrassing, and just crushing. I hid my face. I wanted to be pretty and flirtatious. I didn't want *this*. Why did guys have to make everything so ugly and dirty? I didn't even know something like that could even *occur*- it wasn't in my realm of imagination.

Casey started blackmailing me with the videotape, telling me he was going to show my parents if I didn't do whatever he said. I was devastated. I had only lost my virginity a month prior and had only kissed a boy for the first time a few months earlier. How it spiraled into being blackmailed with a videotape is beyond me. But it did. And it wasn't a very good videotape, because I was *asleep* for chrissakes. But I didn't learn my lesson after my first date. Or my second date. God was knocking on my forehead and I was ignoring the warning signs. I made the decision to hang with these people. I thought it would be exciting and fun and grown up.

Self-hatred was welling up inside me and coming out in other ways. My bulimia had escalated to such a degree that the glands on my neck were starting to swell up like walnuts. One of my teachers sent me to my school counselor, Mrs. Harrod. She was a tough black woman who had a way with teenagers. I think her secret was just asking them questions and showing interest. Most people are put off by teenagers' attitudes and moodiness. Not her. She sat there and grilled me. She wanted to know where my parents were. She wanted to know why I couldn't say the word "NO." She wanted to know how I got such sexy clothes and why I was behaving the way I was with men. She thought I needed medical attention for my eating disorder and needed psychiatric help for my other problems.

She immediately called my mother to find out what was going on in my home. Thank God. It was right after that phone call that my mother finally decided to kick out my father. I wondered why it took my school calling for her to take action. I showed signs of serious problems for the three years prior, which had gone ignored. My mother thought my dad could have possibly abused me, as she admitted years later, but she wasn't sure and she wanted to keep the family together. That meant keeping me in the house with him. And being in the house with my dad was eating me alive.

My counselor later revealed to me that my mom showed up at the school in tears, asking her what to do. She didn't know the first thing about kicking out a husband, making it on her own, any of it. I guess she got some advice and got the courage to do something. Either that or she was kind of forced to act because now someone was watching. At any rate, my mother said she had come home one day and saw a drug dealer in the kitchen with my father and that was apparently the last straw. Within weeks of my school calling, my mother told my father she wanted a divorce and he had to leave the house.

She then pulled my sister and me next to the front door, in front of the Christmas tree. We stood side by side while she blurted out everything in a huge clusterfuck: Our father was a cocaine addict, with a habit that was up to $500 a day, which meant he had stopped paying the bills, including the mortgage. Our house was probably going to go into foreclosure and we would have to move. She had been trying to hide his habit from us, but couldn't do it anymore. On top of that, he was unfaithful to her. He had had numerous affairs. I felt sadder about the affairs than the drugs. I felt heartbroken. My mom kept telling me she was doing it for my sister and me. I started to feel bad. Then I thought, *Wait, aren't you **supposed** to protect us? Is it 'going above and beyond' to protect your children? If my school hadn't called, would you have done this?*

My sister and I were floored. We were not angry with her for wanting to divorce him over all of that- we totally got it. But it was still a shock. I could barely process the information. I had so many of my own problems going on that I couldn't even really think about my dad. I knew he wasn't the same man I knew as a child. I knew there was a new anger to him and a creepy sexual edge to him that wasn't there before. I knew I didn't ever want to be alone with him and did my best to avoid him. Still, I never thought he would be a drug addict and it still surprised me that he would have affairs, even after the way he behaved. It was hard to hear concrete facts about this man who was supposed to be the person I admired, the person who was supposed to protect me from the outside world. It fucked with my perception of reality. Everything seemed to be swirling in my head like a horrible whirlpool.

My mom was a basket case. She was especially mean to me during that time. She told me that she was going to kick me out along with my dad. She told me to just go with him, wherever he was going. My dad was around for another month or so, as if he didn't believe he was being kicked out of the house. One day my mother was in her room crying. My sister and I were sitting in the living room, feeling uncomfortable. My father took me aside and told me she was crying because of *me*. Although I did feel she didn't like me because I blew the lid wide open on our family problems, I didn't buy it. My dad was manipulative and hurtful. I wished he would hurry up and leave.

One night I went out with some guy and I think we went to a drive-in or something, I can't remember. We were drinking and hooking up and I didn't get home until very late, probably three in the morning. Before I left, my mother told me if I didn't come home by my new curfew (I was thinking, *you are trying to implement a curfew? I am so far beyond that, I am in deep fucking trouble here!),* she would put all of my belongings on the front lawn in garbage bags. I wasn't sure where she got the idea, but she was starting to mention "tough love" a lot, so maybe she had received some pamphlet on it and this was one of the suggestions.

I was too chicken to tell the guy to get me home on time. I was scared I would look childish or unsophisticated or whatever, so I waited for him to take me home when he felt like it, which happened to be three in the morning. I entered my room wearing only my tight black dress with white skulls all over it. When I flicked on the light, I saw that my room was completely bare. Everything off the walls, all the furniture out, no clothes, no belongings, no nothing. Just a bare mattress remained. My beloved stuffed animals, my favorite stacks of books, and framed pictures of old movie stars- they were all gone. I panicked. They were my only comfort. I was really into "things" as a way to comfort myself, which was never healthy, but that is the way I was. I started screaming at my mother that I needed my birth control pills and she tried to remind me that I broke the rule. I was thinking, *What the hell are these flimsy rules? These are so ridiculous and they are coming way too late. The damage is already done. These rules will not protect me, I have already suffered and have been abused and wronged and stripped of my dignity and my soul and my innocence. I need guidance, I need help, I am very lost and I am in trouble. I am sinking, I am drowning, I am up to my neck in quicksand. You are offering me what should be a rope but instead is thread that will snap if I try to use it. I am wayyyy past where you think I am; I am in deep, deep trouble. A fucking curfew?* But truth be told, it was good that she was trying to discipline me. I needed that. The reason it didn't work is because of the inconsistency. I had done what I wanted for years and then suddenly there were rules that night.

My mom went outside in her nightgown and glasses, and came back with a few trash bags so that we could find my pills. When I opened one of the bags, I became enraged. My trinkets that were ceramic or glass were broken into pieces because they had been shoved in with shoes, books, and anything that was in sight. It was as if my existence was just thrown away, as if I didn't matter. It was as if I was dead and my things were not going to be opened again. I fished out my birth control pills and popped one, in tears. At least I wouldn't be *pregnant* during all of this misery. I wanted to change out of my clothes and into pajamas, but I didn't know where to find pajamas. I sat around crying in my bare room for a few hours. I then became so livid over my belongings being broken that I lost it. I went to the kitchen, puffy-eyed, and examined the knives. I thought, *Oh my gosh...I can't control myself. I am going to kill my own mother.*

It hurts to write that, but it is what I felt. I was going to take a knife and stab her; that is how mad I was. I found myself crying again because I was scaring myself. I couldn't control my anger and I couldn't control my hand. I picked up the knife and stared at it. Then I put it back down. I went into my mom's room- I didn't know why I was going in. I don't know what I wanted or how it could have helped me. I looked at her sleeping on my dad's old side of the bed. There was no one on her side. His side was closest to the bedroom door and the bathroom. I saw the old headboard in the dark, with its big mirror and the stained glass cupboards on either side. She loved stained glass. There was a tissue box above her head and an alarm clock and other necessities that would grow as she got older into a jumble of earplugs, pills, lotions, and pens.

I looked at the lump sleeping in the bed. The lump that single-handedly shattered any comfort I had left in the world. I became full of rage, enough to make me snarl, snarl like a fucking panther. A feeling shot through my body- it was a feeling of pure wrath. I punched her as hard as I could, in the general vicinity of her face. She jumped up out of her dead sleep and I remember seeing the whites of her eyes in the dark. She looked like a scared animal. I actually felt remorse at that moment and wished I hadn't done it. But at the exact same time I wanted to kill her. I beat her with my fist as hard as I could and she tried to hold up the blanket, as if that would be a shield to stop me. She was screaming my name, begging me to stop.

All of the screaming woke my younger sister, Becky. She quietly went outside, where the rest of the garbage bags were hidden. She took out the things she knew I liked most and lined them all up in my room. My white stuffed cat, Nicky; my big fat Warner Brothers book, my pictures of Rita Hayworth. She pulled out some other things she knew I loved and quietly put them out in the midst of my hysteria and screaming. I always loved my sister for that. She knew what to do. It did calm me down.

Unfortunately, I never retrieved a large portion of my belongings. My mother swears to this day that she really only meant to teach me a lesson so she moved everything out and off to the side of the house. Goodwill thought it was part of a donation and took it all. I was kind of confused as to how Goodwill could make house calls so late at night, because I left at like seven p.m. to go out, but hey, what do I know. Regardless of that, regardless of *anything* my mother ever did or didn't do, I was deeply, deeply wrong for striking her. I don't care if she beat me to a pulp or abused me herself. Striking a parent is an abominable act and I am still gravely ashamed. I am telling the truth in this book, so that is why I mention it here. It affected what was left of my future relationship with her.

My sister says:
"I feel like I understood this all back then, especially the curfew part. It's just really, really sad you went through feeling that way and had no comfort. None. And the bags on the lawn- I remember being stunned. I don't remember when she put it all there, like, I don't remember being there watching her bringing it out - but I remember trying to bring it back in and she stopped me. I remember feeling *so* badly. That was a horrible time."

CHAPTER FIVE

The Mental Ward

In January of 1989, my mother wrote me a letter that pissed me off, but also kind of relieved me. It said that we were moving away from our neighborhood because she knew I was in trouble with a bad crowd. What really happened was that our house was in foreclosure because my dad hadn't paid the mortgage in months. Luckily, my mom ended up being able to sell the thing at the last minute. Anyway, she didn't mention that. She stuck to her story that we were moving because of me, and hell, I *did* need to get out of that neighborhood and away from my new crowd. She said that Jeff Hunter came to her and told her I was in trouble with some older guys. I was pissed at him for butting in. He was only an afterthought to me at that time, even though he was my world six months prior. I think I told him my happenings in passing, but I didn't want to deal with his angry girlfriend if we were caught speaking to one another. I was mad at him for telling her about me, because she still yelled "Whore!" at me any time she saw me at school, no matter where we were or how many people were around. It hurt more once I wasn't a virgin, because I *did* feel like a whore and she was basically rubbing it in.

It felt like I was living on one little AAA battery instead of the usual four D batteries. When in my room, I screamed at the top of my lungs and laid my ear against my stereo speakers that were on full blast. I had dreams of demons and devils and evil things. I drifted in and out of hallucinations. Then I stopped grooming. I stopped the skimpy clothes and started wearing men's T-shirts. I wouldn't brush my hair, wear shoes, or even turn my shirts right-side-out. I went to school with inside-out shirts that were backwards, with the tags sticking out in front, under my chin. I lost the will to live, so it didn't really matter *what* I looked like. I still possessed enough vanity to wear makeup though. I felt as if my being pretty was the only power I held. But as for the rest of me, I looked homeless.

The kids at school left me alone, except for the random gangster girls bussed in from South Central L.A. who shouted at me and called me a crazy bare-footed bitch. The Latin cholas left me alone, raising their penciled-in eyebrows and shaking their heads. I was so tired, depressed, and suicidal that I feared none of them at that point. I would have beaten the shit out of or tried to kill any one of them who stepped to me. People stayed away-even Jeff's hateful girlfriend shut up after a certain point.

My mom made a plan to move us all into our grandmother's house. We had nowhere else to go. When everything was packed and being moved, my sister and I had our belongings in these little train cases. Mine was covered in stickers on the inside and it held my favorite cassette tapes, some makeup, rocker jewelry, and little knick knacks that made me happy. It was a little tiny piece of luggage, but it had my *life* inside. What was left of it, anyway.

We moved in with my grandmother that February. She still lived in a small house in Canoga Park, which was the house where my mother grew up. I normally loved and felt comforted by the house, but this time, it felt dark and sad. Canoga Park was not a bad neighborhood in the 1950's and even in the early 1980's it wasn't *that* bad. But by 1989, the homes in that particular neighborhood had a lot of security bars on the windows and the surrounding area had become infested with illegal aliens. The neighborhood wasn't as safe as the one we had just left.

I got my mother's childhood room, and my sister got what was the TV room (and Aunt Billie's room before that), and my mother shared a room with her mother. When I opened my closet, I saw 1950's nursery wallpaper with lambs and ribbons on it. It was pretty, but my taping pictures of L.A. Guns all over it soon destroyed it. My bedroom floor became quickly covered in clothes and shoes and the bathroom was soon full of wet towels. Within a month or two, the kitchen had roaches that scattered when a light was turned on. We were slobs and my poor grandmother said nothing.

***

One day, I started scratching my private parts and couldn't stop. I laid in my bed and cried non-stop because it hurt so badly. There was no down time; it felt like someone had my skin in a vice grip and was pinching me as hard as they could for hours and hours. My eyes watered, my teeth clenched. I was taken to a doctor at some point and the mystery was solved: I had a horrible, horrible case of VD. It hurt worse than pretty much anything I have ever been through. They put me on some big horse-pill painkillers and tried getting rid of it, but it became so painful I had to go to the emergency room.

I was referred to a doctor who I couldn't stand. One time he was trying to treat me with a Q-tip of acid and he accidentally spilled the entire bottle between my legs, into my butt crack. I screamed in pain. It burned me so terribly that big pieces of my skin were falling off in clumps when I got home. I think the thing I hated most about him though, was the fact that he constantly told me I was pretty, and he always wanted to examine my fifteen-year-old breasts. But instead of having me lie down and put an arm behind my head as he felt in a circular motion (the proper way to do a breast exam), he had me stand against the door as he lifted up my shirt. It was just a man squeezing my breasts and getting off on it. I knew it wasn't right and wanted to scream but I was defeated and exhausted. Who was there to tell? I actually did tell my mother once, but she thought I was being dramatic and ignored me. I even brought it back up to her a few years later and told her it was still bothering me that he was a practicing doctor. This was another scenario where I wanted her to cock a rifle on a mountaintop and vow to shoot the nuts off anyone who touched her child in a sexual manner. Instead, she told me to write a letter to his higher-ups and then went on with her day.

A few years later, I wrote a letter to the American Medical Association and never received a response. I even went back into the doctor's office by myself after I could drive, to try to complain. At that point, they told me he no longer worked there. You would think he got in trouble- but guess what he does now? He has his own practice in Encino. He is an infertility doctor. He probably suggests he screw people's wives to see if there are any problems.

Needless to say, I was pretty unhappy with my life and health problems there in 1989. I didn't know how to deal with my pain and my anger. I started hurting myself: beating myself in the face, hitting myself with things, and sometimes asking other people to hurt me. I know now that self-injury is a coping mechanism, but back then, I just felt so *grotesque* inside that I felt I deserved abuse. I had a lot of self-hatred. Guys picked me up and tossed me across the room like a lifeless corpse and I hit the ground in pain, but I was somehow relieved. Other times I tried to strangle myself, but I couldn't do it. I was too chicken to actually kill myself, but I had no desire to continue my life, so I lived as if I were not alive. I lost all hope for myself. I never thought of the future; I didn't think I would make it that far. I never, ever considered that I would live to be in my thirties. I thought I would die either that year or within the next few years and I didn't care; it didn't scare me. I did not fear death for the first time. I even prayed for death sometimes. I cried and I

begged God to please, *please* kill me. I just wanted to die.
Too many things had happened at once. We left our childhood
home very abruptly, my father was a drug addict and was no
longer a part of our family; I had been date raped, videotaped,
blackmailed, contracted a painful venereal disease, was bulimic,
suicidal and failing school. I was in a lot of trouble and couldn't
seem to get it under control by myself. I knew I got myself into
each mess. I knew I chose to dress and behave the way I did. I
knew I had no one to blame but myself.

I stayed at my grandmother's house with my mother and sister
for another three years, but we all avoided each other and were
not a family. My mother and I especially hated each other. No
one should treat a parent the way I treated her. I was really
horrible toward her, but it was because I was hurt inside. She
told me that the only reason I was still living with her was
because I was a minor and it was the law. As soon as I turned
eighteen, I would be toast. Instead of telling her it hurt me that
she seemed to have given up on me, I decided to be a raging
bitch to her instead. My sister and I did not really get along too
well either, but I don't remember hating her; I remember there
were good times and bad. I don't recall ever consoling her
through her own troubles though; I was too selfish. We all
handled it in our own way. My mom shut down. I acted out and
was wild, vocal, and angry. My sister escaped to the homes of
her friends, who had more normal lives.

My sister says:
"I remember hearing Mom locked in the bedroom, screaming at
the top of her lungs. Just screaming and screaming. I thought she
was going to kill herself. You don't scream like that unless you
want to die. I tried to knock on the door and help her but it was
locked. She told me later she *was* going to kill herself. She had a
lot on her plate at that time, and I wasn't on that plate. She
stopped raising me."

My dad became a transient, living off other people's generosity.
He wasn't cut out to be a father, the head of a family. He wasn't

cut out to follow the rules. Maybe he was cut out to, but refused to- I never really found out. Just like his hippie days before we were born, he 'lived off the land,' his favorite thing to do. He was always running from the law, the IRS- the government in general (oh- and the Hell's Angels were also after him for some reason). He felt a horrible guilt for not being a father to us, but he couldn't or wouldn't make it up to us.

***

One thing that I did not like about living in Canoga Park was that I had to wake up at 4 a.m. to go to school back in our old neighborhood. I was given the option to transfer somewhere closer to my grandmother's house, but I chose to finish out my high school years at the school I was already attending. I didn't want to start over somewhere else. I had just gotten used to my school's layout and felt I was dealing with the kids' reaction of me better than I had when I first got there. I didn't want to have that nightmare all over again with a new set of kids.

My mother made an arrangement with our former neighbors, the Lauderdales, who agreed to take me in three hours before school started each day. I slept in a leather chair in their dark, heavily draped, tobacco-scented living room for two hours. Then, at 7 a.m., they woke me as they left the house to go to their jobs and I walked to school and spent another hour hanging out with the smokers at The Wall before school started. I didn't mind the mornings though. The bad part was *after* school, when I had to take public transportation home. It took me an hour. I got on the RTD bus and took it down one of the big main streets. Then I had to wait twenty minutes or so for the next bus, which took me to a street that was a block from my grandmother's house.

Waiting for the public bus to arrive was sheer misery, especially when it was either ninety degrees outside and I was dripping sweat in the direct sun, or it was freezing and I didn't have warm enough clothes. There was always some crazy, fat man in a stained shirt yelling at an imaginary person, or guys who looked like serial killers rubbing their dicks against me when the bus was crowded and we had to stand. That was the worst. I had to shove several men for doing that. I was about to write that it was scary, but I was pretty tough- it didn't scare me. If I would have had a knife on me I would have sunk it into one of them with no problem at all. I remember always being starving and having to sit on a bus bench in front of a Subway sandwich shop, where I could smell fresh bread baking (no matter that their bread always smells better than it actually tastes, just like movie theater popcorn). It was torturous. I wanted to hold up the store and steal a tray of the bread and then eat it right there at the bus stop like a ravenous maniac.

The second I got home, I dropped my books and went straight to the kitchen to make myself my favorite dish: Rice-A-Roni, either chicken or beef flavor. The sodium content was in the quadruple digits, but who cared? That shit was delicious. Sometimes I watched *Married...with Children* on TV later in the evening, but the hit shows of the time didn't really interest me: *21 Jump Street, The Tracy Ullman Show, It's Gary Shandling's Show, COPS*. I recall going to see the movie *Heathers* with Karen, but other than that, I didn't do much. I spent most of my time listening to music, and not the popular music of the day, which would have been Al B. Sure, Paula Abdul's *Forever Your Girl* album, Milli Vanilli, Bobby Brown or New Kids on the Block. I did like Nenah Cherry's "Buffalo Stance," but that was about it. I could barely stomach the rock bands of the time, like the Bulletboys, Warrant, and Winger. I mostly listened to my Faster Pussycat and L.A. Guns tapes.

Faster Pussycat, who I had been introduced to through *The Metal Years*, wore lots of scarves, and a little makeup and hair spray. Despite the fact that they were uglier than a monkey's asshole, their songs were catchy and upbeat and I thought they were putting me in a better mood. L.A. Guns were pretty hard looking; they wore black leather pants and had black hair, black eyeliner and lots of tattoos. They were not cutesy. I felt they most represented me. I found their look attractive and their music was my favorite. I could listen to it for hours and hours without getting tired of it.

I saw a band in my rock magazines named D'Molls and I thought the singer was cute, so I got their tape. That is how I picked bands at that time. Shoot, at *all* times. D'Molls were definitely designed for girls out of the Poison template: bubblegum music, lots of color, hairspray, and lipstick; looked like trannies. I ended up liking their music, despite the fact that they seemed to know only one chord on the guitar. They sang about Hollywood and girls gone bad and all of the usual stuff. I didn't need deep, depressing Metallica sort of music about guys losing their limbs during wars. I wanted something light and carefree- and I got it.

***

For a few months, I was relieved to be away from my old house because Casey and his friends couldn't find me. No one knew where I lived. No one had my phone number. I had a chance to have a clean slate and escape the bad crowd I had entered. But then I grew bored. (I know, I was an idiot.)

There were two guys in Casey's crowd who were a little more clean cut than the heroin addicts and such. They were identical twins named Fritz and Andy. They weren't dirty, they weren't druggies, they still lived at home with their mother and they still went to high school. They were only two years older than me, unlike the other guys who were four or five years older. They were tall, rich, and spoiled. They had inheritances coming to them when they turned twenty-one because their grandfather had invented some important shit of some sort. They lived relatively close to me, but in a nicer area. I called them and gave them my new number. I convinced my mother they were harmless, so she let me see them.

Andy had shoulder-length dark hair, flipped over to one side. He was very soft spoken, calm, polite and somewhat feminine; I wouldn't bat an eyelash if I heard that he was gay today. Fritz was more masculine, not to mention friendly and outgoing. His hair was bleached blond, and he kind of resembled Anthony Kiedis from the Red Hot Chili Peppers. He wasn't afraid to get into a fight. Andy was a big old queen but I was in love with him because he was sweet to me. Fritz was just plain hot. I couldn't decide who I liked better.

They dragged me around with them to get-togethers and parties, and while they were not as big of assholes as the older guys with whom I had been partying, they were still teenage guys, and they tried getting down my pants every chance they got. There was a point when they started to get into a competition over me. One of them would call and pick me up, and I would go and hang out with him. When that brother went to pick up more beer, answer the phone, or leave the scene at all, the other brother always snuck over to me and persuaded me to leave with *him*. And I always did! I didn't have any sense of loyalty to either of them. I was easily persuaded and loved the attention, even though I highly doubt their competition had anything to do with me- it was clearly between them and their own egos.

One day Andy grilled me on what music I liked. I tried to pick something that I thought would go over well, something universal, so I told him I liked Guns N' Roses. He rolled his eyes and said that they were too "hesher" and that he liked bands like Hanoi Rocks. *Hanoi Who*? I thought. Then I remembered briefly reading about Hanoi Rocks in *Circus* when it covered Vince Neil of Motley Crue accidentally killing Hanoi's drummer in a drunk driving accident. Andy showed me a poster he had bought- it said "Self Destruction Blues" and had a picture of Hanoi's platinum blond frontman, Michael Monroe, exaggerating a wink. He was deeply tanned and had bright blue eyes and teased hair. Hmmm. So this was what was cool? Not being too mainstream? Liking things that were a little more obscure? That made sense. It surely was more 'Hollywood' to have eclectic musical taste...I would have to check them out.

Within the next few weeks, I went to the music shop down the street and looked through some Hanoi Rocks tapes and records. I noted that they dressed in vests, hats, glittery sashes, scarves, and tight pants. They wore lots of makeup and had hair-sprayed hair. That part was all fine and dandy. It was their music that was totally bizarre. I randomly picked *Back to Mystery City* out of the albums that were available. When I got it home, I listened to it and was disturbed. The song "Mental Beat" put me in a bad place in my head and "Malibu Beach Nightmare" reminded me of that awful night on the beach with Jamie. But if Hanoi Rocks were obscure, underground, and cool, then I was convinced I had to start memorizing some songs. I wanted to nonchalantly start singing a tune around someone cool and have him or her say, "Hey- you know that song?" (This actually did happen at some point.) In all fairness, I eventually got the rest of their music as the years went by and fell in love with quite a bit of it, but at that time, I was being nothing more than a poser.

As my tenth grade year came to an end, I started to feel a little better. I hung around my school friend Abby a lot more. She was very tough and mean to many people, but was nice to me. She could be sarcastic and she could be cynical, but I really treasured her. She had been through some abuse in her life, most recently a brutal rape in Hollywood, where she had been a runaway. We both had been through hard times, so finding each other was a blessing. I got a little more confidence just having a friend to confide in and we even started to have fun. We both started to lighten up. We even started laughing and giggling and being regular girls.

I got a second wind that summer and created a new look for myself. It wasn't too drastically different, it was just more creative. I dyed my hair bright purple and colored my eyebrows with a dark purple eye shadow that perfectly matched my hair. While the other girls wore their hair permed and teased, I wore mine ironed perfectly straight and long (I did this with a clothes iron on an ironing board). My new signature look was purple, turquoise blue and black/white polka dots. I had blue nails most of the time and loads of silver bracelets. I had a turquoise blue shirt that stopped just under my boobs and turquoise short-shorts that I wore with lace-up Grecian sandals. I had a skin tight, purple spandex skirt that stopped just under my butt, which I wore with a white top with black polka dots. All of my outfits were from Contempo Casuals, which I thought was comparable to Christian Dior or something- I thought that shit was haute couture. I was proud of my outfits! I had a long, sheer black scarf with white polka dots on it that I tried to wear as a headband but it always fell out. I loved that sash. I also wore this drug store perfume that came in a round white bottle with a black exclamation mark sticking out of it. I didn't care that I smelled like a 1970's douche- I liked that bottle! Any birthday or holiday money I received from faraway relatives usually went toward that perfume.

The summer of 1989 was all about the new movie *Batman* with Michael Keaton, Kim Basinger, and Jack Nicholson as The Joker. It was Batman everything: shirts, cups, stickers and Happy Meals. Disney's *The Little Mermaid* also came out that year, along with *Bill and Ted's Excellent Adventure, Say Anything* and *Steel Magnolias*.

I had to attend summer school to make up my failing grades, so I took Biology with a bunch of kids who were younger than I was. I brought a 1 ½ inch plastic brown cow to class every day and set it on my desk. I called it HowNowBrownCow. I was just trying to get attention and I got a lot of it. All of the younger boys in the class called me a witch and drew cartoons about me, but I didn't care. I just told them to watch out or I'd put a hex on their asses. I became popular in the class, although I was more likely just infamous.

One day, the biology teacher decided to show a boring movie, so I thought it would be perfectly logical to crawl out of the class on my hands and knees (in short shorts, at that). As I was doing so, I looked up toward the class across the hall and saw a delicate boy with fluffy blond hair and gamine features watching me. He approached me later on, in passing, and introduced himself as Justin Sandstrom.

I knew immediately that I could not date him, because I felt his innocence and his big heart. I knew I was too internally warped and was not capable of having a regular relationship with some nice boy my age. He was polite and sweet, lived with his parents- probably the kindest person I had ever randomly met. He acted as if I was some goddess and I felt very flattered. He said, "I didn't know girls like you actually *existed*." I gave him my number to pump my ego initially, but we ended up becoming very close friends after I explained why I couldn't date him.

I told him all of my secrets and he told me about his life, which wasn't completely innocent. He told me about how he was turned off by girls who came on really strong. He told me stories about sleeping with his ex-girlfriend when her parents weren't home, going to dances, and all the stuff he did with the girls he dated. He always tried to tell me I was very special and deserved better that the guys I dated, but I couldn't comprehend that. I felt destroyed inside and I didn't see an end to that, so I was trying to accept it and move forward.

I turned sixteen that September and was feeling much better about my life. I was going into the eleventh grade and I was excited to take drivers education that year to learn to drive. I signed up for the stage crew for the school plays. I had Abby as my friend at school and I had Justin to talk to on the phone every night. I didn't feel so alone. My hair was brilliant purple and I loved it. I thought things were finally looking up. But that wasn't to last.

My dad, who we hadn't seen for nearly a year, suddenly started showing up around my grandmother's house. He snuck into the shed in the backyard and slept there a few nights, watching us through the kitchen windows when it was dark. He hid in the bushes and watched us go to school in the morning. One night he knocked on a window and it scared me because I couldn't see outside in the dark. I opened the window and promptly told him to get the fuck out of my yard or I would call the cops on him for trespassing.

My sister and I were both confused. Some nights she thought she might want to see him; other nights she didn't. We tried to respect that one of us might feel one way and the other another way at any given time. We didn't know *what* we thought. It put us into an absolute tailspin, mentally. We acted out in different ways. She started shoplifting and having crying spells in school. I became very angry and full of rage again and wanted to run away.

I let my dad in the house on one of those nights. He crawled in on his hands and knees, crying. He told me he saw God in the street when he was on acid. He started pouring out all of these disturbing things. It was very hard on me and really did a number on my mind. He was clearly in a lot of pain. He kept telling me he didn't want to live. He was full of regret and apologized a thousand times, begging forgiveness. He knew he made a mistake and ruined the family. He said he would do whatever it took to make it up to us, and that he loved us. We felt bad for our dad. It was hard to see him in that state, the former head of our family so vulnerable. It left me raw, thinking that there was no one really in charge of us. My mom was a walking corpse and could barely talk. I was scared.

Seeing him in that state was a lot worse than not having a father. I regretted letting him in the house that night; I realized I wanted him to leave me alone so I could heal. But he was relentless in wanting to talk to me and make things right. I got up and walked out of the house while he was in mid-speech, without my contact lenses on. I couldn't see anything and to make it worse, it was dark out. I didn't care, I just kept walking. Tears filled my eyes and my heart overflowed with pain. He followed me and tried to talk to me. He said we could live together; he would get us a place. I said no, I was running away to Hollywood.

I started walking faster in the dark. I saw blurry streetlights through my tears. I just wanted him to leave me alone and he wouldn't. I suddenly got this rush of adrenaline and thought, *This is it. I am going for it.* I ran straight into traffic on a busy street. I somehow didn't get hit. My dad ran out, grabbed me, and pulled me back to the sidewalk, while horns blared and cars screeched. I got out of his grip, turned around, and tried going down a different street. I finally just collapsed onto someone's front lawn and started bawling there in the dark. He sat down next to me. I started yelling at him. I told him the horrible things that I had let happen to me because I had no respect for myself, because I thought I was only good for one thing. I told him that is what he taught me. I yelled it in his face. The things that were coming out of my mouth were shocking me, but I couldn't stop. I yelled, "It's because of *YOU!*" He screamed really loud when I said that and then started crying really hard. It was horrible to hear a man cry. The next thing I knew, a bunch of tiny kittens came out of the bushes and started crawling all over us and meowing. It was surreal. I thought I was having a dream.

He came by a few weeks later. I couldn't look at him. He apologized to me, saying cocaine was a very sexual drug. I knew inside that he was talking about something filthy and I couldn't bear it. I couldn't think about what he was apologizing for, even though I had made reference to it when I was screaming at him. I made my mind not think about it. I was picking at my big purple candle and *wishing* he would leave. I just let him ramble on; I didn't answer him. I remember feeling like I used to feel when my mother would force me to listen to a sex talk, learning about menstruation or something. Just really uncomfortable, no eye contact, picking at something and not responding whatsoever. I was *praying* he would just hurry up and finish the speech. I kept telling myself it didn't happen. *It didn't happen. It didn't happen. Don't think about it.*

I heard a song around then that always made me cry because it struck something really weird in me- "Janie's Got a Gun" by Aerosmith. It was about a girl who killed her father because he had abused her. I often had that same fantasy. Although I felt sorry for him on some days, most days I loathed my father. I wanted him dead. I was so deeply hurt and angered by him that I would have killed him myself if I could have. I shopped around through some of my rougher guy friends to see how much putting a hit on him would be. I found out someone would do it for five thousand dollars. I didn't have that kind of money. I wished he would stop coming to the house and disrupting my life, so I could have a chance at being happy.

I started to get a lot of anxiety for the next couple of months. By the time Christmas came, I was back in a deep depression. Christmas, a time I adored, would not be the same this year. My family was broken apart. We were living at my grandmother's. Most of my belongings were gone. And the yuckiest thing of all was that my father gave a half-assed admission to molesting me. It absolutely broke apart my soul. At the time, I told myself I was depressed over a guy or something. I think it was Andy (*please*).

I saw a commercial for the Rudolph Claymation special that they showed on TV every December. The next day at school, I felt a stinging pain in my heart, like heartbreak. I missed watching cartoon TV specials with my sister; I missed being a child. I didn't want to be a teenager; I didn't want to be in all of the situations I got myself into. I wanted my old dad back, the one who played church hymns on his guitar and bought me Beach Boys records. I wanted both my parents to be normal and still married. *What happened to my dad? Will my mother ever look me in the eyes again? What **happened** to them!?* I was going down some stairs at school between classes, when my mind started to go. I sat down on a step and put my head in my hands. People walked around me. I started blacking out. My fists clenched. My nails were making marks in my palms because I was squeezing so hard. My eyes were crushed shut and tears were pushing through. My mouth was open and nothing was coming out. A girl I hated from P.E. asked me if I were okay. She was the only one who did.

The next thing I knew, I was screaming and crying at the top of my lungs, running through the halls. I couldn't control it- I didn't know where it was coming from. I remember seeing a kid

I knew from grade school stare at me in fright. I don't know how much time lapsed, but I remember being in a different spot when a bunch of security guards came up in a group to restrain me. I was kicking and screaming at them and it seemed they couldn't get control of me. Or maybe they were trying to be gentle with me and were having a hard time. They dragged me into an office where I continued screaming at the top of my lungs for a half an hour straight.

They didn't know what to do with me. Someone sent for Abby, who came in, made everyone leave, and tried to talk to me. They tried to arrange for me to be institutionalized but Abby was vehemently against it. She begged them not to lock me up and started crying on her own. She had been locked up before and she didn't want it to happen to me. My mother was called and when she came in, Abby started yelling at her. Something happened with the insurance company- I think it might have been that they wouldn't cover me coming in unless the police were bringing me in after a threatening incident, but I hadn't threatened anything? I don't know. All I do know is that I couldn't get a hold of myself. My mom was cold, aloof, and annoyed, which made me feel worse.

A few days later, I was at the breakfast table with my sister, mother, and grandmother. My mother wasn't talking and she wouldn't look at me. I said out loud that I wanted to kill myself. She said, "Just *do it* already and stop talking about it; I am sick of hearing it."

I wanted to smash her into a billion pieces. I remember thinking, *I knew it! She doesn't love me! She doesn't care if I die!* She used to be so proud of me, smiling at me with love in her eyes. Her eyes were flat, dead, and black now. *I am her first-born child...what happened? Could she really have lost all feeling toward me?* I wanted so badly for her to take me in her arms and say, "If you died, I would never recover. I love you so much; you are my world. Please don't ever do anything to hurt yourself; you are precious to me." But that isn't how it went. She told me to go ahead and kill myself already.

I reached down for her milk in a swift movement, to dump it in her face a la Alexis Carrington from *Dynasty*. She had been a victim of my anger before, so she quickly tried to block what she thought was going to be a punch with a punch of her own, and the milk went splattering all over both of us. In a burst of adrenaline, I jumped on her and started kicking her as hard as I could. Then I punched her with all of my might, cursing like a demon. I heard my grandmother's cracked voice begging me to get off my mother. Either my grandmother or my sister grabbed me by the back of my shirt and tried to pull me off her. My mom was just kind of balled up and trying to protect herself. I don't remember any damage she did to me in return or if she even tried to retaliate. I just knew I felt enough anger to break through a brick wall. I felt as if I could punch a hole right through her.

I was acting out of impulse that day. I now know as an adult what an incorrigible act it is to strike a parent, no matter the reason. It is with absolute shame and disgrace that I recall this incident.

Sometime shortly thereafter, the cops came and arrested me.

My sister says:
"I remember that fight; it's when things got totally out of control from like, then on. I was just frozen, watching. You stormed off afterward. Mom was crying and called the police on you. I ran to find you. You weren't crying but you had a lot to say. You were positive Mom hated you and you were just plain old pissed off. We talked for a long time and I told you Mom called the police. You didn't try to run but you wanted to go and tell her off and I tried to keep you from doing that. My heart was racing and I couldn't believe it escalated to that. I wondered what took things to that point. I didn't know everything; I was barely there. Then the police came and took you away and it seemed like you were gone for months. It was a living hell that whole time."

When the cops picked me up, they asked me if I was on cocaine. They revealed that my mother told them I was on it. I said I wasn't. They said they would be testing me so it would be best to admit it. I said I truly was not on any drugs. They handcuffed me outside of my grandmother's house; the house where I always felt so safe and wonderful as a kid. I always loved going there. It was sad to have had a scene such as this take place there, in front of the wood fence and the birds of paradise bushes; in front of the sidewalk where, with a key, my mother wrote "Linda Marie" and my uncle wrote "Scotty" in the wet cement.

I sat on my handcuffed hands in the back of the cop car, embarrassed. When we stopped at stoplights, I didn't look out the windows. I could feel people staring at me. Finally, we arrived at some back entrance of a hospital. I was taken into a room where they drew my blood and gave me a urine test. They gave me some orange juice because I was getting a little dizzy. I cooperated with everything they were doing and deliberately acted very calm, just so my mother would look like she was overreacting. I knew not to mess with the police. I wasn't a *complete* idiot. They took me to a ward on the second or third floor. It was a psych ward with unbreakable windows and security guards and what not.

I was assigned to a very passive and soft-spoken shrink with a specialty in eating disorders named Dr. Bernstein. He was not a good match for me because I didn't respect him. I found him to be a huge pussy and treated him awfully. Sometimes I just sat there for the whole hour and picked at his distasteful couch, while he asked me incessant questions about my father's and my relationship. I shunned the questions. I always told him, no, nothing happened with my father. I wouldn't even let my mind wander in that direction because it was such a disturbing thought. I pushed away all thought of it and was angry when he continued to ask. I wanted to talk about the guys I was dating and I wanted to shock him. He had no change of expression no matter how deranged my stories were. He diagnosed me as manic-depressive and put me on Lithium. I felt cool that I got to be on a drug. I couldn't wait to tell Abby.

After a week or so, I figured out the ward through some of the girls. They reaffirmed the obvious: *I had to act stable.* I had to draw pictures of rainbows and sunshine in art therapy. I had to behave. I had to show them they were wasting a space on me; that someone else who was severely troubled and out of control needed my spot. I knew it was crucial that I do the best acting job of my entire life: I had to act like I was normal.

It was devastating having my freedom taken away. I couldn't listen to my music. I couldn't get on the phone and call Justin or Abby. I couldn't go watch TV. I couldn't do much of anything that wasn't supervised. I had to eat shitty food, go on dorky supervised outings in a van, take a paper cup of various white pills, and be signed in and out to do everything. I didn't like that my eyebrows were growing together in a unibrow and that my legs were so hairy (we couldn't have razors because we were always on suicide watch). A unibrow can really put a bitch over the edge- I felt like killing myself just over that alone. Anyway, I knew I needed to get out of that place and get back in school if I didn't want to flunk a grade and suffer the humiliation.

All of the teenagers in the ward had to march down to a little schoolroom to receive our studies each day. I enjoyed my writing assignments and I loved looking through the books they had available, because they had some really crazy erotic novels in there, of which I am sure they weren't even aware. I found them back in the depths of the bookshelves, and then curled up and read away, looking studious.

I desperately wanted to be out of the ward for Christmas. I wanted to drop kick my mother for abandoning me in that place, but I had to get out, no matter the cost. I ended up staying only a few weeks and was let out a few days before Christmas. My dad called one night and asked to talk to me. When I got on the phone he said, "I heard you were in a mental hospital." I tried to tell him how awful I felt to even have gotten to that place, but he started laughing and saying, "Ohhh, poor *baby*," in a sarcastic tone. He said his friends were making fun of him for having a mental daughter or a crazy daughter, or something like that. I was so hurt that I couldn't even react. I started mentally calculating how long it would take me to save up five G's.

I no longer had the option of fitting in at school, especially after my breakdown. I knew a lot of people in the school smoking section had heard the news of my whereabouts, because I received a huge purple card, created by Abby and signed by like, fifty people. I was embarrassed because it said "Hope you get out of the loony bin soon" or something like that. So needless to say, I wasn't going to be getting any dates or making any new best friends any time soon. Frankly, I wasn't attracted to the selection of boys anyhow. Actually, that isn't true- there were one or two I found attractive, but I knew that I wasn't normal and never would be. There was no way I could date like a regular person. The other girls had socially acceptable clothing, standard parents and knew the rules of how to behave around boys. I had bypassed the innocence of dating, I had never had a boyfriend, and I had already had sex. I knew I would scare the shit out of some poor boy if I accepted a date with anyone who wasn't tattooed. It was okay with me though; I didn't want to be like the other kids in school and be into Vanilla Ice, MC Hammer, C & C Music Factory and Bel Biv Devoe. Kids stared at me with my straightened purple hair, blue nails, and big boobs. I carved a heart in my ankle and filled it with ink from a pen. I pierced my ears a bunch of times with a needle. Although I had gone through a ton of shit, I *still* wanted to be a Hollywood chick, but my plans kept failing. I needed get back on track.

I started to make more trips to the record store down the street, and I soon realized that they carried local Hollywood magazines like *Bam* and *Rock City News*. Bingo! Those magazines were a gold mine. They were a great window into what was going on down on the Sunset Strip. I saw pictures of tons of people on Sunset Boulevard watching bands play at places like The Roxy, the Whisky a Go Go and Gazzarri's. The women were beautiful. Most had really long hair, made up faces and wore cool-looking tight dresses. They looked like my Barbie dolls. I couldn't imagine what stores *sold* clothing like that; I certainly didn't see outfits like that in the stores at the mall. I saw ads for the Hollywood Tropicana, a mud-wrestling bar. The girls had dark tans, sequined bikinis, teased blond hair, and silicone breast implants.

The guys featured in the magazines were gorgeous. Many of them had beautiful faces solely because of makeup, but that didn't bother me. I saw tattoos, I saw long black hair, and I saw skinny legs in tight black pants. It was like a dream to see that many attractive guys in the same place. They all appeared to be wearing a brand of clothing called Lip Service. It was made up of crushed velvets in black and purple and sometimes a hint of burgundy. The main Lip Service logo was a cross and skull. They made pants with the logo print and jackets with a big skull in back. Some of the guys wore floppy velvet hats or shirts with the logo.

I stared mostly at pictures of a band named Tryx and another called Pretty Boy Floyd. They were local bands who encompassed what I found attractive and hip. I studied their interviews and learned their names, their likes, their influences. I cut out their pictures, put them on my walls, and dreamed of seeing them play live at a show.

I loved Tryx because they were creative and stood out (and maybe because I loved kids' breakfast cereal).They each wore a certain color, head to toe. One guy (the singer, Jessie Star), was in red leather, with a red stripe in his dyed black hair; another was in turquoise (Roxy DeVeau), another in purple (Tracy Dahne), and another in pink (Cody Marks). They even had color-coordinated tattoos. I think the pink guy had a Pink Panther, the blue guy had a Smurf, and so on. I couldn't figure out who was the cutest. I read all of their interviews and longed for the day I had a car so I could go to Hollywood to see them and all the rest.

I spent the remainder of the year looking at those magazines every week. I began to learn the names of the popular people. Screaming Boy Mandie from the Glamour Punks. Stevie Rachelle from Tuff. Theodore Love from Imagine World Peace. Paulie and Sunny from Swingin' Thing. The 'Miss Gazzarri' dancers in bikinis with a sash over their breast implants, like Miss America. With each issue, I became more consumed.

I had to get there.

CHAPTER SIX

The Tattoo Shop

I studied *Rock City News* with a hunger. Soon I knew what I
should look like, what crowd I should try to break into and the
spots in which I should be seen, if I ever had the chance. I knew
the names of the clubs, the bands who were in rotation and who
was up-and-coming. I knew the labels of the clothing I should be
wearing and the stores in which I should be shopping. I had a
pretty clear picture of what I was going for. I also knew it was
not going to be easy to make it into a scene so obscure and so
based on a coolness factor. I knew good looks were always
welcome, so I could be on the fringe at the very least. But it was
clear you had to have more to hang with the Big Dogs- you had
to be kind of a 'name.'

I wished I could meet some Hollywood people so I could tag
along with them when they went out, but it was very rare to run
into someone from that crowd outside of Hollywood. And I
knew I was very far from getting a car of my own and driving
there myself. I was sitting around waiting, waiting, waiting. I
would lie on my bed at my grandma's and look out the window

while listening to Hanoi Rocks, Jetboy, and Roxx Gang records, daydreaming about the Sunset Strip. I always had on men's boxers and my cut-up Faster Pussycat shirt. My room was jam packed with pictures of all of the bands I liked. There were stacks of tapes and records, bins of makeup and perfume bottles, and random pins and stickers all over the place. I don't think I had made my bed once since we moved in. I just crawled under a pile of clothes and went to sleep each night.

It was the beginning of 1990 when I saw a real live Hollywood guy in Canoga Park. I nearly shit my polka dot biker shorts. I was tripping over myself because I knew I had to act and act fast. I couldn't pass up my ticket to Hollywood, my ticket out of misery in the Valley. I originally saw him in a fast food parking lot and I knew right away he was from Hollywood. He had long, dyed black hair; tattoos, combat boots and Lip Service clothing. *Ding Ding Ding! We have a winner!* I watched him get into his car that had a cartoon skull painted on the doors. Then I saw something that made my heart skip a beat: his bumper sticker. I knew the bright pink script on a black background meant none other than *Riki Rachtman's World Famous Cathouse*, located in Hollywood! It was frequented by Guns N' Roses, Faster Pussycat, L.A. Guns, and many other rock stars and beautiful women. The guy had access to the Cathouse! I had been reading about it in magazines since I was fourteen. I never thought I would *meet* someone who *went* there. I started sweating and wanted desperately to talk to him, but he was getting in his car to leave and I couldn't make my feet run over there and act like a fool. I was mad at myself. How would I ever get to Hollywood?

A few months later, I was coming home from school on that hateful bus. I looked out the window at a stop light and I saw something that intrigued me. It was a little tattoo shop! Tattoos were very Hollywood. I was not discouraged by my unfavorable dealings with Casey, who I met because I saw *his* tattoo shop bumper sticker. Tattoos were a symbol of rock and roll, of rebellion, of *guts*. I knew I had a higher chance of meeting a Hollywood guy in a tattoo shop than anywhere else in my town (it was either that, or I would be walking into a room full of Hell's Angels or Marines).

I decided to check it out one day. I wanted to take action. I needed to do this! I got off the bus before my usual stop and crossed the street toward the tattoo shop. It felt thrilling and dangerous. It felt bad ass. It felt *adult.* When I walked in, the first thing I saw was a black-haired tattoo artist working on someone's arm. He looked up and I recognized him as none other than the guy from the parking lot. I couldn't believe my luck. I could hardly breathe and left the store after barely looking through a few racks of assless chaps. My heart was pounding as I got back on the bus to go home. I had to make sure I came back. I *had* to meet the hot tattoo guy and get my ticket to Hollywood, the town where I belonged. But what would be my reason for going back? I had no business at a tattoo shop…unless...unless I…*needed a tattoo.*

I know, I know, I was pretty lame. And don't ask me how I got money for a tattoo, because I can't even remember. I just know that in March of 1990, I went back to that tattoo shop with balls of steel. I thought, *Okay, I am not going to blow this. My ticket to freedom is **in this shop***. *My new life could start because of this shop. There is a hot guy in there and I could flirt with him and get to go to Hollywood.* I had to make it happen.

I waited for a day that I felt pretty. I think it was a day that I liked my makeup application and/or hair styling and outfit. I was nervous all day at school thinking about getting a tattoo in front of the hot guy. What if he wasn't even there? What if he WAS there, and I cried in front of him because the tattoo hurt? What if I were too nervous after getting my tattoo to talk to him about Hollywood? I would be stuck with a tattoo and nothing to show for it. What if he had a girlfriend?

After school, I took a deep breath and got off the sweaty, smelly, crowded bus in the crisp March air. I entered the shop, hearing L.A. Guns blaring. My favorite band! Playing there! Right *there*! It was a sign! I couldn't believe somewhere else in my neighborhood was playing that music, as they were not as mainstream as other bands. My adrenaline was pumping very strong. I wanted to drop to the floor and do a few push-ups and jump back up.

I was greeted by the parking lot guy. He had bright, electric blue eyes. My heart felt like it would jump out of my chest. He locked eyes with me and I felt weakened, but made myself continue. I somehow got the words out of my mouth that I wanted a tattoo. He gave me a book of tattoo drawings to look through, to decide what I wanted. Oh…I hadn't *thought* of what I wanted! I couldn't let on that I didn't even **care** what tattoo it was…I had to pretend I was really there for a tattoo, and if that were true, I would've at least had something in *mind*! Crap…

I pointed to the first feminine thing that I saw: a very plain sketch of a fairy. It was not elaborate and didn't even look professional, but it was either that or skulls and flames, so I quickly pretended to be in love with the drawing. It looked like a drunken retard drew the thing.

"I drew that myself," said the guy, who introduced himself as Jimmy.

I announced that I wanted it on my ankle, over the heart I had carved. He asked me if I was eighteen and I said I was, hoping he didn't want I.D. He took my word for it.

So there I sat with my ankle in the Hollywood guy's hands. He had on rubber gloves, and started to dig into my ankle with a tattoo gun filled with ink. I was never so happy. I know: I was crazy. But a L.A. Guns song was playing. A couple of cool Hollywood people were in the background. Lip Service clothes were on racks in front of me. And the tattoo didn't even hurt. I don't know if that is because I had developed a very high pain tolerance or the ankle just isn't sensitive, but I remember thinking, *What's all the stink about tattoos hurting? People sure are babies*. You would think that I ripped a beer bottle open with my teeth afterward, but I didn't. My euphoria of being tattooed did not end there.

Jimmy said, "If I do a good job, can I take you out?"

And I am ashamed to admit my answer, but, I will tell you. I said, "You can take me out if you do a *bad* job."

Classy.

Jimmy called me a day or two later and we went on a date (I don't remember where), and we were inseparable from that day on. I spent all of my time with Jimmy, who, despite the long hair and tattoos, had been educated at an upper-crust Catholic private school. It was something he kept secret, along with his upper-middle-class upbringing in the suburbs and his former blond crew cut. He had created a new image for himself, just as I had. He lived in his own apartment (wow!) on Coldwater Canyon and was a graphic artist; he had created many of the ads I looked at in *Rock City News* and *Bam*. Tattooing was something he did on the side (he had a picture of Drew Barrymore in his shop, getting tattooed near her bikini line).

Jimmy was not just a frequenter of the Cathouse. He was in the inner circle; part of Riki Rachtman's close group of friends. There were always articles and mentions of Riki and the Cathouse in magazines, but he was most recognizable from MTV, where he was a host for the rock show *Headbanger's Ball*. I knew his crowd was the in-crowd. Axl Rose of Guns N' Roses was one of the Cathouse members (who reportedly got him the MTV job), as was Taime Downe of Faster Pussycat. There was also a guy named Shannon Hoon, who was in a band called Blind Melon. He was friends with Axl through his sister or something. There was a guy named Tip, a guy named King T and some other dudes I don't remember. The members of Riki's inner circle wore leather jackets with a skull and a Cathouse logo on the back, as opposed to the T-shirts that were available to the public. You couldn't just buy one of those jackets- they weren't for sale. You had to be in that inner circle to get one.

After dating Jimmy for a few glorious months, I threw a wrench into my life. Once again, it was due to my own impulsive behavior. I got into a venomous fight with my mother, who I still hated with the fire of a thousand suns. I was still deeply wounded and seething at her for telling me to just go ahead and kill myself and I somehow wanted to give her a chance to give me a different answer than the one she gave the time before. I took a knife, walked out of the house with it, and told her I was going to kill myself. I guess I wanted her to chase me and say, "No! Please don't! I love you so much and I would die if you did such a thing!" But instead, she called the cops, remaining bitterly cold. I knew in my heart I would hate her for the rest of my goddamned life. And I did.

I remember going into my grandmother's room, lying on the bed and calling my good friend from Middleton, Todd Lewis, to tell him I was about to be locked up again. He kind of helped me to cool down. Next thing I knew, there was a cop in the doorway. I was about to be dragged back to the psychiatric ward. I thought *Awwhh shit.*

I wasn't *really* going to hurt myself. I knew the whole thing was going to be a big waste of time and a huge disruption to my life (most of all my new relationship) but *I* was the one who had cried wolf. So I had to deal with what I had started. I asked the cops if I could go to the bathroom first, before I went through the long process of being hauled off, tested for drugs, and put into a holding tank. I really did have to go to the bathroom, and everyone was reluctant about letting me, in case I was going to kill myself in there somehow, or climb out a window. When I came out, they handcuffed me and put me into the back of their police car in front of all of the neighbors. I was taken back down to the same hospital to have my freedom taken away. Again. (*Sigh.*)

I was on suicide watch at the hospital and I was bored to tears. At first, I shared a big room with four girls who were younger than me. I broke down one night in that room, laying on the floor and crying to a staffer named Lori, an anorexic looking, redheaded lady with a Brooklyn accent. She tried her 'tough love' bullshit, which made me cry harder. She was **so** cold and rude, thinking that it was the only way to deal with someone like me. I *longed* for somebody, anybody, to put their arms around me, hug me, and tell me they cared about me. I felt so trapped. My mother had used that same tough method with me and it only hurt and angered me further.

The people in the hospital ward came around with a little tray full of white paper cups that contained various pills for each of us, just like the last time. I never knew what the hell I was taking. We had to take what they gave us because they checked under our tongues to make sure we swallowed everything. It could have been cyanide for Pete's sake, but you had to follow the rules or stay in there even *longer*. When my mother came to visit once with my sister, I pretended to be very spacey and very drugged. I wanted her to feel guilty, to feel bad for handing me over and letting them drug me. I detected a *hint* of concern, but nothing came of it.

I spent my days doing whatever was asked of me. If you disobeyed, you had to go into seclusion, and if you got physically out of hand, they would strap you down with restraints. I never had that happen to me; I was sure to be well behaved. I got the picture the first time and was not about to stay in there longer than I had to. I had things to do, a life to live, rock stars to meet. Debbie, a chubby, good-natured girl, was restrained one time for a totally ridiculous reason. She was not a threat to anyone- she was a kid. I was **so** frustrated for her, I knew she was just having personal feelings that she wanted to express and she couldn't. She had to learn to play by the rules to get out, just as I did.

I was soon moved out of the big room with the younger girls and into a small room that had two beds. My roommate was a girl my age named Eden. She had dyed black hair just past her ears and was sort of punk/goth/alternative. The type I would've hung out with at school. She was really cool. Eden and I used to get up in the huge window overlooking a busy street and take off our clothes and dance in our underwear. Sometimes we put lotion on our butts and then stuck them on the glass to make butt prints. We held up colored signs that said, "We're crazy!" That was one of our thrills, that damn window and the rush of acting like crazies.

One day we were all taken to a pool to go swimming. All of the girls were allowed to wear two-piece bikinis except for me. They banned me from the two-piece. They said I looked too sexual. It made me feel bad and dirty toward myself. I did not have a stripper bikini; it was a regular, store-bought bikini. No one had boobs the size of mine, of course, but that wasn't my fault. That was my body. It reinforced the thought that I was a blatant sex object even if I didn't want to be, and it made me feel that anything that happened to me was my own fault for looking the way I naturally did. That was kind of the story of my life at that time.

Eden and I had a crush on a guy who worked in the ward who was only a few years older than us. Not a *crush* crush, but more of a boredom crush. His name was Tad and he was pretty hot, for a guy who wore Dockers and didn't have tattoos. We would summon him, ask him useless questions, and then check out his ass. He was always a little nervous to come into our room alone and managed to remain professional around us. I entertained the thought of trying to seduce him out of having nothing better to do, but I decided I was really into Jimmy. I missed him terribly while locked up. One day he called the payphone for me. He said that he had spoken with my mother and she told him I was only sixteen. *Gulp*. I had told him I was eighteen when he gave me the tattoo, and I had never corrected myself. I didn't expect to still be dating him! I thought for sure he would dump me for the lie, especially since he was twenty-one. But he didn't.

118

Jimmy and I continued dating when I got out of the hospital. I really clung to him and spent a great deal of time with him in his apartment. The cool thing was that he clung back to me. We both seemed to be starved for affection and we were more than happy to shower it on each other. As the year went on, Jimmy became my first boyfriend and we entered a serious relationship. He still went out all of the time, to both the Cathouse and Riki Rachtman's other club, Bordello, but I wasn't afraid of competition. He was smitten with me and we were crazy for each other. Looking back on it, it was my first time being in love. Was it comparable to the love I have for my husband now? No. But for a sixteen-year-old it felt very real and my heart was twisting and turning with every argument or crying spell. Every song reminded me of him and we were very big into baby talk and romance. It was us against the world. He and his eyeliner, tattoos, and long black hair, and me looking the part of a rock and roll girlfriend with a bikini model's figure, tiny clothes and of course, my tattooed ankle. We were a perfect match.

Just my luck, none of the time we spent together was in Hollywood. We hung out at his place on Coldwater Canyon watching movies and then he moved to a condo somewhere else, where we spent a lot of time by the pool and drinking with friends. We made dinners and were just homebodies. I loved him, so being with him, wherever that was, was fine by me. The guy didn't have a dime, which was evident when he made me several dinners of white toast and spaghetti, costing under $3.00 per dinner. Don't get me wrong, it was somehow totally delicious.

While I enjoyed most of my time with Jimmy, there was one thing irking me. I desperately wanted to start going to the Cathouse with him and his friends. But I was banned from both of Riki's clubs, Bordello and the Cathouse, supposedly because I was underage. Please. This was Hollywood. I knew Jimmy could get me in. I started to become a little bitter toward him. He loved me, but he wasn't about to ruin his standing with the most prestigious crowd in town. None of the guys brought their girlfriends out and he wasn't about to be the one pussy who brought his girlfriend everywhere. We got in several fights that summer because I felt kind of trapped. I could only go places when Jimmy decided to bring me, and he didn't want to bring me out with him very often, if at all. I couldn't let on just how desperately I wanted to go to Hollywood, so I let it go. I had fallen in love with the guy.

I started to hang around my childhood girlfriend Cristabelle around that time, on days I wasn't with Jimmy. She was fifteen, a year younger than I was, and she wanted to go out and have fun. She had long, thick blond hair, dark eyes, and an athletic body. She wore well-made clothes and there was an expensive, powdery scent in the air when she walked by. She lived with her parents in an affluent area of Sherman Oaks, south of Ventura Boulevard. Her parents drove a Mercedes and a BMW and had a *gorgeous* home that literally overlooked the San Fernando Valley. There was a cobblestone driveway in the front leading up to a very landscaped two-story house full of antiques. There was a formal sitting room which we weren't allowed to enter, a maid named Luisa, and two or three white Persian cats and kittens who padded around the slate flooring in the foyer. The backyard had a huge swimming pool and a patio full of white padded lounge chairs.

Leaving my run-down neighborhood to come to that house was always like going to an expensive day spa. There was food, beauty products, clothes and every amenity I could think of. But most of all, I was *safe*. That is the main thing I felt. *Safe*. I felt protected by Cristabelle's family. If something happened to us, we would be rescued and have a full legal team behind us. When something happened to me at home, I was on my own. You can bet your left tit that if Cristabelle's gynecologist tried getting fresh with her, there would be a cop arresting that doctor the very next day and he would pay for what he did. If we got a flat tire, or if someone tried to scam us or we were abandoned somewhere, we would be saved. Before Jimmy was in my life, I was left places and no one would come get me. People tried to take anything I did have, and did horrible, horrible things to me. But nothing bad would happen to me when I was with Cristabelle. That was one of the main things I looked for in a friend as the years went on. If a girl came from a solid family, I was very likely to make friends with her.

Cristabelle's room was a cloud of pastels. It was full of designer clothes, perfume bottles, and scented candles. Little fairy and angel trinkets were dotted about the shelves. Pictures were matted and framed on the walls; it was very different from the haphazardly taped magazine pictures on my own walls. Her bedding was always so soft: she had a thick, white goose down duvet, egg foam under the soft sheets and six goose down pillows. My own bed contained precisely one flattened pillow and it was so old that cavemen probably used the thing. I never slept as well as I did when I was at her house. Next to her bed was a bubbling aquarium that hummed us to sleep at night. There was central air always keeping the place cool in the summer and warm in the winter. It was heavenly.

Her bathroom was my favorite, because it had two sinks in which we sat to do our makeup. There were thick pink towels, movie star lighting around the mirrors, and body lotions in every floral and fruit scent lined up on shelves. She had expensive makeup that she didn't bat an eyelash at letting me use. I most liked her huge stash of Borghese that she crammed under her sink as if it was garbage. It would've taken me a year of lunch money to save up and buy my own. My favorite products in that bathroom were the glorious conditioners and hair products by Joico. They smelled delicious and were in pale lavender bottles. She had so many bottles of conditioner in her shower! Nexxus, Paul Mitchell, Sorbie, KMS, Mastey- I wanted to try all of them. I felt like a queen getting made up in that bathroom; it was so lovely. I was used to using Infusium 23 in my hair and makeup that I stole from the local Sav-On drug store; none of this salon quality hair stuff or department store cosmetics. Those things were not even *available* in my world. I had never set foot in a store that sold things like that.

She had a walk-in closet full of clothes and shoes. She sometimes let me borrow this lime green Betsey Johnson top, with tons of pink and red cartoonish flowers on it. I *adored* that top and had a good night whenever I wore it. Wearing Betsey Johnson, a *real* designer who had a shop on Melrose that I could never afford, made me feel pretty and confident.

Cristabelle was just as interested in going Hollywood as I was. She wasn't into the more obscure bands; she was more interested in mainstream bands like Slaughter. I could tell it was going to be a passing fancy with her, because her dedication to the project (as I saw it in my head) just wasn't strong enough. But I didn't give a shit, I needed a partner in crime. Neither of us had cars or could drive, so she decided to beg the only logical person: Jimmy.

I acted nonchalant during the begging- it was crucial that I didn't appear too eager. I let her do the dirty work and sat back, not wanting to ruin my validity with him. I was crossing my fingers she would somehow flatter him into taking us. He finally caved and said he would take us to the Rainbow. I nodded calmly while she screamed and jumped up and down. In my head I thought, *The Rainbow! The famous Rainbow Bar and Grill!* I wanted to fall back onto my bed and kick my feet really fast in the air. I knew from my magazines that there was no other spot that contained so many rock stars per square foot. All of the bands I loved always referred to it in their magazine interviews. It was on the Sunset Strip, next door to The Roxy, which was another place I dreamed of going.

My plan was in motion, baby!

CHAPTER SEVEN

The Sunset Strip

Sunset Boulevard. What was the big deal, you ask? Well, technically, it was only a street that ran from downtown Los Angeles to Malibu (it dead-ends at the Pacific Ocean). The famous spot known as "The Strip" was/is the mile and a half portion of it from Doheny Drive to N. Crescent Heights (incidentally, the intersection of Sunset and Crescent Heights was a special spot for my family: my great grandparents owned a beauty salon there back in the 1940's). The first buildings went up around Sunset Plaza in the mid 1920's. The area wasn't part of the city of Los Angeles back in the day, so it wasn't as heavily watched by the police. Alcohol was served there during Prohibition and casinos popped up around the area because it didn't count as part of the city (you could gamble in the 'country' but not the city). It was the seedy, crazy part of town, which attracted many people working in the film industry. The area became more glamorous in the 1930's and 40's when more restaurants and nightclubs popped up. In the 30's, there was the black-tie, French-themed Café Trocadero, where everyone went to Jitterbug under hand-painted murals of the Paris skyline. Fred

Astaire, Bing Crosby, and Jean Harlow frequented the spot among hundreds of other big names. In the 40's, there was the green silk-draped Ciro's (which later became The Comedy Store), where many stars dined, danced, and got themselves into the gossip columns. Humphrey Bogart and Lauren Bacall, Lana Turner, even President Kennedy dined at the Baroque-decorated club. There was the Latin-American themed Mocambo, with its light blue interior and bright red columns, which had glass cages of live parrots lining the walls. Frank Sinatra and Ella Fitzgerald performed their acts there and patrons included Howard Hughes, Elizabeth Taylor, and Bob Hope. Although that old Hollywood heyday was over, the Sunset Strip was the still the most glamorous spot for a girl into old film stars (and current rock stars) to set foot.

I was nervous, sitting in the car with Jimmy and Cristabelle. The traffic was completely stopped in a big jam the whole way up The Strip. It was very dark out but there were so many lights twinkling from cars' taillights and nightclub signs that everything was lit up in reds, blues, and pinks. I looked out of the car window and saw crowds of cool people, all talking and laughing while passing one another on the sidewalks. It was like a huge street party. Some people were yelling to their friends across the street, and others were jaywalking through the traffic jam and shouting at their friends in cars. I saw *tons* of cute guys, pretty girls, and lots of backlit marquees advertising bands that were playing at this place or that place. Eight by ten pieces of neon paper were stapled to every phone pole and littered the ground like huge chunks of confetti in hot pink, acid green, lemon yellow, and bright turquoise blue. They were band 'flyers.' Band members passed them out to everyone walking by to try to get them to go to their performances. The flyers had the show date and time on them, along with a promo picture of the band.

I really wanted to get out and walk around in the crowds, but I didn't want Jimmy to come with me because he always seemed to be getting into altercations when he went out to Hollywood.

He very often came home with a black eye or a smashed jaw, due to some disrespectful utterances muttered by drunken club-goers. He told me stories of what he could remember: Some guy said he looked like a fag, or someone messed with one of his friends and he had to stand up for them. Many of the instances sounded completely foolish and few warranted actual fights from what I could decipher. I hoped the fact that we would be inside the Rainbow would tame some of the violence that might be provoked out on the streets.

I wore a very risqué outfit that night, something along the lines of what I had seen in the local magazines featuring Cathouse girls. I borrowed a black bejeweled bustier from Cristabelle and paired it with a tiny black skirt, high black shoes, and huge hoop earrings. Cristabelle wore a tight purple velvet dress with a spiked belt and huge cross earrings that sank into her long blond hair- she looked very cool and at least had her stomach covered; I had a completely bare midriff. I assumed everyone would be half-naked and I wanted my debut to be perfect.

Jimmy valeted his car and we got out and went up to the crowded line at the Rainbow. It looked like a small English Tudor house with a big vertical sign that was striped in rainbow colors with black lettering over it. I could hear rock music brazenly blasting from the open front door, "Rocket Queen" from Guns N' Roses. I was shaking. I thought of the things I had heard about the Rainbow, such as the fact that John Belushi ate his last meal there. I knew Led Zepplin used to hang there, as well as John Lennon, Ringo Starr- even *Elvis* went there. But even before that, the place was once a restaurant with some other name - Judy Garland's director husband Vincente Minnelli owned it. He proposed to her there. Judy *Garland*! She was in this establishment! And Marilyn Monroe met Joe DiMaggio there on a blind date. Marilyn *Monroe!* Charlie Chaplin and John Wayne even ate there. But more important to me was the fact that in the 1980's, the Rainbow was the hangout of Mötley Crüe, Ratt and Guns N' Roses. It was a combination of old Hollywood history and new Hollywood - and I was standing there in front of it! I was beaming (*secretly*, of course).

I can't remember if Cristabelle and I had fake ID's at that point or they let us in without ID or what. I think that, technically, you could eat in the restaurant if you were under twenty-one; you just weren't supposed to drink. Anyway, I was sixteen and she was fifteen, but no one gave a shit. (And may I please note for the record that I am sure this fine establishment is much different today and plays by the rules- we are talking a long time ago here. Ahem.) Okay, so, we finally walked inside, past a man in a suit with a carnation in his lapel. It was very crowded, very dark, and the music was even louder. I hung onto Jimmy and held Cristabelle with my other hand, as I passed mutton-chopped Lemmy Kilmister from Motörhead in a denim jacket. I was afraid I would get lost and never see the light of day again. There was a main room with a big, blazing fireplace and about twenty big, red leather booths filled with people. Rock and roll memorabilia was crammed onto the walls: gold records, guitars, autographed pictures. It was kind of like the Hard Rock Café in a way, except that the rock stars actually hung out at the Rainbow. The place looked like an Italian restaurant underneath all of the paraphernalia; there were red glowing candle jars and big pizzas at each table. People could barely get out of the booths, because every inch of walking space was taken up by crowds of rockers. It was wall-to-wall *packed*, to the point that your body was up against other people, not unlike the RTD bus that I took home from school. There was a downstairs bar behind the fireplace and then there were stairs heading upwards to another story. Upstairs, there were bathrooms, and then *another* stairway to go even *further* upstairs to a dance floor and another bar. It was as if there were a million dark *tunnels* in there. I remembered hearing that the little secret loft upstairs (that they called the 'Lair of the Hollywood Vampires') was the spot where Alice Cooper, Keith Moon, and their buddies partied when they came to town back in the day.

As I looked around, I realized that I was actually a little *too* sleazy looking. The girls were not that naked. They were in dresses and what not, but they were not showing as much as I was. I got it wrong and I was embarrassed, for the *millionth* time in my life. I got drunk because I was *really* nervous. How many doors would I walk through completely overdone, until I got the hint? Geez. I felt a little better after a few Long Island iced teas- that was when I asked Jimmy for his Lip Service jacket and I decided to cover myself.

I couldn't believe I was there. The one and only Rainbow Bar and Grill, meeting place of every rock star on the planet! It was in all the music videos. And there I was, *me*, amongst crowds of cool people! I looked at a collage on the wall of different stars partying. I wanted to savor the moment. It was pretty sketchy how we kids were having cocktails, but hey, that's Hollywood. If you look good, you're in. So anyway, as the night went on, the parking lot between the Rainbow and The Roxy started to fill with people. I didn't know until later that it was the spot where many people scored drugs at 2 a.m. We walked through the parking lot at closing time (the Rainbow played "Sweet Child o' Mine" as their "last call" song around 1:30). I was feeling bold and brazen after several cocktails and decided I wanted to show off, so I took off the jacket. Immediately, a bunch of guys whistled at me and started to make comments about my boobs. Jimmy started yelling at them and challenging them to a fight, which I talked him out of. I was like, *What, are you going to take on ten guys by yourself!? Am I supposed to be your back up here in my high heels? Ignore it!* He started fights with any man who whistled at me, which was basically everyone. Even *blind* motherfuckers were whistling at me. Old men, young men, gay men, monks; the whole *world* was whistling at me and this poor guy tried to defend me. The thing that really sucked for him is that he couldn't fight! He was always getting beat up. That never stopped him though.

Jimmy didn't want to take me anywhere in Hollywood for a while after that. Cristabelle was asking and asking when we could go next, and I didn't have an answer. We decided we had to take matters into our own hands. We were determined to get down to Sunset by ourselves and party on the glittered sidewalks. It was too delicious to pass up, too exciting not to return.

Cristabelle got us a ride down there one summer night. We got to The Strip, parked somewhere, got out, and started walking up the street. I was finally trotting up the world famous Sunset Strip. I no longer had to read about it in my bedroom. I didn't have to look at it from a car window. I was there, breathing in the cigarette smoke, perfume, and the scent of leather. I was exhilarated and scared at the same time. I watched musicians passing out their colorful flyers in the warm summer air, smiling and being friendly. Probably because they kind of *had* to if they wanted people to come to their shows, but still. It dawned on me that the Sunset Strip crowd was different from what I saw of the Cathouse crowd. I thought they were one in the same, but no. The Cathouse guys were a little older, darker and biker-esque. They were not into the glam look. They were more into the L.A. Guns look: black leather pants, dyed black hair, maybe a little eyeliner (but no other makeup) and a lot more tattoos. Nikki Sixx and Tommy Lee were more Cathouse. The Strip was younger; a colorful candy store full of cartoon characters in more costumed attire. They wore *lots* of makeup, had *lots* of hair spray in their hair and most of all, lots of color in their clothes and accessories. They were a lot more happy and light. They were less threatening. They were more about the party.

The night was magical. It was a freak show combined with a rock video combined with a beauty pageant. I had never laid eyes on so many creative, extraordinary people. Because I was wearing black that night, no one even looked at me, boobs or not. There were beautiful, tan, blond girls in pink and sexy brunettes in white. There were so many better bodies than mine, so many girls with longer hair, longer legs and bigger smiles. This wasn't gonna be easy. I realized at that moment that I had never seen pictures of the people on the actual Strip. The local magazines showed pictures of people inside clubs watching shows- and it was all in black and white film. It was a *lot* crazier in real life. I started to take many mental notes.

As we walked down near the Rainbow, an old guy pulled up in a sparkly, bright purple Excalibur; it was one of those long cars that had a spare tire on the side, real old fashioned looking. He got out of the car in a purple hat and a sparkling purple jacket with a lit-up beating heart glowing through it. He had long, frizzy white hair. He looked like a wizard or something. And if *that* wasn't weird enough, a cat jumped onto his shoulder from inside the car. He was walking around The Strip doing card tricks and that cat just sat quietly on him the whole time. It was truly bizarre. The guy's name was Fig and the cat's nametag said "Figgy."

Most of the guys on The Strip were stunning. Some had bronze tans and long, super pale champagne blond hair wrapped with a pink scarf. They had exaggerated beauty spots penciled in above a lip, eyes lined in blue or black and bubble gum lip gloss on their lips. Some wore scrunchies in their hair (it was 1990 y'all) or rainbow plastic charm bracelets on their wrists. Other guys had their hair half up and half down, like a girl. Some wore clips in their hair, or bandanas tied into a bow on top. Some were wearing blazers in dark pinks or purples and wore polka-dotted or striped headbands. I saw a guy with long, straight, flamingo-pink hair who wore checkered tights under his shorts that were cut off at the knee. Another had turquoise blue hair and a leather jacket with bright candy airbrushed on the back. They were amazing. It was as if I were back in my ten-year-old bedroom, looking at a bunch of pink and glitter and neon. It was a potpourri of 1980's New Wave, circus clowns and *Vogue* spreads.

There were other types too. There were black-haired guys with a punk vibe who wore bondage pants and torn T-shirts. Many of them had tattooed arms like the Cathouse guys, but the difference was that their tats were not skulls, flames, and devils. They were cartoons like Bugs Bunny or Betty Boop. They were about as hard core as a unicorn.

I heard some of their names through the crowd. There was a definite theme going on with the names. Lots of Jamies, Billys, Bobbys, Rikkis and Johnnys. I thought, *Damn, I haven't heard these names since "Cool it Now" by New Edition*...I also heard some other girly names like Candy, Holly, and Ginger. I could have sworn they were names of guys, but I wasn't sure. There was sort of a scale of gayness, for me at least. Some of the guys looked *way* too much like women. They were too close to being transsexuals. I would have felt gay if I had hooked up with them. Many of them were walking a fine line, but still man enough to want to screw as many girls as possible.

Guns N' Roses and Poison had recently made it big by first playing The Strip, along with Ratt, Van Halen and several others. Bands from all around the country came to L.A. to play the same club circuit in hopes of drawing attention from record labels. There were bands from Detroit, New York, Boston-everywhere. Many musicians moved to L.A. alone and created their own bands once they got there. They went through the want ads in *Rock City News* and *Bam*, and auditioned potential bandmates. Some bands were looking for serious musicians, but many were looking for guys who had the right look. Once they got something together and named their band, they got to work on practicing for shows and promoting.

It felt like Halloween on The Strip when the bands passed out their flyers, because they each had their own little theme. I felt like we were all trick-or-treating. There were bands with a beachy theme, some with a gypsy theme, and others with a kids' cartoon theme. I saw variations of punk and glam, vampire and glam, and plain old beauty school dropout glam. They each had their own vision, their own brand, and their own marketing and publicity ideas. I was a big fan of candy and toy packaging, so I really appreciated the work the bands put into their themes. I loved the bubble letters, stars, glitter, candy, kiss marks, lightning bolts, and leopard skin. I felt like it was what my teenaged life had been missing, this creativity, this imaginativeness. This scene was not just music to me, and it wasn't just about cute guys- it was about people who were into their art, into their creations, into making something out of nothing. People who not only loved music, but who recreated themselves, who deconstructed clothes to make a new look, who made their own rules and their own scene. It was wild, it was shocking, and it was adventurous. The creativity level was at such a high that it was electric. I had a deep respect for these interesting people (not to mention fire in my underwear for a few of them), because they had left their hometowns, come to Hollywood, and were convinced they would survive. There was only a small percent of the population who actually thought they could get away with something that risky- it was a certain personality type, the type that left their comfort zones and marched straight into the unknown, completely exposed. And it was that spark that rose from the crowds of people on Sunset.

One of the first bands Cristabelle and I saw passing out flyers was named Drop Dead Gorgeous. Two of them were really handsome, but wearing red lipstick. They had really long, black hair and wore all-black clothing, but were still masculine somehow. Their theme appeared to be glamorous vampires. One of the guys was named Loren. He looked right past me and was instantly taken with Cristabelle. I thought *he* was drop dead gorgeous and was immediately jealous. *Painfully* jealous. She got into flirt mode and snagged him, straight away. I felt kind of down and defeated the rest of the night. Was I pretty enough for this place?

Cristabelle ended up dating Loren in the coming weeks. One night we went to their show at the Coconut Teaszer, which was on the corner of Crescent Heights and Sunset Boulevard. I believe it was painted purple at the time, in honor of The Zeros (an all purple-haired band) playing there. Even though it wasn't close to the other clubs, it was one of the spots that all of the bands played (same thing with the Troubadour on Santa Monica Boulevard). The Teaszer had a big flight of stairs that you had to climb to get into the front door. It was super dark inside and there was a tiny little stage that was really close to the ground. It felt like someone was just doing karaoke in your living room. There were all sorts of nooks and crannies in the place, kind of like the Rainbow. There was an outside patio overlooking the huge intersection, a dance floor off in another room and a few different bars. I was less nervous than I would have been in The Roxy or a place with a bigger stage and more people in the audience, but I was still kind of scared. Scared that I looked like a geek, scared that I wasn't acting cool, all of that.

Drop Dead Gorgeous played their show and we tried to show support without looking like morons. I was thinking, *Should I bop my head to the beat? Should I smile? Not smile? Lean against something? Not even watch?* We ended up standing there looking like bitches. We thought we looked older if we didn't talk or smile. Out of the corner of my eye, I tried to look around the room to see if I was dressed like any of the other people. I guessed I was in a way- but I was playing it too safe. I was in black again and went unnoticed. I couldn't seem to strike a good balance- I was either way overdressed or invisible.

I was secretly mesmerized by the guys in DDG and very interested in seeing how they operated in the daytime. How did they live? Did they have regular jobs? Did they hang upside down like bats to sleep? I found out soon enough. Cristabelle and I started to go over to their place so she could see Loren. They all lived in a one-bedroom scumbag apartment on De Longpre in Hollywood. It was in a bad area- total crack central, not to mention a major pick up place for male hustlers. Anyway, I used to sit on their couch and just stare at all of them getting ready to go play a gig. They'd all get around the one mirror in the place and get real serious while they applied their makeup.

They had pictures of The Munsters, El Vira, and Traci Lords all over the place. I guess those were their inspirations, and fine ones at that. In the daytime, they all laid around in shorts with their stringy hair sticking to their bony backs. Well, they all had bony backs except for the singer, who was rather chubby, bless his heart. He must have been able to sing somewhat, I don't remember. He wore vests over white frilly shirts and had long, frizzy hair.

I used to love the rush of excitement before Cristabelle and I got to their door. Kevin, the cute bassist who loved the red-headed 1980's teen singer Tiffany, lit up when I came in. He would look at me and say "GOOD GOD." He always bluntly flattered me. I started to wear skimpier clothing to try to elicit more compliments from him. Once I got a reaction from him, I would then feel guilty and cover up with a black jacket in case word got back to Jimmy that I was some wild woman about town. I didn't want to publicly disrespect him.

Cristabelle and I started going to The Strip every weekend. While we were getting ready we listened to Slaughter's *Stick it to Ya* album, namely the song "Fly to the Angels," and Mötley Crüe's *Dr. Feelgood* album. There was a band called Nelson, who had a hit called "After the Rain" (I didn't like them), that always played on the new station *Pirate Radio* (100.3). The song "Epic" by Faith No More was big and so was "What it Takes" by Aerosmith. We lounged by Cristabelle's pool during the day, me in a zebra print bikini and a pink scrunchie in my dark hair, and she in a neon orange bikini and her blond hair piled into a bun. Sometimes we listened to the regular mainstream music, like Madonna's "Vogue" or Mariah Carey's "Vision of Love," which Cristabelle belted so loud that it shriveled the goddamn plants. Laying there in the California sunshine, daydreaming about The Strip and eating sugared raspberries from a cut crystal bowl, I felt that my life was as good as it could get.

I started to notice the ins and outs of Hollywood pretty quickly, as I was always sort of a spy wherever I went. I was good at spotting details and trends. The Sunset Strip scene was nothing like hanging around Jeff Hunter in the Valley. There was a definite set of rules to follow. First off, very few Hollywood guys would ever have a name like Jeff. If they did, they would change it to "J.J." or something 'cuter.' They rarely had natural blond or brown hair. That was the kiss of death. Their hair had to be *platinum* white blond or dyed jet-black and at *least* past their shoulders. The colors could *not* be natural, only unnatural colors, which included streaks of pink, purple, or blue. If you had *any* sort of curl in your hair, you were "out." It had to be straight. Many ads for musicians looking for bandmates said straight out, "no 'brown hairs'."

Most guys on The Strip that year were considered Glam Rock. They wore eyeliner at the very least and at most a full face of makeup, including the beauty spot and lipstick. Glam guys were very skinny and not muscular in any way. Their bodies were almost all the same: very long stick legs in tight black pants and lanky, slouching torsos in colorful, glittery shirts. They rarely had chest hair and no one ever had facial hair. If you are thinking...*wait...they sound like girls*, you would be correct. They looked exactly like women. I don't know what that says about me and all of the other girls mesmerized by them, but think what you will.

If you were a guy with curly hair, you were fucked. If you were not skinny, you were fucked. If you were hairy, you were fucked. I realized at that point that Drop Dead Gorgeous, who I thought were so great, were on the 'not cool' list for having a singer who was plump with brown, wavy hair. You had to look like a supermodel, just to be a GUY on The Strip. So you can imagine how difficult it was to be a *girl*.

Anyone could go to The Strip. It was public property. But to get in with the in-crowd? You had to have something they wanted. And that was either: 1) beauty, 2) status, or 3) money. Usually, the face was most important, followed by youth and a hot body. There was no reason for anyone fat or unattractive to be present. If there ever was a fat person hanging in that crowd, you can bet your left ball that they had money. I know, I know. I sound like a jerk, but it's true. A few fat chicks were wealthy enough to buy their way in. The guys were always poor and were very money grubbing, so if a girl was three hundred pounds, and was willing to shell out money for the musician's expenses, she was allowed to hang out. It would be low profile, of course, so as not to upset their image, but they would not turn down money. It was not just buying drinks. Oh hell no. It was literally paying the guys' rent, or getting an apartment and letting guys live in it for free and keeping the fridge filled. One fat chick in particular was named Esmeralda and had very wealthy parents. She bought one platinum-haired glam rocker a *Corvette*. I am serious.

Most musicians lived with some sort of boring girl who wouldn't give them too much trouble and was generally just happy to be in their presence. Those girls would always fall in love with them and that made it difficult for the guys to date any one, or even hang out with girls like me.

The girls that became actual *girlfriends* to the guys on The Strip were usually beautiful *and* rich. Just being beautiful was not enough. I had it pointed out to me very bluntly, by a popular guy about a year later who had just discovered me in his crowd at a party.

He walked up to me and said, "I like your lips. I like how the top one protrudes like that. You're beautiful. You want a boyfriend?"

"Yeah," I said, seeing where it went, because he was such a sought-after person.

"Where do you work?"

"A beauty supply store."

"How much do you make?"

"$5.50 an hour." (I added on fifty cents, like that would make a difference.)

"Never mind," he said, and walked away, leaving me standing there.

In most crowds, men are chasing after females and the females are picking and choosing who they want. In this crowd, it was a very high ratio of women competing for a tiny ratio of men. The men were pursued; they had women throwing themselves at them. I saw how disposable the women were and I didn't want to be like that. I already felt bad enough about myself for my earlier mistakes with men and I knew it could be a landmine of even *worse* situations if I didn't watch out. I luckily had a boyfriend, so I didn't have to get into any situations with guys at that point. Regardless, I could tell it would be very hard to be a respected woman in the Sunset crowd. It seemed pretty impossible, laughable even. I was nervous about how I would carry out my plan.

One night, Cristabelle and I ran into a guy I used to know through the Casey crowd named Michael Michelle (he was called 'Mikey' at the time, but for all intents and purposes, I will use the name Michael, because that is what it changed to). He told us that everyone was going to the Swingin' Thing show at The Roxy that weekend. They were the new "it" band and all of the cool people would be there. Cristabelle and I agreed that we had to go. I was secretly thrilled that I could finally watch the main players in the cliques first hand. I could stand among them myself. *This was it!*

We showed up at The Roxy, trying to act all cool and unimpressed. I was terribly excited to be there, but I was sure I had to hide such foolishness. We went inside and it was super loud and very dark. The people I could see appeared to be smiling and colorfully dressed. Beach balls were being passed around in the crowd by tan girls with long blond hair and chalky pink, almost white lips that kind of glowed in the dark. They were in little Marcia Brady outfits of peach, yellow, and rose. They didn't look as sleazy as most of the other girls I saw. I later found out they were all from a beach town in Orange County called Huntington Beach. I looked around at the rest of the audience. It seemed as if every big band was there networking. Michael and his friends were walking around talking to people, not really watching the show. No one who was cool would go to the front of the stage; they stood back by the bar and socialized.

Swingin' Thing's songs were about surfing and doing it with the lights on. They even sampled the Beastie Boys' "The New Style." I gathered that I wasn't supposed to be paying attention to the band so I tried not to stand there staring, but inside, I thought they were really talented and different. I actually liked them. They didn't sound like suicidal Scandinavians or angry bikers. They were cute, happy, and sexy. I looked out into the crowd. Everyone was drinking, laughing, and tossing the beach balls. I was *sold*. I don't think I have ever been so sold. I definitely felt they were more my cup of tea than what Jimmy was doing. He could go ahead and go out without me. I had found *my* place, my very own scene. I wanted to be nowhere else.

Jimmy was still going to his own spots, and after a while Cristabelle stopped wanting to go out as much as I did, so I started hanging with Michael. Now I don't know if this is because I was unintentionally visualizing what I wanted until it came into being or what, but very shortly after running into Michael on The Strip, he moved into a condo only a few blocks from where I lived with my grandmother. A guy named Dusty owned the place and needed roommates, so Michael moved in along with a guy named Razz.

Razz was a big part of my Hollywood life. I met him through the Casey crowd as well, and had even hooked up with him prior. He had the look of a musician: very, very thin and very tall, with (let's all say it together now) long, black hair. How do I put this…His hair was not exactly luxurious looking and his skin was not the smoothest I've seen. And, I am sure he wouldn't disagree with me in saying, he had a big fuckin' nose. He was not your typical Adonis. In spite of all of that, he somehow thought he was fabulous and hot. He was *so* confident with his looks that everyone else believed him and treated him as such. He carried himself as if he was a god, often looking down on others for *their* looks. He had no problem getting girls and was dating some of the most beautiful women I had ever seen. It was fun to be around him when I looked good and it was hell when I was not up to par.

If I looked good, he fawned over me and praised me and paraded me in front of everyone saying, "Isn't she *hot*?" But if I had gained weight or I had split ends, he would let me know immediately. I felt like I was having a sit-down with my boss when I was told these things about my looks. It made me nervous.

Razz couldn't be bothered with anyone who didn't have "the look," whatever that was in his head. He called everyone 'honey,' as in "You just don't have the look, honey" (said with raised eyebrows) and he wore women's perfume. One of the greatest nights ever was when he pissed out of a fourth story window at the palm-tree-lined Studio Club on Wilcox, right over the entrance to the building. We were all shocked, and he responded by saying, "That's Hollywood, babe," in his drawn out, bored voice. When he walked out of the doors later that night, he slipped, literally catching air, and then landed straight on his back in a puddle of his own urine. Everyone said, "That's Hollywood, babe!" between guffaws and cackles.

Michael was also very confident, but in a more friendly way. He didn't make me nervous or scare me like Razz often did. He was a tiny little guy with super long, black hair and lots of makeup and colorful clothes. He was always laughing and joking and hanging out with whomever was up and coming, or whomever was deemed "in." He was very social and outgoing but excluded anyone who wasn't cool. He always dictated the in crowd. Razz would not be seen with a girl who didn't look like a supermodel, and he had to have some sort of respect for a guy to befriend him, even if it was just his look, so he wasn't as easy-going about things. Regardless, they pulled together an in-crowd for the Sunset Strip, linking different people from different bands together and hand picking pretty girls to join. And most important of all, they were more than willing to pick me up and let me tag along with them to Hollywood on the weekends.

It would usually be early evening, the sun still out. After getting ready, I laid there on my messy bed, listening to Hanoi Rocks or Faster Pussycat, arms propped up, waiting to see Razz's little red Mazda RX7 slow down in front of my house. Once I saw that bright red car, I ran outside, excited for the night to begin. Razz was usually wearing sweats and a scrunchie around his wrist. He always started out the evening going over how cool he was, reminding himself of his status as if to pump himself up for the night. It would go something like this:

"Honey, let me tell you something. I can't be *bothered* with someone who doesn't have the look, you know? I mean, *I* have the look. I look like a rock star. I'm tall, I have great hair, I have the clothes, I have the connections. It's only a matter of time before I am doing something big."

When we got to the condo, I took a seat on the couch. Dusty had a fluffy white Persian cat that looked like it should be eating Fancy Feast out of a Baccarat goblet. She chased shadows while the guys chatted about their love lives. Razz would reiterate how beautiful his chicks were (and strangely, I would find that he was not exaggerating), and how he dated nothing but the best. I nodded. Michael would tell me about girls who he had crushes on, asking if he should call or not call or why they were ignoring him. His voice was a pinched, nasally, Valley Girl voice- it sounded like this:

"Like, whot should I deewww? I like, *like* her. I think she goes out with a lot of other guys. Should I tell her I like her? Or maybe I should try to make her jealous…thot would be kewl…"

Then it was on to a beauty discussion. Michael and I discussed the plucking of brows and if it were normal to see a lot of hair in the drain when you took a shower. Sometimes Razz would cook dinner and yell in a shrill voice, *"Michael honey! Dinner!"* I would then wait for them to get ready for the night out. They drank their beers in the shower and blasted Yaz or Dead or Alive (Michael's two favorite bands). I loved the getting ready time. They sat around with their hair wrapped in petal pink towels, drinking more beer and gossiping. Then they applied their makeup with a steady hand, lining their eyes and applying lipstick, beauty spots, and mascara. Their hair took a while because it had to be teased and hair-sprayed.

We all drank until we had a buzz, piled into a car that was blasting music and got on the 101 freeway heading south. It took about twenty minutes to get to Hollywood, so we continued drinking beers in the car. It was very exciting, all smashed together on each other's laps, laughing, singing, and smacking each other. We zipped around traffic- Franklin to La Brea, La Brea to Fountain, Fountain to La Cienega, La Cienega to Holloway, Holloway to Sunset Boulevard. Once we got there, we parked on a side street off The Strip. We drank more beers in the car then got out in the dark and walked through the crowds, saying hi to (their) friends, stopping to drink with different people. We went in and out of the Whisky, The Roxy, the Rainbow, and Gazzarri's, not to mention the sushi bar across the street from the Rainbow, Ten Masa. Every one of those places was always filled past capacity and we could barely move. We continued through the night, getting increasingly drunk and doing reckless things like crawling over fences, getting in fights, peeing in bushes or being thrown out of bars. I felt like I was going to the biggest and best rager of the century every single weekend. It was non-stop. The vibe never died down.

Even though there was chaos coming from all sides of me, I felt in my element within all of this craziness. I felt so happy to be around people who weren't staring at me because they thought/heard some horrible thing about me. I felt happy to be in a group of guys who laughed and partied with me like I was one of them. When I went back to school, I walked with my head held up high. I was in a crowd that those kids could never penetrate. They would be laughed right out of the clubs. It eased my nervousness at school and even made me friendlier, because I felt *happy*.

Little did I know, I was about to get even happier.

CHAPTER EIGHT
Valley of the Dancers

Jimmy was peeved by my weekends with the guys, but I convinced him they were old friends and it was platonic. I told him I looked at them like brothers (brothers that wore makeup and pink). Although it annoyed him, there was nothing he could do if he didn't want to take me with him when he went out to his hangouts. The guy had worked hard to get to where he was socially; it took him a long time to create a name for himself and gain credibility. He had endured who knows how many days of rejection before being accepted into the personal lives of these cool people who were featured in magazines and on television. If taking *me* along with him was going to get in the way of that standing, then there was no question in his mind: I was simply not going with him. It wasn't up for negotiation. I wrote in my journal that summer:

Jimmy is painting this huge mural on the wall at the Cathouse and they say they are making him 'alumni' next. I guess I am happy for him, but it seems like they are stringing him along sometimes. It is a really big deal for him to be in that group

*along with Axl Rose, Taime Downe, Riki, etc. They get to wear a
special leather vest and be studs I guess. It seems similar to
rushing a fraternity. I guess to be initiated, you have to sneak
into the Universal Studios lot, climb up to the window of the
house used in the movie* Psycho, *slap a Cathouse bumper sticker
on the wall inside the window, and then take a Polaroid picture
of it. Apparently they have all gotten away with it, but I know he
is gonna get caught. He will do anything for them. He would
probably even dump me if they asked him to.*

I don't know if it is because I finally stopped asking him to go to
his hangouts and it worried him, or he knew it was going to be a
great show, but Jimmy finally invited me to the Cathouse one
night. He said I could bring Cristabelle. There was some special,
secret performance that was going to occur, during which some
of the guys from Guns N' Roses were going to jam with some
other famous guys. I was finally going to the friggin' Cathouse. I
could check it off my mental checklist. The thing that sucks is
that I was always drunk for these great performances of world
famous bands, so I can't even tell you if they were great or
horrible. I just remember keeping my eyes straight ahead and not
looking at anyone, trying very hard not to let on that I was a
sixteen-year-old that had no business being there. Inside, I felt
really lucky and special, and was delighted that Jimmy took me.

Jimmy moved from his condo into a house with one of his
buddies, who lived only fifteen minutes from my grandmother's
place. I saw him after school sometimes, and in the daytime
during the weekend. We left our separate social lives out of the
equation and spent our time being lovey-dovey and romantic.
He was a great guy, but he had his issues, like most of the people
in Hollywood. For one, he drank entirely too much and did
stupidly dangerous things like running across the freeway in the
middle of the night, dodging cars. And, like I mentioned
previously, he was *always* fighting. One time he knocked on my
window in the middle of the night with his pale face full of
blood. He was shitfaced drunk with his head kicked in. His blue
eyes were dazed looking, his black hair caked with dirt and

blood. He said he got knocked out by some guy and while he was on the ground, a girl kicked his head with her boot.

While Jimmy went out with his buddies and got into trouble, I continued to frequent The Strip with Razz and Michael on the weekend nights. We went to see bands like Jailhouse, The Zeros and Blackboard Jungle. I started to go there every single weekend, each weekend being more exciting than the last. I didn't seem to notice that I never paid a dime for a cocktail or an entrance fee. I just thought everything was free. Now that I look back, I see that other people were paying for me. While Razz and Michael were relatively popular with the doormen and often *did* get me in places for free, I am sure that Razz opened up his wallet more times than I realized.

It didn't take me long to realize that it irked Razz and Michael that I had a boyfriend. If a guy who they were impressed with thought I was cute and asked them about me, they had to tell him I was taken. They always rolled their eyes when I said that I wouldn't cheat on my boyfriend. I knew I would be a much bigger asset to them if I were single. I was sort of hurt knowing that they would offer me up like a sacrificial lamb if it would increase their social standing, but I also knew that it was all I had to bring to the table. I couldn't chip in for the twelve packs we drank before we went out, I couldn't drive and I wasn't putting out to any of them. There was no other way for me to pay my dues.

I turned seventeen that September and entered the twelfth grade. I was finally a senior. I signed up for journalism, the stock market club, and the literary magazine. I still had my long hair dyed bright purple and I took to wearing Jimmy's Cathouse shirts to school with Lip Service shorts and purple suede cowboy boots. I *loved* my style; I finally felt comfortable in my own skin.

There was a girl in my journalism class named Tricia Griffith. I had seen her around school and remembered that she was not liked by many people for one reason or another. She was rather obnoxious and had been beaten up by girls at school just for having a big mouth. She was half Iranian and half British, the Iranian appearing to be dominant. She had large, dark eyes with black eyebrows; smooth dark skin, and a prominent nose. Her hair was peroxided orange, the color that appears when someone with dark black hair tries to go blond. It was quite frizzy and damaged looking, with ragged, fried ends. None of that mattered to the guys though, because her body was slammin'. She was tall and thin, with long legs and big boobs.

I was minding my own business one day, writing some stories in my journalism class, when she came through the door cracking gum and crowing about her life in Hollywood. My spine stiffened and I straightened my Cathouse shirt. *Whoa, whoa, whoa* (cue the sound of horses being pulled by their reins) ...*Slow down there tiger,* I thought. I knew for a fact that she *had* no Hollywood life, or I would have seen her. I was the only one at school in the Hollywood crowd at the time, and I didn't want some loud bitch walking around squawking about how *she* was part of the scene. It was *me* who owned it, not her. Please.

I was torn between arguing with her and befriending her in order to keep my enemy close and snuff out any competition. She spoke of her French glam rocker boyfriend named Pierre. *Pierre*? I thought that name was ridiculous. No popular Hollywood guy would give himself a name that didn't end in Y or IE or at least have some Z's in it somewhere. It wasn't cutesy enough. Even Jimmy's name walked a fine line, but at least it ended in the "ie" sound, which was a literal requirement.

Journal Entry 12/1990

That BITCH named Tricia is talking about glam bands and Hollywood again, the things that are MY domain! It makes me feel faint and gives me a lump in my throat to hear someone I despise so much talk about something I completely love! I saw her "glam" boyfriend drop her off at school the other day. He *was so ugly. He had a shoulder length 'fro and wasn't even skinny! Some Glammie. She would **die** if she knew what I did this weekend. I was with Jimmy over at Riki Rachtman's apartment with Taime Downe and the rest. I have to hide that I am any sort of fan though; I have to be very unimpressed. Dammit, I want her to know how great my life is! I **have** to brag to her! No one else could appreciate what I get to do and who I get to meet!*

One day Tricia saw the bright strawberry red Swingin' Thing flyer inserted in the cover of my clear notebook and asked to see it. We started talking about the band and then about our boyfriends and what clubs they frequented. I found out that although she was still in high school, she lived by herself in an apartment. I was impressed. Her parents were in England, where she resided previously. She talked a lot about the Hippodrome, a hot nightclub in London. She also talked about Carnaby Street or some street that was similar to Melrose. I secretly rolled my eyes. I thought, *Europe? Please!* That was no Hollywood! Who would want to be in *London* when they could be kicking beer cans and stepping over bums and trash in Hollywood? There was NO comparison as far as me or my in-crowd friends were concerned. I had quickly forgotten how much I worshipped London as a young teenager because I was so caught up in my scene.

She then said she had never been inside an actual Hollywood club. I perked up. *I can show off!* I quickly invited her to the Swingin' Thing show at Gazzarri's that weekend. She wanted to bring her boyfriend, which I thought was a no-no, but I couldn't change her mind so I invited Jimmy. I thought, *She and her dumb boyfriend will realize how cool I am and how outdated and ridiculous they are, and I will be queen of the world; residing on a throne of leopard skin and crushed velvet.* It was all a ploy for me to pump my own ego and nothing further.

I knew her big boyfriend Pierre was not the most attractive thing on earth (his lack of hair styling knowledge was no help) and he drove a beat up black Trans Am. Jimmy was thin, had the right look and had recently bought a new black IROC Camaro (they were the shit back then). It was as if he was the upgraded, cool version of her boyfriend. I felt I was cooler than her from the get go. I know, lame, but I was competitive.

So anyway, off we all went to Gazzarri's. I loved that place. It was all black inside with big paintings of all of the former "Miss Gazzarri" dancers painted on the wall like cartoons. The girl's bathroom was a gold glittery box with a star on the door, like a little dressing room. We all ended up getting along famously. I still didn't exactly trust Tricia, but I wanted to show off. She was no Karen- I wasn't going to tell her my secrets or do facial masks with her. I just kept her in my little black book as a go-out friend. She was a classic *Frenemy*.

That December was the highlight of my year. Jimmy was invited to a private Ratt show at the Whisky a Go-Go on The Strip. I couldn't believe my luck! *Ratt*! My teenage crushes! I was *so* excited. We had press passes, as we did for all shows and concerts we attended. It meant that we were in the VIP room, backstage, partying with the people on stage. I nearly shit my Fredrick's of Hollywood G-string that night at the Whisky. Not only did I see Ratt play, but I was personally introduced to Nikki Sixx of Mötley Crüe and his wife, Brandi Brandt. You may be thinking *so what*. But keep in mind: I had been staring into the heroin-possessed eyes of Nikki Sixx all through the ninth grade. He single-handedly threw me over the edge with desire and led me away from the teachings of my Christian school. I can pinpoint it on my lust for Nikki Sixx. Was this a good thing? No! Was I happy to be face to face with the guy whose picture was in my school locker two years prior? *Fuck yes*. Nikki Sixx was tall with perfect white teeth, green eyes and a gorgeous face; I could barely look at him. I felt like fainting straight backwards. Brandi was beautiful and doll-like, dressed in black with long dark hair and scarlet lips. They were both totally polite and said hello, shook my hand and what not, as if we were at a personal friend's cocktail party.

So if seeing Ratt play in an intimate setting and mingling around the Sixxs wasn't enough, Riki Rachtman brought over lanky, blond Duff McKagan of Guns N' Roses, who was with a blond chick. I was like, *No, no, I **cannot** be meeting Duff McKagan right now, in a setting of his peers at a Hollywood show. This just **can't** be happening.* He was tall and hot and I could barely look at him either. He had a drink in his hand, a cigarette in his mouth, and a Sid Vicious chain around his neck. The girl was platinum blond with a heart shaped face, cherry colored lips and a white dress. They smiled, shook my hand, and were just as cordial as the Sixxs. I noted to myself that being introduced by someone with credibility was the ultimate way to meet these guys. I wasn't lifting up my shirt to a roadie in an alley. I felt important; I felt part of the crowd. So I was seventeen, so what? No one knew. We were in *Hollywood*. It was such a thrill! I am pretty sure I met Warren DeMartini of Ratt and his brunette wife, but I don't remember if I was introduced or if I just saw them. The night was so spectacular that I honestly felt like I had just taken twenty-five hits of crack. I was completely high on adrenaline. Fireworks were going off inside my head, confetti was sprinkling down in my brain. I wanted to do thirty backflips right there in my cheetah print pumps.

Jimmy and I continued to hang around Riki and his girlfriend Diane the rest of the year. Diane was very small and tan with really long, golden brown hair, green cat eyes and huge boobs. She was gorgeous. She had a gap in her teeth and a smoky voice. She did a lot of sexy posters- I often saw her picture taped up in guys' lockers at school. She was always in a see-through football jersey or a bikini or something. She was very sweet and friendly toward me. I liked her a lot.

Riki knew *everyone*, naturally, so if Jimmy and I went to a barbecue at his place, we were always graced with the presence of at *least* one rock star. Riki's huge cat, Baby, sometimes walked around in a little cat-sized leather Cathouse jacket when I was there. I think Jimmy painted it for him if I am not mistaken; he made it look like the others. It was fricking hilarious. With the exception of possibly staring at that big-ass cat, I am pleased to say that I never did anything inappropriate during that time.

I somehow managed not to screw it up and embarrass myself. I was never caught even *looking* at any of his famous guests or acting as if I were impressed in any sort of way. Again, it was imperative that I remain unimpressed, and I was determined to stay in character. I couldn't let on that I was only seventeen, or, more importantly, act like I *gave* a shit. I stayed quiet and calm all of the time so as not to reveal my age or lack of coolness. But I wanted to scream from the motherfuckin' rooftops and twirl on the hills like Maria from *The Sound of Music*.

One night I was walking to a club on The Strip with my friends and I heard some guys yelling from the traffic jam in the street. I looked over to see a big car full of jocks from my high school. I heard one guy yell, "So THIS is what you do on the weekends!" To them, anyone on Sunset was a prostitute. I thought they were such pussies for just staying in their car and being too afraid to get out and join the chaos like I did, but admittedly, it wasn't for everyone. They would not have been embraced without "the look," of course. They were jocks. Jocks looking to heckle some freaks. I worried that they would go back to school and announce that all of the rumors about me were true: I was a drug addict/hooker/stripper/porn star. Saying I was going into nightclubs would be too cool, they would have to make up something horrible. And my outfit didn't help matters: I was wearing a tight, low cut dress with cut-outs on the sides.

That New Year's Eve was fun. Cristabelle and I went to a historical Hollywood theater called The Palace, off Vine Street. It was a big old Spanish-Revival style building that had been there since the 20's. It had operated under several different names, but the building itself was used for radio broadcasts in the 40's, and television broadcasts in the 50's and 60's. In the 70's and early 80's it was the West Coast version of Studio 54. By the beginning of the 90's, it was still a magnificent venue and it was about to host my favorite band: L.A. Guns. I remember having the night of my life watching them play- it was awesome. Razz snuck me into the dimly lit and crowded VIP room (by dragging me straight through without stopping). He was hanging with Kristy Majors of Pretty Boy Floyd most of the night, chatting, laughing, and boozing. Billy Idol even came over to chat with them for a minute, I noted through my buzz.

Razz started dating a new girl named Missy around that time. His roommate, Dusty, was dating her co-worker, Sabrina. The girls were strippers- but one thing I learned in Hollywood was not to call strippers *strippers*. They called themselves exotic dancers, or just plain *dancers* for everyday use. I was *fascinated* by these particular dancers and their friends. I honestly could not stop staring at these chicks. They had very long blond hair ranging from sun-streaked highlights to platinum white. They were suntanned, like the beach girls from the Swingin' Thing show, and they wore very bright colors- mostly pinks (neon pink, taffy pink, hot pink, fuchsia), and metallic gold or silver. They were very bubbly and friendly- I didn't expect such pretty girls to be nice to me. They called everyone "babe" and didn't appear to have a negative bone in their bodies.

I idolized Missy the most and immediately formed a girl crush on her. She looked like Brigitte Bardot: lots of long blond hair, dark eyes lined in black 1960's eyeliner and pale pink lipstick. She was very tall and thin with big boobs and a huge movie star smile. I think the best thing about Missy, besides the fact that she was totally friendly and sweet to me, was that she took no shit from guys. My jaw dropped as Razz chased and chased her while she remained nonchalant and aloof. I sometimes saw him a blubbering mess, crying over her in the corner with his hankie. He couldn't have her to himself and he couldn't stand it. She was dating Stephen Pearcy of Ratt and it pissed Razz off to no end. He was so plucked! He tried to get her to be exclusive and she refused.

Missy was also a bit of a daredevil, which I found interesting.

Razz told us that she was driving him through Laurel Canyon one night and she was speeding so fast that her car spun out, bounced off the side of a mountain, and flipped upside down. They were wearing seatbelts, luckily, so when they looked at each other, all they saw was hair hanging down. We were like, *Oh my gosh, Razz! Were you okay?* He said, and I quote, "Honey, my makeup wasn't even *smudged.*" Other times Missy sped along the shoulder of the freeway if there was a traffic jam, or purposely ran red lights if she was in a hurry. She basically didn't give a fuck about cops, tickets, or getting in trouble, because she so easily got *out* of trouble by being so pretty.

Missy's friend Sabrina was also very wild, but in a different way. She was this tiny thing and had the same basic look as the others (tan, pale blond hair). Her stage name was 'Summer' and she was bisexual; something that came out after she got wasted. She appeared to be an instigator and was always making out with her friends, who went along with it if they were wasted enough. It wasn't a big deal to them, it was all laughable. I was intrigued by their nonchalance.

One night Sabrina tried hitting on me. I thought: *This is Hollywood. This shit can't be uncommon.* We were all drunk and happy in a dark VIP room, weaving in and out of people I had seen on MTV. Sabrina started to grind on one of the other girls on the dance floor. She was wearing a skintight, neon pink dress with long sleeves. Her bright blond hair was glowing. I thought she looked neat. Then the next thing I knew, she started trying to grab me, telling me she wanted to dance. *Shit,* I thought. I thought she and her friends were really cool, but I didn't know how to dance and even if I did, I didn't want to grind with her. I didn't know what to do. I didn't want to insult her but I also didn't want to look like a dork. She was hinting that she wanted to "get together" and asked for my number. I stalled and acted as if I had to pee, remaining friendly. I hoped she would be too drunk to remember what she was saying and wouldn't be mad at me the next day. Luckily, that is exactly what happened. She ended up getting in the car and making out with her friend,

Rachel, the entire way home.

I started to observe Missy and her friends closely. They were always having masses of roses sent to them and had lots of guys following them like puppies. They chased *no one*. Guys chased *them*, even in Hollywood, where the roles were switched. I had kind of just accepted that the guys were on a pedestal, but after meeting Missy and her friends, I saw it didn't have to be true. They didn't sit around waiting for guys to call. They didn't get heartbroken. Guys were all over them while they were just bouncing around town, happy as could be. They didn't want to be tied down. I thought...*Wait...THAT is what I need to be doing*. They couldn't be bothered unless they were with the *most* popular people and were going the *coolest* places and having the *best* time. Somehow, they pulled this off without looking bitchy.

Things and people were very quickly deemed "out" if it wasn't to their liking. That club is out, that drink is so out, and that color is out. I watched them in their tight Barbie dresses and long bleached hair, tripping on the new drug *Ecstasy*. They were dating stars like Vanilla Ice and David Lee Roth. I was not in their league. I was a regular high school student by day, trying to lead a normal life of writing commentaries for the school paper, making lopsided pots in ceramics and playing tennis in sweat shorts. I felt like a spy. It was hard to make conversation with the school girls my age who were going to the movies on Saturday nights in their high-waisted paper bag pants and teased bangs. I had no idea what a normal girl's life was supposed to be like. And even stranger than that: I was terrified of the normal kids. I wouldn't have known what to say or do on a date or what to do at a typical teenage house party.

Razz, Michael, Missy and her blond dancer friends became the new in-crowd on The Strip. I was the youngster in the crowd. They loved me. The girls were maternal toward me and kind of coddled me. One of the things I really liked about dancers is that they liked to hang around other pretty girls. Most girls I knew wanted to be the *most* pretty, so they wouldn't hang with another girl who would take attention away from them. That was kind of standard. But dancers were one big happy family of really gorgeous girls who were not threatened by anyone. They thought I was cute and treated me like a little sister. Being around them was like wearing a big, fluffy, warm fur coat; I felt protected and comforted in their presence. I sensed they were very tough people underneath their beautiful doll faces and candy colored dresses; I knew they could take care of themselves.

I decided to revamp my image at that time. I stopped wearing black and cut back on the purple because it was too dark in a crowd. Once I realized that I had to use color to bring attention to my image, things started to fall into place. I started to wear a lot of bright pink. I had a long-sleeved hot pink top that stopped just under the boobs and showed my flat stomach, which I wore with some matching little shorts. I also had the outfit in white. I bought a tight, bright green shirt and black hot pants. I wore swirly, Pucci-like tops in bright colors and sixties headbands. The shit was crazy. In a sea of blonds, I was the hot new brunette girl in pink with the blue eyes, long hair, big boobs and bare midriff. I darkened the beauty spot above my lip. I changed my lipstick color from a dark berry color to a cartoon pink. I was getting the hang of it. Was it tacky? Of course! I was amongst walking Barbie dolls of both genders. I had to get in on the craziness or be left in the glittery dust.

The place to get these over-the-top outfits was a store on Hollywood Boulevard called Playmates of Hollywood. I went there on a sunny spring morning with Jimmy, walking over the stars on the Walk of Fame. We turned in toward the two floor-length shop windows that always had really crazy displays. They were like Bergdorf window displays on acid, with a 'shrooms chaser. The mannequins weren't like the regular mannequins you see; they were more curvy and busty. One month it would be an *Alice and Wonderland* theme with tiny blue skirts and Queen of Hearts bikinis. There would be a Mad Hatter tea party full of various colorful lingerie and stage costumes, with some huge playing cards and trimmed hedges behind them. Another month the theme would be hell, or an S & M dungeon full of red leather bikinis and bondage costumes, complete with tasseled whips. Or they would do a *Wizard of Oz* theme with glittery red platform heels, tiny blue and white gingham bikinis, and a yellow brick road. One bikini would be silver for the tin man; one would be a deep, shiny emerald, and another would be black leather, worn with a witch hat. There were displays of summer barbecues featuring teensy, cut-off shorts, red checkered bikinis and little polka dot outfits. Sometimes it was a Parisian boudoir setting, full of pale pink lace lingerie and black satin ribbons.

I was inside the bright pink dressing room at Playmates that particular day, when I heard Missy's voice on the other side of me, telling whoever she was with that she loved the gold bikini. We both came out of the dressing rooms at the same time.

"Babe!" she squealed, and hugged me. Her hair was wet, she wasn't wearing makeup, and she smelled like chocolate cupcakes. She was with another pretty dancer who had her light blond hair up in a messy bun, wearing no makeup and pastel pink sweats. They were trying on "work" costumes. My excitement in seeing Missy quickly turned to horror when I realized I was with Jimmy, and I would have to introduce them. I didn't want him seeing the girls I hung with, and I was afraid Missy would find him uncool. I went ahead and made the introductions; Jimmy stiffly shook her hand and she was polite. She didn't seem to care either way, but I could tell he was pissed off. He later said that he could see me getting into trouble with her. He was right. I wanted nothing *more* than to get in some trouble with her. I wanted some of her sunny, blond sunshine; some of her power.

So there I was. I had my new look, a new attitude and new friends. The next thing I knew, the unimaginable happened: people started to know my name. I started getting lots of invitations to go to even more cool places. I was on the VIP lists and was invited to be a guest at the shows. I saw my own face in

Rock City News, the magazine I had once combed through to find out who the cool people were. My picture was added to the collage of photos on the wall at The Rainbow.

I regained my initial teenage confidence through the attention I received. I became very bold, very brave; I wasn't so broken. The only bad thing about that time was that I had to be completely wasted to live the life I was living. I had to be buzzed just to walk out the door in the outfits I wore. I had to drink to calm my nerves when hanging around rock stars and other cool, older people. I basically had to be drunk in order to walk into the rooms I was entering. It wasn't as if I was walking into high school dances on the weekends. I had made it into the exclusive, obscure crowd for which I was pining. I was constantly beaming. I felt like kissing babies, shaking the hands of the common folk and cutting ribbons at the opening of new towns. I was on cloud nine.

Could it last?

CHAPTER NINE

Cat Fight

One night, Brent Muscat of Faster Pussycat started hanging around our crowd. He was a friend of Razz's, so he was always kind of around in the background. He confided in Razz about his songwriting and his life and what not. His band was bigger by that time; he was more famous in my scene than he was when I was younger and had only seen him in *The Metal Years*. He came to the condo to have beers while everyone got ready and I stupidly called Jimmy from Razz's room to tell him I was leaving for Hollywood. Brent saw that I was all nervous talking to my boyfriend and wanted to cause trouble amongst us laypeople. He started playing around with me while I was trying to talk on the phone, grabbing one of my legs and trying to lift it up into the air until I screamed. I was trying to remain composed to talk to Jimmy, but Brent was determined to distract me from the call. I remember saying, "Can you hold on just a minute, Jimmy?" and then slamming Brent in the head five times with the phone receiver, as he laughed and tried to block me, the coiled cord becoming tangled around us. When I got back on the phone, Jimmy was furious. He didn't know who was in the background, and I knew it wouldn't be long before he found out.

The next weekend I was back with my friends in the hot tub at Dusty's condo. I sat there in my zebra print bikini from Marshall's, cursing myself for not being prepared with something cooler to wear. Through the rising steam, I looked at the tags on some of the dancer's bright string bikinis; they were all from a place called Ziganne's of Hollywood. *Ooooh, another place I need to check out!* I saved up weeks of lunch money and got a ride there one day. It was on Hollywood Boulevard, not far from the huge Art Deco Frederick's of Hollywood building that housed a small museum of movie stars' lingerie. Once again, the Walk of Fame was on the sidewalk I was using to get there. I looked down as my feet walked over the coral pink granite stars laid inside a dark gray background. They each had a little symbol to show the honoree's field: music, TV, film, etc. Some stars had bouquets of fresh flowers on them and others I had to go around because tourists were taking pictures next to them. I got a little heartsick when I walked over James Cagney's star. I loved *Yankee Doodle Dandy* when I was a young teenager. I smiled and looked at the other names over which I was walking: *Alfred Hitchcock...Count Basie...Alan Hale...*

I stopped at a glass storefront full of headless mannequins wearing brightly colored string bikinis. This had to be it. *Wow!* It was so cool looking. It was clearly the place for stage bikinis- I recognized the styles from pictures of the mud wrestlers from the Hollywood Tropicana and dancers at The Body Shop. I went inside and looked through racks of brightly colored string. Many were sequined or day-glo and they were all in really teensy tiny styles that barely covered your private parts. Some were breakaway, so they could be torn off. My boobs were real and not perfect hard balls, so the little spider web bikini tops in glowing violet didn't look good on me. All of the bikinis were unlined and would be completely see-through if they got wet, but they weren't for swimming; they were for working the pole on a stage. Why I thought that was so glamorous I do not know. I looked through clear drawers of sequined pasties out of curiosity: they were in every color from bright magenta to rainbow sparkles. Boxes of glue sticks were next to the drawers; for keeping things in place. They were regular kindergarten glue sticks; I was surprised that the girls used that on their skin. There were huge, puffy feather boas hanging in colorful bunches on the wall. There were purple chandelle boas with hot pink tips, baby blue ostrich feathers, and dense black swan feathers. Some of the boas were so thick that they looked heavy. I felt like I was backstage in a Vegas showgirl's dressing room.

All of the crazy bikinis intimidated me; I wasn't quite that confident. I looked and looked through the racks and ended up picking an all-white bikini. It was pretty standard: Brazilian cut bottom, triangle top. I looked decent in the thing, so I bought it. It was so tiny that the bag they gave me was only big enough to hold earrings. I was happy to be ready for the next hot tub night; at least I would fit in with the girls.

Lo and behold, I was invited to Dusty's to drink and go in the hot tub again on another night. Brent Muscat joined us that night and took to teasing me about having a boyfriend. Any sort of attention flattered me of course, but I could see he was just doing it because it was bothering me so much. When the night was over, I changed out of my bikini and back into my normal clothes. I wasn't carrying a purse, so I had nowhere to put my bikini. I stuffed it in a pair of black socks, and when Brent drove me home later, the ball rolled out into his car. Razz told me later that Brent thought I did it on purpose and was convinced I liked him. I certainly did not do it on purpose- I was dying, hoping there was no yucky crust in my bikini bottom.

Jimmy came over the next day. We were washing his car in the driveway when my mom came out the screen door, a little too delighted. Right in front of Jimmy, she said, "Some guy named *Brent Muskrat* called? And said you, uh, *left* something in his *car*? He said he will come by and drop it off." Jimmy looked at me and said, "You *left* something in *Brent Muscat's* CAR? What were you *doing* with **him** in the first place?!" I scrambled to try to explain myself.

On a weekend soon after that, Razz called me and invited me to a party at their place. I said I couldn't come because Jimmy was over and he told me to bring him along. I really didn't want to bring Jimmy into my private little world. I was nervous the guys would rat me out for doing something flirty or risqué or inappropriate; probably the same reasons he kept me from his crowd. But on the other hand, I kind of wanted to get the tension out of the way. If Jimmy finally met them and saw that they were 'harmless,' he wouldn't get so mad at me for going out with them every weekend. I finally realized that they would have to meet, so I could put the whole thing to rest.

Jimmy and I walked up to the door and Razz answered. I held my breath. When he first saw Jimmy, he made a horror-stricken face to me when Jimmy looked away, as if to say *THIS is your boyfriend? The guy who you are choosing over all of the prime cuts of meat we are presenting you with?!* I was very uncomfortable and wanted to turn around and leave. Razz then said, "Come over here, you bitch, and gimme a hug!" Jimmy appeared annoyed that he was taking such an informal tone with me. I went over to Razz and he whispered under his breath, "I do *not* approve." He made so many faces of disgust, that I was sure Jimmy would catch him. He didn't. It crushed me that Razz was critiquing the person I loved so much. After about five minutes of Razz snickering, I told Jimmy we should go. On the way home, he commented that Michael seemed like a dick and Razz seemed pretty cool. He had no clue.

Jimmy did something out of left field that winter. He somehow ran into the vampire bats of Drop Dead Gorgeous, the band Cristabelle and I hung out with over the summer. He said that they had parted ways with their singer and were looking for a replacement, and that he thought he might give it a shot. *Wait...what!?* I didn't know Jimmy was interested joining a band- I didn't even know he could sing. He had been content with being an artist and a scenester, but it seemed that he was now entertaining the thought of being a musician. I was pissed. Why did he have to pick *that* band of all bands to join? The offer fell through after a few weeks; the fit wasn't right in one way or another, and I breathed a sigh of relief. But my relief was premature: Jimmy decided *he* was going to start a band. When he told me, I immediately choked on my Rice-A-Roni. My eyes were watering as I tried to dislodge a piece of vermicelli from my windpipe. Did he ask his own buddies from his own scene to be in his band? No. He asked Tricia's overgrown ape of a boyfriend to be his bass player! My jaw was hanging open for so long that ten flies must have flown into my mouth. Couldn't this guy pick people other than the ones *I* knew?

***

In January of 1991, the United States went to war with the Middle East. The news called it "Desert Storm." I was actually concerned, in between drinking beers. I pictured myself in black and white film: there I was, clad in a 1940's dress and sergeant hat, singing "The Boogie Woogie Bugle Boy of Company B" while bombs went off in the background and sailors cheered in the audience. When I was at school, it hit me harder. We were assigned commentaries in journalism class, so we sat around watching the grainy night-vision footage on an old TV as we click-clacked on our typewriters. I was afraid of things I had never considered before. What if it got much, much worse? What if we were bombed? What if there was a draft? What if we had to start rationing food? We were children of the 1980's- we had never seen a *war*. Something that could bring hard times, something that could even bring death- those thoughts were new to us. I thought of the people who were actually fighting for our country and I was stunned at what heroes they were. I didn't know anyone like that. Everyone I knew wore more makeup than the entire cast of *Cats* and had pants so tight they had moose knuckles.

Okay; two things happened around then that set me back. And let me please state for the record that now, twenty years later, my thought is this: You can't blame your parents for your own bad behavior. It is up to you to control your own actions, to turn away from bad direction. You can't go be an asshole and say, "Well, my parents were jerks, so what do you expect from *me*?" That is bullshit. A cop out. But back then, as a seventeen-year-old, it was hard for me not to hate them and blame them for every single one of my problems.

One day after school, I was sitting at a bus stop in a bad part of town. I sat there waiting for the bus, hungry and tired; wishing I could be one of the lucky people who were in cars, driving straight to their destinations without stopping for thirty other people in the same vehicle. I looked up at a truck and saw one particular man's head looking at me. I focused on his face. It was my father. We met eyes for a split second and he saw that I noticed him. Just when I thought he would stop and give me a ride home, he turned his head and kept driving. I couldn't believe he left me sitting there. I watched as his truck got smaller and smaller. I had dealt with a lot of crap from him through my short life, but that really got to me. It crushed me pretty hard to see that truck pass me by.

That incident set me off and put me into another bad depression. I had troubling episodes of mania and violence in the following months. I started feeling really worthless and was basically full of rage inside. Jimmy and I started arguing, but not just arguing like regular people. We argued like typical Hollywood people: violently. One of the times, I dove at him and choked him as hard as I could, and then started socking him with all of my might. I could practically kick his ass. He crouched over and let me go at it. He never hit me back. One time he shoved me against a wall, but that was it (in my crowd, that was basically standard). I felt such guilt after my violent episodes that I crawled out of the room, locked myself in a bathroom, and beat myself with anything I could find: a brush, curling iron, whatever.

The second thing that affected me was that my mother threw me out of the house for not having a job. I know that I should have definitely had a job after school, but the way she went about the whole thing really hurt me. She told me that I had, like, a *week* to get a job and if I didn't have one by then, I had to get out. It was almost as if she knew I couldn't get one that quickly and was just trying to get rid of me. I was surprised at the whole thing, taken aback at the suddenness of the situation. I was out partying all of the time- I wasn't some great teenager. I am sure she had to do what she had to do, but her delivery was just so...detached. I just remember being really hurt looking at her eyes. They were dead. Flat. Black. She had no emotion whatsoever. She didn't care where I went. I just had to get the fuck out. Bye bye. So I went and lived with Jimmy until I got a job.

I tried not thinking about my parents, but I couldn't help it sometimes. I felt like, *Damn, the two people who are supposed to love me and care for me no matter what... don't give two shits about me. My mom told me to go **kill** myself and my dad not only laughed at me for being institutionalized, but he just drove by and left me sitting at a bus stop in a bad part of town.* Now mind you, I forgot all about this stuff when I was buzzed and out with my friends, but from time to time, I had to face my situation. I had these intense feelings that I wasn't mature enough to deal with in another way. I was so deeply hurt by these people that it stabbed at a spot really, really deep inside of me- a spot deeper than I thought my body could go.

Tricia and Pierre went with Jimmy and me to see a Tryx show at The Roxy the next weekend. Tricia was interested in walking down the rest of the Sunset Strip and seeing the Whisky. When our guys started talking, we left and walked down there. We didn't discuss what we would say to our boyfriends when we got back, I just assumed we were going to tell them what we did- I didn't see it as anything wrong. When we got back, they asked us where we went. At the same time, we answered two different things. I said "the Whisky" and she said "Nowhere." The guys were like, *Uh, which is it?*

"Tricia," I said, laughing, "We went to the Whisky, come on."
She looked at them with a straight face and said, "No, we
didn't." I wanted to strangle her in her white lace-up rubber
dress.

I called her the next day and asked why she lied and she said she
didn't lie, she was trying to save her relationship. She said Pierre
was highly jealous and she couldn't tell him she was at another
club without him there. I told her that I understood, but by doing
that, she was making *me* out to be a liar. She said she valued him
over me, sorry, but that was the way it was going to be. I hung
up thinking, *oh **hell** no; this bitch needs to slow her roll.*

I asked Jimmy to take me over there so I could talk to her. He
told me not to do anything stupid, because he was in a band with
Pierre and he didn't want to ruin it. *Yeah, yeah, yeah,* I said. He
took me over to her place. She was very cocky right off the bat
and wouldn't talk to me in the parking lot. She insisted we go by
the pool, where people were hanging about. *Fine.* I followed her,
looking at her tiny, cut-off denim shorts and little, red halter top,
like the girl in Warrant's "Cherry Pie" video. I tried to talk to her
and reason with her and she was bitchy, smirky, and rude. I sat
for about five minutes and stared straight ahead, trying to
compose myself. I looked down at my shoe. I should have been
thinking, *Why am I wearing these awful half boot/half shoes?*
But instead, I thought *I am going to beat this bitch with my
shoe... I have to calm down....Jimmy will be pissed.* Then after
some time I said, "I can do what I want to do, or what other
people want me to do." She cocked an eyebrow, smirked and
said, "What do YOU want to do?" while chomping open-
mouthed on some gum. I said, "You know what? It's no wonder
you have no friends- you are-" I didn't finish my sentence. The
cocked eyebrow did it. I immediately jumped on her, ripped her
head back by her hair and started socking her in the face. She
curled up into a little ball and tried to protect her face, but I
pounded right over her hands.

She was screaming, squawking, and shrieking. I could hear the

sound of my fist slamming her face over and over and over.
Curse words were coming out of my mouth that I didn't even
know existed, like the kid in *A Christmas Story*. I even scared
myself a little bit. In mid-pounding, a lady came out of an
apartment and screamed at me to get off Tricia or she was
calling the police. I didn't feel like being arrested again. I
stopped, but I wasn't done. I got behind Tricia and ripped her up
by her hair. I put my mouth in her ear and said, "If you fucking
scratch me; if you even THINK about touching me you fucking
bitch, *I will kill you.* I will beat you into the fucking ground, *do
you hear me*?" and she nodded, with her hands up in the air.
Then, the best part: I said, "I have a job interview tomorrow and
I don't need to be all scratched up." Always thinking ahead.
Then I threw her scrawny ass across a bunch of lawn chairs. She
went flying. I was thinking, *Damn, either I am really strong or
she is really light.* I think it was both. We composed ourselves
and walked out of the same gate, her in front of me. She stopped
and turned around toward me, her hair looking like a firecracker
had been set off on her head. Blood was peeking from one of her
nostrils. She screamed "GAAAT OUT!" in a crow-like voice
and pointed in the general direction of a maze of paths in her
apartment building. I quietly walked past her, saying nothing. I
let her have her dignity. I guessed she needed that.

I walked back to the parking lot and got into Jimmy's car. He
had no clue what had happened until I showed him my hand. It
was swollen and red. I was afraid he would be pissed at me, but
he just told me that I wasn't using the right part of my hand to
punch. He showed me how to make a fist and tried to tell me
how to tuck my fingers so they wouldn't get hurt. We went back
to his place and I iced my hand.

Tricia dropped out of school with only a few months to go until
we graduated our senior year. She never got a diploma. A small
twinge of guilt hit me. I had affected her life; I had prevented her
from achieving a milestone. But as always, I quickly washed it
away with some booze. Life wasn't easy. Tough shit for *her*. It
wasn't *my* fault that she was afraid to come back to school, or

whatever was wrong. I know...I was an asshole. I really was. The girl was bitchy, yes. But she got beat down pretty badly over something pretty trivial. I didn't know how to deal with anger. I didn't know how to solve issues with people without being violent. I couldn't control my impulses. I definitely would not do that today, but my mindset at that time was one of extremes.

I made it to my job interview (with no scratches) and got a job at a beauty supply store. The girl who hired me, Gwen, told her manager on the phone: "She is really pretty, I can't believe she doesn't already have a job." *Pretty?* I thought. Was that my qualification?

Gwen was a total bimbo. It was totally exaggerated to where I thought she had to be kidding. She was in her early twenties and bottom heavy, with big pores and blond hair. She giggled at everything. She showed me briefly how to run credit cards and how to count the drawer. Then she showed me how to bring the money to the bank in a deposit bag and drop it in the merchant's slot. I had to put a certain amount in the store safe for the next day's drawer. As I tried to remember it all, she said, "Did you get all that? Good. See ya!" and bounced out to play tennis. I was like, *Wait! Come back!* but she never did. I ended up figuring it out after much trial and error. I remember customers having to help me run their credit cards. They had to get behind the counter and show me how to do it.

Razz and Michael came into the store in their little rolled-up sweats and visors and stole the beauty products right in plain sight. Razz walked around filling up a basket with nail polish and hairspray as if he owned the joint. Stealing beauty supplies for *myself* felt justified for some reason, but I felt weird letting Razz just rob the place without batting a mascara-caked eyelash. I didn't want to get fired. I worked there part time in the evenings and on the weekends. I enjoyed being around all of the beauty supplies and cosmetics. I always gave myself manicures and tried on the makeup, leaving my germs all over products that

I eventually sold to other people.

The store was soon bought by a discount chain and stripped of all the good products. Gwen was gone with the old storefront. By that time, I was an old pro, ringing up bottles of Clairol hair color without even looking. I eventually memorized every code to every type of hair color and could key it on the ten key without even getting off the phone to stop my gossip. I didn't even greet the customers. I just talked about getting drunk and cute guys to whoever was on the other line and the customers had to stand there and listen. I only stopped to look at them when I figured out their total and it was time for them to pay me. Then it was back to gossiping. I was a totally rude employee! One time I even fell asleep on some cases of perms in the back.

I had to wear a smock that said "Ask me! I am an Expert." I looked at the thing and thought, *The only thing I am an expert on is partying.* People were always coming in the store with hair dye issues, namely fixing a color they didn't like. After studying a color wheel and some pamphlets, I decided *Okay, I am an expert now. Ask away.* I started helping people with color corrections, toners, bleach, peroxide levels, everything under the sun. I understood the acrylic nail supplies. I tried out the waxes and provided transsexuals with instructions on waxing their nether regions.

My father showed up on my sister's birthday that year. It was hard on us because we hadn't talked to him in a while. I tried to be nice to him and forgive him because he was so pathetic. He kept telling us how miserable he was. I got sick of hearing it after a while; I just wanted it to stop. He didn't ask us how we were or what was going on in our lives. While we were glad to know he wasn't having the time of his life being away from his family, we were hurt that he was not interested in knowing who *we* were, who we had grown into or how his departure had affected us. He tried to curse a lot and act tough to try and relate with us, but we were embarrassed and disgusted. I knew I couldn't trust him and distanced myself from him, emotionally.

We always reacted to seeing our father, even if we didn't realize it. My sister insisted it wasn't affecting her, but she cried at school the next day and said she didn't know what was wrong. The day after that, she found herself crying at work with no explanation. Then she was caught stealing at Newberry's. Soon after that, she got in a car accident with her new boyfriend. My sister was out of Middleton by that time and had entered the tenth grade at the local public high school in Canoga Park. It was very different for her. It was in a pretty bad area. One time I was driving by there and I saw a cloud of dust, along with a ton of flashing lights, in my rear view mirror. From behind me came the sound of sirens. A car was being chased by the police and was coming right toward me! I was on a single lane part of the street and there was nowhere to pull over. The car got closer and closer to me. Before it slammed right into me, I pulled my car over onto someone's front lawn and let the whole train of chaos pass me.

My sister was really into the Red Hot Chili Peppers during those years and we laughed at the songs together. It was one of the few things that allowed us to still relate to each other, though we were living separate lives with separate crowds. We always bonded on the Chili Peppers. We sang songs like "Yertle the Turtle" and other funky, weird songs that were very "her." Some were even very "me," i.e. "Stone Cold Bush." It was no surprise she chose that 'funny' music because things were not very laughable in our lives then.

My mother started dating a new guy that spring. He was an old family friend, a friend of my dad's. He was very nice to me and complimentary. My mother didn't like it. I remember she was sitting on the couch with him one day, and she called me over to them and told me to turn around so she could check out the back of my legs because she said she could see cellulite. She started pointing it out to him, as if I weren't there. She asked me what I had been eating. I yawned, filed my fingernail, blew dust off it, and lifted my eyebrows, which translated to *Bitch please. No need to try so hard to make me look bad. And by the way, I am now an old pro at dealing with envious women- this shit is nothing new to me.*

Although my mind was set to only one dial, Hollywood, there were times when things appeared to be more normal, like in my journalism class at school. I got some validation from working on the school paper and started to think about maybe not being such a die-hard party girl. I had figured out that wearing my Hollywood clothes to school was a big mistake. I learned my lesson in tenth grade. By my senior year, people had stopped yelling things at me on the school grounds. I still wanted to show that I was a Hollywood chick because I was very proud of it, but I didn't want to look like a stripper. Well, not at school anyway. I was writing for the school paper, for goodness sake; I had to have a *little* bit of credibility. I tried getting away from too "rocker" of an image. I let the purple fade from my hair, letting it become a more natural brown. I swept it into a long ponytail and wore my big hoop earrings. I couldn't buy a whole new wardrobe, but a pack of white men's T-shirts helped me to hide my cleavage and cover myself better. I still wore Jimmy's Cathouse T-shirts from time to time (one in white and one in black, both with bright pink writing), and his Lip Service shorts with little skulls and daggers, but mostly, I looked pretty normal for the times.

I enjoyed feeling more accepted at school. I even felt like a regular teenager on some days. When I wrote stories for the school paper, I felt important and smart instead of a freak, a troubled kid, or a tough girl. I realized I didn't need to try to separate myself so much from the norm. I didn't need to pigeonhole myself, which would only take away my opportunities. I started to feel better about being a student, and as a person as a whole. I started to feel more valued academically.

Journal Entry 3/12/91

I just interviewed Coach Green, who kicked me out of P.E. in the *tenth grade. He said I conduct a very good interview. I thought he was kidding because he was just grunting and stuff, but he wasn't. He said, "You're very intelligent. You just don't let people know it. You got me talking and now you have filled up that whole paper. Most people couldn't do that." I felt good. I was wearing all black on Friday and it made me feel...dark. Just putting on white made me feel more alive. I told Jimmy I didn't like wearing his black Lip Service jacket with the skulls and crosses on it any more. He was insulted. I mean...I used to find it so cool, but now it looks evil to me. I told him that I got much more respect dressing like a normal teenager and I liked being respected. He got defensive and said, "Hey, I don't care **who** likes me. This is what I dress like!" But I don't like being judged as dark and evil, especially when it doesn't really represent me. Jimmy made me feel like a sell-out, like I was turning my back on my own kind.*

The article I wrote for the school paper ended up in a showcase in the office building. I was stunned. I wrote:

It feels good to work on a newspaper. Proofreading it, cutting out misprints with an X-Acto knife, and pressing new letters in their places. Kids were watching me from the other side of the glass as if I were important. They were pretending to look at dictionaries. It is different from being on the literary magazine. I didn't use to think so, but this is real. We sell ads, lay out the pages, do interviews, and actually report things. The literary magazine is heavily edited by someone who decides what is creative enough, what is 'art'. I consider art to be a very personal thing- it has to be determined by each person individually. I don't think the magazine has enough different viewpoints. I am witnessing a lot of censorship going on there. There is a very artistic guy named Roger, who is probably the most talented and creative guy at school. He keeps writing poems that the teacher finds inappropriate. Every couple of days he comes up with a new one and she shoots it down for being too racy. It sucks that he has to hold back his talent and censor himself, when those are his thoughts and feelings. I respect him

*because I want to write things that are raw and truthful and I
don't want to hold back either.*

*Roger just wrote on the chalkboard above me, 'I lost my spleen
to a heartless surgeon.' He must be referring to the teacher
editing his stuff. Here is the conversation he is having with Mrs.
Kego:*

*Kego: "Roger, that is so graphic! If this were a college
magazine-"
R: "What's wrong? Okay. I can change it to 'the sheets are
damp'..."
Kego: "It's so graphic! Couldn't you veil it a little better?"*

***

I went to Razz and Michael's and drove with them to The Strip
every weekend, rain or shine. One night we sat around the red
restaurant booth in their game room eating hot dogs, thinking of
which cartoon characters we would be. They said Razz was
Icabod Crane, Michael was Doonesbury, and I was Betty Boop.
Then they all got ready, complaining that their hair had a wave
in it or needed a trim. They decided whether to make their hair
stick straight, a little poofy, or maybe just poofy on the bangs.
They each did their makeup and piled on bracelets and necklaces
and spritzed on colognes and perfumes. Sometimes I went over
and just laid under the covers with Michael while Razz and their
new bandmate Holly practiced songs on their guitars (they never
ended up playing anywhere, from what I can recall). Holly had a
bloated face and pretty bad skin. He tried to keep his skin
covered with his hair, which was an outright disaster in and of
itself. It looked like an explosion of burned straw.

Michael and I thought of funny things that happened that week
and laughed so hard we rolled up in little balls and held our
stomachs, out of breath. One of the things we couldn't stop
laughing about was when some girl backhanded Razz in the
mouth for being rude. He flicked her in the mouth, twice, and
then once on her ear. He was so proud of himself and told

everyone about his flicking, which was of course feminine and wimpy. We also couldn't stop laughing about the story of Holly falling asleep in the middle of hooking up with a girl. She got pissed, smacked him to wake him, and it startled him. He jumped ten feet in the air and said, *"Huh!? What?! Where's the fire!?"*

A new guy came into the crowd named Stacy. I don't remember if he was there before me and I just never saw him, or he was out of town for a while or what. He just kind of showed up one night. I know he was from New York and was a friend of someone's, but no more details come to mind. He looked like Howard Stern, but with tons of makeup on. He wore super red lipstick, lots of pearls, crazy polka dot clothes, and platform boots. Michael always said he looked like Herman Munster and often did the impression of Herman getting mad and jumping up and down and saying, *"Darn Darn Darn Darn Darn!"* while the whole house shook (does anyone remember that? Just me? Okay then). Anyway, I detailed one of the nights with Stacy in my journal:

Journal Entry 4/8/1991

Stacy Star from Stars from Mars walked in the door with like, ten-inch platform shoes, red lipstick, and pearls. He is easily seven feet tall. I am surprised his head didn't smack the door jam. Even with all that makeup and shit, he still sounds like a tough New Yorker, with a deep voice. Razz said, "Hey, ya big-nosed fuck! What's up! Dude, does your nose get in the way when you kiss a girl?" Stacy looked at him without missing a beat and said, "Does it get in the way when I kiss YOU? ...Well then."

We tried to cut through the Bel Age Hotel parking lot to find a place to park on a side street, and some guy wouldn't move his car. Holly, the New Yorker that he is, jumped out of the car to fight the guy and security broke it up. He should probably change his name from Holly to something like Carmine.

*Not too long ago, the front of the Bel Age was full of screaming girls because New Kids on the Block were staying there. They are real popular with teenagers right now. Well, **normal** teenagers, anyway.*

CHAPTER TEN

Sucker

I was over at Razz and Michael's one day for a barbecue, when a very hot guy walked through the door with a twelve pack of beer. He had long, silky black hair with the top part dyed dark blue. He was super confident with great skin and sexy eyes. I thought, *Oh no...I didn't think I would be meeting HIM.* It was one of the guys from Tryx: Roxy DeVeau. My pupils turned into cartoon hearts.

I knew exactly who he was because I had his picture pinned on my wall at my grandmother's house and had been staring at him constantly since 1989. I know, I know. It is stupid. But back then, Tryx was a group I had heard about before to getting to Hollywood. They were very colorful and had a really cool look that I dug. I appreciated their creativity and I also thought they were really attractive. I realized at that moment that the reason that none of the other guys I had met in Hollywood, no matter how cool or 'famous' they were, were a threat to my relationship, because I wasn't truly attracted to any of them. I thought a few were cute, but there was no one that worried me.

There was no one that I thought "oh shit" about. Except this guy.

Next thing I knew, I was chatting with him while shaping ground beef into hamburger patties over the sink. Later he asked me to help him do his eyeliner before we all went out; he wanted me to hold his eyelid open so he could line the inside of his eye. I got nervous, and pounded so much beer that I was lightheaded. I thought, *I wish hadn't beat up Tricia so I could tell her about this; she would shit her G-string.* I calmed myself down by thinking, *He won't want me. There will be someone prettier, someone better. I won't even have to get into that situation.*

I was wrong! Roxy started hanging out with us every weekend, so I saw him a lot. He started to flirt with me and we had major tension. He kept trying to get me to kiss him. I said no. *No, no, no.* I knew if I gave in, two things would happen: 1) He would lose interest and 2) I would lose my boyfriend. It was a lose/lose situation that I had the sense to foresee, but still, it was *painful*. I lusted after this guy *hard*. He didn't make it easy on me. He was always pulling me onto his lap or trying to pull me into corners to "talk."

Razz knew I actually liked Roxy. He flipped his hair and raised a plucked eyebrow into an arch. "You dig him, don't you?" he said in a drawn out voice. "*Please*. I could tell. I *know* you. He is a pretty sexy guy, huh? Look, he digs you. You dig him. Why don't you just go with your feelings, you know?"

I said, "No! Don't let me *near* him! Be my friend!"

He said, "Listen, I *am* your friend. And you are *my* friend, okay? You come over here and you don't fuck anybody. I like that."

Holly, who had a bad stutter and a thick New York accent, really made fun of Roxy, especially the part in his hair. He always said, "I haven't seen a part that big s-s-s-since Moses parted the Red Sea. Tell him to bring his b-b-b-b-big Dumbo ears over here. But tell him to stop scamming on all of our women. It's not cool."

One night Roxy gave me his leather jacket to wear on The Strip, which was unheard of, because popular Hollywood guys always wanted to appear single. This way, they could get a lot of girls to think they had a chance with them and buy tickets to their shows. It was not unlike a stripper who pretends she is single so the guys think they have a shot. They are selling a fantasy. Anyway, I was secretly giddy to be wearing a Tryx jacket over my bright yellow dress; it was like wearing the hot quarterback's letterman jacket or something. A small part of me thought...*What if this leaks back to Jimmy? This is kind of public*...and another part of me told that part to shut the fuck up.

I thought I was in the clear as far as wearing that jacket. We got separated in the crowds and parties later that evening, so I wore it home and of course looked through every crevice of it. His wallet (empty- no surprise) was inside and so were his keys- I knew he would have to come get that jacket if he wanted those items back. I found his ID, which said his real name, Brian Charles DeVeau, and a Florida address. I stared at it like a psycho- I probably sniffed the damn thing, knowing me. The next day Jimmy showed up at the door and I panicked, throwing the jacket in my sister's closet and burying it with her pile of dirty underwear and socks.

While I was sitting on the couch talking to Jimmy, I felt like that jacket would come walking out of the closet itself, just to haunt me. I tried to calm my guilt and tell myself I was in the clear. Then the doorbell rang and I felt my armpits shoot sweat. *Shit!* I held up a pink fingernail toward Jimmy and smiled a weak smile as if to say, *Just a minute, this is probably someone selling vacuum cleaners. Let me just get rid of them so I can continue spending time with you, the love of my life.*

I opened the door a sliver and it was Razz, with his hair in a scrunchie and a striped shirt that was hanging off one shoulder. He was chewing.

"We are down the street eating hamburgers in the car. Roxy

wants to camp out because he thinks you want to see him! Go out there."

"No! Get out of here!" I hissed through clenched teeth. I wanted to drop a piano on his head and squash him.

I went back in the house and Jimmy kind of laughed and said, "Do youuuu want to tell me what's going on?" He promised he wouldn't get mad. I thought...*Oh shit...here it is.*

I said, "It is totally lame- it is nothing. It's going to sound worse than it is-"

He sounded like a dad catching his kid having a huge party.

"I can't *imagine*. Just tell me the story."

I was brief. I told him I was holding this guy Roxy's jacket for him real quick, but we suddenly lost contact and I didn't want to just throw it somewhere because it had his keys in it. Jimmy was quiet. He sighed and rubbed his eyes. Then he looked up at me and said:

"You would *never* hold *my* jacket. Never. You don't hold people's jackets. I know you. Second, why would you keep that jacket with you, unless you wanted him to come get it?"

Shit. What was with all of the psychology? Had Jimmy been hanging out with my shrink? He had me figured out. Was I that obvious?

"I know what it looks like..." I said, as he calmly stared at me and crossed his leg, bracelets jangling and boot buckles clicking. His bright blue eyes were piercing mine like lasers. I could swear that if I looked closely at his pupils, they said *Lying Ho!*

Later that night when Jimmy was gone, Roxy rang the doorbell. I looked out the peephole and quickly ran and ripped his picture off my wall, yellowed and full of Scotch tape. My mom was walking out of her room because she heard the doorbell. I jumped ahead of her, flew out the door, and slammed it behind me, nearly knocking ten crucifixes off my grandmother's wall. I knew my mom would totally find a way to tell Jimmy if she saw something fishy and I couldn't let that happen. Roxy's car was running and the passenger door was open so I quickly got in, despite the fact that I was wearing Joe Boxer shorts with little ants all over them and a pink pajama top with an ice cream cone on the front. I didn't even have shoes on! I thought he wanted to talk in the car or something but no, he drove me to Razz's.

When we arrived, Holly was sitting on the couch in a black Ramones shirt, having spasms from alcohol. Michael was spinning a basketball on his finger, talking about how much he thought he looked like Pete Burns from Dead or Alive. Razz was playing Gene Loves Jezebel on the stereo and talking on the phone in his pink sweatpants. Roxy and I went onto the patio to talk.

He got right into it: "People tell me you like me, but when I see you, you ignore me."

"I stay away from you because I don't want to start liking you."

"Really start liking me? *I like you*, okay? But you won't believe anything I say."

"I could imagine us together for about ten minutes and then never seeing you again. Then I would get all attached to you and get all psycho- I don't want you to hurt me."

"I would not do that to you," he said. "The way you keep someone around is not to sleep with them right away. So, you don't have to! I just want to *kiss* you."

We were standing there amongst potted plants and the fluffy white Persian cat with little bells on her pink collar. I knew the situation could go terribly awry, and I mustered willpower from every pore in my teenaged body not to make out with the guy. I think the main thing keeping me sensible was the fact that I was sober. Goodness knows what would have happened had I been pounding beers. I told him flat out that I just didn't trust him and he was pissed.

"I am not making promises, all right?" he said, his dark eyes flashing. "Look. I don't want to tell you what to do, but you're frustrating me. I think that you need to decide what you really want. I can tell this is bugging you. What I really think, is that you should just kiss me. Then you can decide. Do I *excite* you more than your boyfriend?"

I turned red and told him he was going too far and that he should take me back home. I marched off to the car, but inside I was fantasizing that we would fall onto the sand on a beach and make out while waves crashed around us like the scene in *From Here to Eternity*.

As we were driving, he said:

"You are living a fake life."

I gave him the side eye as he continued: "You don't do what you want. You are staying with this guy because you can't imagine what life would be without him. What is wrong with doing what you really want? Look, I could get you to have sex with me, because I know you want to."

"*What*?" I said, looking over at him. Who did he think he was? "Do you think you have some magical *powers* or something? You couldn't get me to have sex with you; I won't even *kiss* you for God's sake."

"I could. Believe me. I *know* you want to. But I am not doing that."

I got out of the car, walked back into the house in a huff, and slammed the door. Boy was he right. I wanted to sleep with him in an awful sort of way, I ain't gonna lie. The guy was sexy. I also knew very well that it would be a stupid groupie thing to do, and it would surely end the relationship that I felt was keeping me out of trouble. I started thinking about the show Tryx was playing that weekend. I didn't want Roxy to see me there and have his ego blow up as if I were some fan of his (if only he knew). I didn't attend the show, but the next night I went to Ten Masa. Gerry Gittelson, the columnist for *Rock City News,* popped up out of nowhere and said he heard I was dating Roxy from Tryx. I immediately told him I was not, and prayed it didn't get back to my boyfriend.

Journal Entry 4/14/91

*I don't want to give up Jimmy. I am scared of life. I am scared of being in another relationship; trying to figure out who's safe and who's not. I don't want to ever be without Jimmy because then I will have to be on my own with all of these men and I will get weak for one of them and ruin my life. I will **crumble** without Jimmy.*

Speaking of Jimmy, he invited Cristabelle and me to the Cathouse again. We were in a VIP area that was roped off and surrounded by bodyguards. Stephen Pearcy of Ratt was there, he smiled at me. Tracii Guns from L.A. Guns and Taime Downe from Faster Pussycat were also there and they all played songs together. The night after that, Jimmy trashed his whole house and cussed me out, shaking the whole time. He doesn't want me hanging out with the guys on the weekends. He is afraid I will hook up with someone, namely Roxy. He is starting to look like a chump to his friends, I think.

Anyway, the next night I took Cristabelle and my sister out with me. We stopped by Brent Muscat's house and he had dyed his bangs bright pink and was doing laundry. He said Jimmy was "weirding out" on him at Bordello so he started throwing cigarette papers at him. I was embarrassed for Jimmy because he was a fan of Faster Pussycat, but I went and put my arm around Brent in front of Holly and Razz and said, "Cigarette papers. What a man!" and laughed. He smiled real big and hopefully felt taken down a peg.

Razz said, "Come on, you know you are going out with Jimmy against your will."

*I said, "I am **not**, Razz."*

We all went to The Strip, which was very crowded. Bobby Berry and Pepper Sweet from the band Strawberry were in front of The Roxy with a ton of neon pink clothing, colorful plastic charm bracelets and lots of clown makeup. Bobby's stage name is actually "Boppin' Bobby Gene" but Michael started calling him Bobby Berry and that is what we all call him now. Pepper and he were carrying huge orange and green water guns and TV cameras were following them while they tried squirting my feet. I shot them an evil look that said, "Don't get my fucking shoes wet or I will slice your glittered balls off." Bobby has black hair down to his waist and plucked eyebrows. He is actually really beautiful when made up- he does a good smoky eye. He loves looking at Cosmopolitan magazine- that is where he gets his beauty tips. If you listen closely, he has a Texas drawl- he says 'y'all' when he is buzzed. Sometimes we go to their place to drink beers before we go out. It is full of toys, Cap'n Crunch cereal boxes, cartoony stuff, and of course, lots of women's magazines. Bobby thinks if he does these face exercises from Cosmo every night, he won't age or something. He always does facial masks and moisturizes.

Pepper has straight, shoulder-length white-blond hair and wears red lipstick. Instead of a beauty spot, he draws an "X" above his lip, which is weird, but creative. He says it is the anti-beauty spot. He is my age and works at the Hostess bakery during the day, where they make Twinkies and stuff. We are probably the youngest people in this crowd right now. So anyway, back to the

story of the night. I found Razz, Holly, Stacy and Roxy and they
wanted to use the old tickets from Roxy's Tryx show the week
before to get into the Swingin' Thing show, but no one wanted to
face getting caught, so I walked up to the door man, handed him
all of the tickets and we all walked right in. Swingin' Thing was
half over and everyone separated into the crowd. A bit later, I
saw Roxy at the bar with a blond pulled up close to him.

Swingin' Thing played a great show and threw out the beach
balls into the crowd as we all tried stealing each other's drinks.
After the show, the whole crowd poured out in front of the club
and gathered under the lights of the marquee. Razz was telling
Jessie Star of Tryx that they should touch foreheads, saying "Big
*foreheads unite!" and Jessie said, "Is my forehead **that** big?"*

My sister Becky, Michael and I piled into Cristabelle's car to
leave, but we were missing Razz and the rest. We were yelling
his name but he couldn't hear us. Cristabelle was forced to pull
her car out into traffic on Sunset because there were people
behind us honking. I got out of the car in the middle of traffic to
run and get him; she said she would pull up the road a little and
wait for us. People were "wooo-hooo"ing me from their cars,
yelling stuff about me and whistling at me. I ran onto the
sidewalk, toward the Rainbow. Guys were grabbing me in the
crowds, but I kept going, dodging drunk guys left and right,
slapping people's hands off me. I got to the Rainbow and
realized that not only could I not find Razz, but I was all alone
out there in a skimpy lavender and pink leopard print outfit. I
was scared.

Then I saw a bright neon light: Bobby Berry. He came over and
agreed to walk with me to find Razz. His made-up eyes looked
tired and I noticed he had a five o'clock shadow under his
makeup. As we wove in and out of the crowds, I realized that all
of the good-looking people had left to go to parties and all that
was left was people who were not the standard patrons; people
who were drunk and had decided to finally get out of their cars
and take a look around, maybe beat up a few "glam fags." We

ran into Pepper and waited for him to pee by the Whisky, his platinum hair pulled back into a headband. I left them and hoped I could find Cristabelle up the hill from the Whisky, where she said she would be. Just as I was about to cry from thinking I was left there, Cristabelle pulled up and I ran and got into the car.

Journal Entry 4/21/91

*I went to The Strip on Friday and after the night was over, we all got into Stacy Star's BMW that was parked above the Whisky. When we got to the stoplight, we saw Weird Al Yankovic at the crosswalk. Missy yelled, "AL!" – apparently she knew him- and he came and jumped on the hood of the car! He smashed his face against Stacy's windshield; we could see his eyes bugging out and his glasses tilting to the side, trying to be funny. Stacy said in his baritone voice, "I don't care **who** the fuck you are, get the **fuck** off my car!" He accelerated a little bit and then stepped on the brakes really hard. Al went flying out into the street like a rag doll. I wondered if he broke some bones, but we peeled out, so I never knew. We turned out onto Sunset. Michael saw us, jumped out of a crowd on the sidewalk, and started running alongside the car with Bobby Berry, banging on the windows. Missy said, "Leave him. He'll be fine. I have left him down here so many times…" So we sped away, leaving him in the street.*

Journal Entry 4/30/91

We all went to El Compadre on Saturday night. It is a dark little Mexican cantina with a mariachi band, candles on the tables, red leather booths, twinkly lights around the edges of the place and chips and salsa at each table. Everybody ordered flaming margaritas. They cut a lime in half, douse it with alcohol, and then light it on fire. It is a little fire ball in your drink. I hate tequila since I puked from it in front of the cops. Razz kept yelling for the waiter to bring me daiquiris in a shrill voice, "Caesar! A daiquiri for the lady!"

Razz told me about a waiter at another popular restaurant- he said that when the guy brought him the check at the end of the night, there would be a line of coke on the little tray, under the bill. Then they would do the coke together.

Caesar kept coming and dumping extra shots in our drinks. Some young girl asked me how I was served alcohol, if I had a fake ID or what- I thought about it for a second and said truthfully that I had no idea. I hadn't thought much about it, it kind of just happened. Michael weaved through the crowds and ended up at another table talking to a guy who fought in the war in the Middle East. When he came back, he was disgusted with himself.

*"Dude," he said in his snobby, nasal, Valley Girl voice and teased out hair, "That guy just got back from the Middle East. He has **shot** people. Dude...he is a **stud**. He fought for our country. We're **wimps**, Razz. We were gonna go hide in **Canada** if there was a draft. That guy fought for our country and he is still alive! He is here partying! What a stud!"*

*Razz rolled his eyes nonchalantly and said, "Could you picture **me** at war, Michael? With my beauty spot, going, 'who do I shoot'?" He sipped his margarita like a woman and considered the conversation over.*

Michael went with me to the ladies room, fixing his hair and using the stall. He had on a magenta blazer, khaki pants, and saddle shoes with polka dot bows on them. One foot was black with white polka dots and the other was white with black polka dots.

Back at the table Holly said, "I used to drink every day...now I drink nonstop! Dude, I am an alcoholic!" I took off with Holly, who was my ride and who is the only person who has never tried to pick up on me, so I trust him. We sat in the car and waited for the others and he told me he had just found out that a very good friend of his had just died of a heroin overdose. I felt so sad for him. We tried to corral everyone back to the car and somehow Michael was pulled into a big brawl with an Arab guy. The next thing I knew, Holly was out of the car socking the guy in the face, probably letting out his anger over his friend dying. Bobby Berry jumped in and was punching people with his neon green bandana in his hair. I was sitting in Holly's car with all of the doors open and the motor running. Security people ran over and so did a bunch of other people. Holly split the guy's nose open with his rings and Michael was being dragged by his long hair (as was Bobby) and thrown all over the place. They were both still punching people. Then the Arab guy pulled out a gun. Everything screeched to a halt.

When it was over, everyone was all pumped up, especially Michael.

"Dude! We brawled! Bobby! You can *fight!* You knocked out **two guys!**"

He couldn't believe it. Bobby had clearly fought before, but kind of hid it because it wasn't 'glam' to be that masculine. He made no comment.

We left and went to a gas station on Highland and Franklin. Some guy looked at our guys and said, "Hey GIRLS." They all jumped out of the car and started brawling again, except for Razz, who looked back at me and said, "I don't wanna mess up my pretty face."

Holly started hitting the guy with a crow bar that he pulled out of his car. He threw the guy on the windshield and started beating his head in. The guy grabbed Holly's arm and started biting him. Michael punched another guy and got punched back. Then one of the guys pulled out a huge knife and everything went silent. I covered my eyes- I didn't want to see a stabbing through the windshield. The gas station attendant was laughing and did nothing. I wasn't surprised because I had seen that place taped off with police tape before; complete with white sheets covering

*dead bodies. Anyway, the fight stopped when that knife was
pulled out.*

Journal Entry 5/12/91

*Michael moved out of Dusty's condo and in with three girls in
Hollywood because he couldn't afford the rent. I got a ride to
the apartment, somewhere on Sycamore. I was the only person
wearing brightly colored clothing in a room of girls sitting
around wearing black and pouting. I was also the only person
smiling, which I consider key. The girls who rent the apartment
are not pretty enough nor are they stylish enough, but they are
now in our crowd by default. We went to pick up Roxy and he
ignored me for the first 45 minutes, which I predicted and didn't
care or worry about whatsoever. Michael just started hanging
with a band called the Brats. They are kind of tough, no pink and
shit. Lots of black. They seemed a little dark, but apparently they
are the new cool guys in town, so all bets are off. We picked
them up and we all went to El Compadre. While I was sucking
back cocktails through red straws, I thought about how that
night was the senior prom at my high school. I was missing it.
But I like where I am. I love my crowd. I love that it is colorful,
unpredictable, and exciting. There are no rules for me. I am free
to run wild. I think I am a little past proms. I don't know if that
is really cool or sort of sad.*

*I won't bore you with the story of Roxy and me. It was the same
cat and mouse chase as always. He was pawing me under the
table while several girls sent me death stares. Here is the
conversation we had:*

*He said, "Look, I will be honest- I just got out of a three year
relationship- I am not going to get back into one. But I like you.
I do." Then he asked me to go to the movies. I found it corny, but
endearing.*

*"Your boyfriend won't even know! I like you! Why won't you
believe me?!*

*I laughed and pretended to be very nonchalant, but I was dying inside. Missy told me he went down on Rachel the other night and then tried to get on **her**. I asked him about it and he said, "Okay, okay- I am not gonna lie and try to deny shit. I do fucked up things all the time. But I like you. I want you to believe me."*

We just sat there and stared at each other. He is such a whore- he doesn't even hide it! He is the worst.

Journal Entry 5/20/91

*The girls who went out with us tonight were totally rude to me because one of them likes Roxy. Who doesn't? Her name is Mia and she is very plain, with this overinflated sense of confidence. She kept trying to drop hints to me that they are sleeping together, which they probably are. She said, "When we are in **bed** tonight" and "When we **wake up** in the **morning**" a bunch of times. The best part was when I was walking and she ran and caught up to me. She put on a really confrontational voice and said, "We have a problem. I am dating Brian. You like him, don't you?" I laughed and said I had a boyfriend. She was so non-threatening to me that I barely even got mad. I looked at Roxy in a different light that night. Anyone can have a piece of him. He isn't hard to get. He isn't even good enough to have me.*

I was finally over *really* liking Roxy. It had taken a few months, but the sting was gone and I felt more in control and less impressed with him. It taught me a good lesson, but then again, it also worked against me. I thought to myself, *Okay, now that I don't like him anymore, I can't get hurt...*

And that came into play one night when we all went out. I had come straight from work and hadn't even showered, so I cringe to think of the state of my lady parts. They were the furthest thing from fresh and clean that you could possibly imagine. You know where this is going (laughs). Roxy and I ended up at a party somewhere and out of nowhere, I started totally making out with him in a kitchen, next to some hanging baskets of vegetables. We went into a bathroom and hooked up- we didn't have sex and I didn't do anything to *him*, thankfully, but he went to town on me. All I could think was *I should have showered!*

After that night, I saw him one more time. He walked right by me with a girl on either side of him, one blond and one brunette. He glanced at me and then kept on walking, as if he didn't even know me.

I never saw him again.

CHAPTER ELEVEN

Big Bang Glamour Cat Scratch Punk Alley Babies

With the exception of that, uh, *indiscretion* in a random
bathroom, I appeared to be playing the game correctly. I was one
of the popular girls, one of the cool people. I had the look, I
knew everyone, and I was confident. I had achieved my goal, no
matter how lame it was. Partying with the right people for a
summer increased my social value even more. It no longer
mattered to me that my family was broken apart and my mother
couldn't stand me. I had a new family who worshipped me. I
was on top. I got a ride to The Strip every weekend, jumped out
of the car, and ran off into the crowds to find my friends. I had a
toothbrush in my boot and nothing else. I was nuts.

Journal Entry 6/6/1991

*I only had four dollars to last me the whole week, and I pitched
in two of it for a twelve pack. Michael and I were walking down
The Strip drinking those beers, when a fight broke out between
Johnny Valentine from the Brats and some shorthaired guys.
Johnny was socked in the back of the head, and then it got*

broken up. Some black girls looked at me and said I looked like I was twelve years old and should be at home watching the Gummi Bears. I was hurt for a second, but quickly got over it when dark haired, blue-eyed Sunny from none other than Swingin' Thing asked me to go to a party with them! I was thrilled! They were trying to pull me into their car and it was starting to drive away when he yelled, "Come on! Come on! Jump in!" I was flattered, but I knew if I got in that car I would end up God knows where. I grabbed my camera (the ONE time I ever brought it to Hollywood) and pointed it toward them. They were motioning for me and hanging out of the car. I thought, 'This will be the ego boost of the year if I can get this shot! The glory!' But my camera didn't work and I looked like an idiot taking a picture of them instead of either going or saying no.

After coming down from my temporary high, I realized that I had no ride home. I was just standing there in the dust with a camera and two dollars. I found Michael and we got in some girl's car to go to a party. The girl made out with Michael and before the night was through, she gave him money! That little snake has all the luck. After the party, we laid on the ground and looked up at the sky for UFOs- then we started slapping each other in the forehead. Eventually, I had to call Jimmy to come and get me. He was pissed.

Journal Entry 6/16/91

The band that Jimmy put together had their first gig at Riki Rachtman's Birthday Bash at Madame Wong's West. It was a twenty-one and over club with a line around the block. Cristabelle and I got in through the side door and were on a guest list. One of the men at the door asked for my ID and I started to say I didn't have it but another doorman said, "No one asked if you had ID." And I said, "He just asked me," and the man looked at his partner and said, "Ahhh, what does he know?"

I had a lot of beer. Razz was there with his good-looking friend,

Darren Tyler, and they were sticking their strong margaritas in
my face. Darren is hot and tall with olive skin and long,
burgundy-tinted hair pushed over to the side. He is currently
dating the wife of someone pretty famous. She used to be a
bikini-clad mud wrestler from the Hollywood Tropicana, and
now she stays home while the famous husband is on tour.
Darren thinks he is the shit and has the personality of a bored
debutante. He had the nerve to say, "Not to be mean, but your
boyfriend is ugly. Does he have some really great personality or
something?" I wasn't shaken because I had heard it many times
before by bigger names than his high-school-going ass. I
responded in a more bored manner than even he could muster,
"I can't deal with your attitude. I won't tolerate it," and then
walked away with my eyebrows up. I didn't want to stand in the
long line for the bathroom so I walked right in front of every
single girl in line and went right into a stall and peed. They were
mad. I did that twice.

I didn't bat an eyelash at checking out another guy at Jimmy's
show because I had just recently done worse: I had cheated on
him with Roxy. I kept trying to tell myself that maybe it wasn't
cheating because I didn't so much as touch Roxy's private
parts…but he had touched mine. And I had made out with him! I
couldn't believe myself.

Cristabelle was truly ready to change scenes at that point. She
was completely exhausted. She started to take interest in the rave
scene and wanted to start going to underground clubs, but I
wasn't ready to leave Hollywood. I had only just begun. I had
found a place where I felt comfortable and happy and I wasn't
about to give it up to start dancing in abandoned warehouses
with a pacifier in my mouth. I didn't blame her for leaving the
Hollywood scene and me along with it. I was totally using her to
drive me around, which was horrible. I wasn't even hiding it.

The guys dared me to kiss beautiful Missy one night on the way
to Hollywood. She turned around from the front seat of the car
and I leaned up toward her, heart beating fast, wanting to be cool

in front of my older friends. All the guys woo-hooed and we laughed after kissing. I felt initiated, cool. I also felt even further away from my peers in high school and realized I had no one I could even share my story with. I couldn't tell Abby; she would think I was gay and be uncomfortable around me. I would have to keep things to myself. I continued my double life of high school student by day and cool rock chick by night.

Next thing I knew, it was time for me to graduate high school. I looked around me as if to say *What? Really? It's...over?* I was actually enjoying my senior year and kind of wished I had paid more attention to it. I was presented with two awards in journalism at a special luncheon- I was stunned going up to accept the plaques. I was thinking, *Me? Really?* I felt proud to have written for the school paper, in which I had pushed my way into the title of Sports Editor (though I knew nothing about sports whatsoever), and the literary arts magazine (where they pulled my story on heroin addicts and featured a story of a black bear on a hunting trip instead). I had improved my tennis game and somehow scored A's in economics and government, of all things. I had become proficient in the stock market club, investing my fake money in stocks each week. I rolled into the class, hung over, and bought and sold stocks like a champ. I was like Gordon Gekko, ready to start corporate raiding up in that bitch. We didn't have the Internet then, so I had to sit there and scan the *Wall Street Journal* every day, but I chomped on an apple and made my picks- I was a born risk taker, so my portfolio beat the pants off of the others.

I couldn't believe I had made it after how hard it was for me in tenth grade and how I had missed most of eleventh grade for being in the mental hospital. I had somehow thrived in twelfth grade; it was a miracle. Jimmy came to my graduation with loads of red roses and my dad even showed up in a bad suit. We had one last family picture taken, my mother looking thin and frail and my father looking rather tanked. My sister's eyes were watering in the picture. She was totally uncomfortable, surprised by my father's attendance. I had a regular smile on my face and looked completely normal. I could bluff better than anyone I knew, and it was no different that day. I looked out at the sunset over the mountains and thought to myself, *I will never come to this school again. I will never see these kids again. It's over.* I felt melancholy.

I spent that summer learning to drive. It was about time! I had finally saved up enough money to buy a car: a pale blue Honda Accord. My mother took me for driving lessons after she got off work each day. She was scared teaching me because I was always blasting music, speeding and making left turns on the tail of other cars without looking to see if it were safe, all during rush hour traffic. It was hectic, but she stuck with it because I would need no further rides from her once I learned to drive. I could take myself to work and community college in the fall. Once I learned to drive, I was *never* home. I went to Hollywood every second I got, driving back home shit-faced drunk, thinking nothing of it.

Missy left the scene at that time, and her girlfriends disappeared with her. She ran off with some guy and got hooked on some of the bad shit. I ran into her one time and she was almost skeletal, with dyed brown hair and black clothes. She was not at all bouncy and happy; she was even a little mean. The dazzle was gone, the smiles were gone. She was robbed of her sparkle. Razz wasn't around as much either because some guy had pulled a gun on the teller who was helping him at his bank and it scared the hell out of him. He was so shaken up that he didn't go out for a while. That left me with Michael, and he was curating a new crowd of his own.

While most of the bands on Sunset tried to be attractive, a few took the shock value route, playing up the fact that they were not "pretty." One of those bands was called the Glamour Punks. They had been around for a few years, but were always breaking up and replacing members, so they were on hiatus at certain points. That summer they had a new lineup and were back in full force, socializing and getting themselves out there. I was interested to see what they were all about.

*As The Strip started to fill with people this past weekend, I saw
the crowds part: The sickly, infamous, overly-made-up Glamour
Punks were trotting up the trashed sidewalk. Michael and I
butted into their group and next thing I knew, I was shaking
hands with Strange, Skitzo, Spazz and Dizzy Damage. It's kind of
hilarious that these guys were all polite and shaking hands. The
singer, Screaming Boy Mandie, ruined all of that by screaming
into my ear as loud as he could (hence the name). He was
smiling these wide, snarling grins to his surrounding onlookers.
His hair is fire engine red with shaved sides and his eyes are
thickly lined, coming to points on both sides. He could very well
be Satan, or the closest thing to it. Whatever image he is trying
to project for his band- it is working. People are interested in
him. The guy has showmanship, he's got something different
going on.*

*Strange was very sweet and didn't seem as hard core as the
others, but he had the look and fit in with them physically:
skinny, long black hair, pale skin, wearing black leather
bondage type pants and a ripped punk T-shirt. Dizzy had his
chin and his tongue pierced and was relatively quiet with sad
eyes. He sort of looked like a punk Johnny Depp. I can't
remember how the other ones behaved. They were pretty
interesting though, something a little different from what I have
been seeing. Their logo is "Hated by Millions, Loved by All"
and they have a really big buzz right now in the magazines.*

The Glamour Punks caused a general fear amongst the super-
glammy bubble gum bands. To be on their bad side was not
recommended because they could beat the shit out of most of the
people there. Michael befriended them, in a smart social move.
He was no fool. It was at that point that our crowd turned from
Glam Rock to a little more edge; we were in with the Glamour
Punks. While other styles of bands still hung in our set, the

Glamour Punks would remain the driving force of the crowd and sit perched at the top of the party scene because there was no one to take them down.

There were not only new guys on the scene, there were new girls, too. I first saw a girl named Birdie Montgomery in August 1991, a few months after I graduated. I was about to turn eighteen and she had just turned fifteen. The reason I knew that was because she was out one night running around in a tight red gingham dress, announcing to the world that it was her fifteenth birthday. She looked like a young Jessica Alba. She had olive skin and shiny, caramel colored hair that was all one length and curled at the ends. She had perfectly shaped brows over huge, dark Bambi eyes and thick, black eyelashes. She had a gorgeous white smile and a beauty spot above the corner of her left lip. I thought, *Oh wow, she is beautiful- but she is really ditzy and young.* I saw her another night later that year when I was hanging out with Bobby Berry. He got one look at her face and said she looked like a live Cosmo cover. He dropped my hand and went straight to her, never returning. Word on the street was that she had been dating one of the guys in Guns N' Roses at fourteen years old- limos sent to her house and everything.

I saw another blossoming rival outside of The Roxy. I smiled at her pretty moon face and noted her very long, straight, gold hair and pink cheeks. She came over to me and asked me if I knew Birdie. Then I remembered some girl telling me about a thirteen-year-old named Ashley stealing her boyfriend and I immediately knew it was her. I stayed clear of her.

I couldn't believe that I was one of the *older* girls on The Strip. I was only eighteen! It had happened overnight- I went from being too young to borderline too old. It was shocking. And with Missy and Cristabelle gone, I was running out of girls to hang out with, so I took a chance and hoped that Tricia might be as desperate as I was. I called her one day and apologized to her for beating her up. What can I say, I was a nice person. No, not really. I needed a sidekick. And get this: She was so bored that she was more than happy to hang out with me again, despite the ass-kicking she received. We were not exactly students of civility.

The band Jimmy formed with Pierre started to garner interest. They recruited a French friend of Pierre's as the drummer (Tricia thought he was the hottest thing she had ever seen), named Andre, and a few other guys to complete the lineup. Jimmy and his band felt they were "this close" to getting a record deal. I secretly didn't want them to make it. I was such a hater. I sat around thinking, *Who would buy his records?* I felt that the only two Hollywood bands that weren't a fad were Motley Crue and Guns N' Roses. Oh...and Van Halen...and Ratt... and Poison...

Jimmy flew to New York with his band to accompany L.A. Guns at some show, and they met with Polygram records. He said he was riding around Manhattan in limos and was put up in an expensive hotel. While he was doing all of that, I started hanging around a friend of Bobby Berry's, named Harmony. He was tall with teased, platinum blond hair, a great square jaw, rounded white teeth, and light baby blue eyes. He was a truly beautiful human being and had no attitude whatsoever- he was almost like a Golden Retriever puppy or something. Coolest guy ever.

Harmony talked about art galleries, beauty products, Thai food, and Catalina Island at midnight. He liked Ragtime and the ballet, Madonna and lobster at Gladstone's. He worked in a sex shop selling dick stretchers and dildos, and he used to wear false lashes, garter belts and teddies in his old band. He idolized Morgan Fairchild; he thought she was a goddess. He wanted his jaw to look just like hers. I was like, *Dude, it already **does**. Morgan Fairchild wishes she could look like **you**.*

In hindsight, I can see that he may have been gay and not out of the closet. His wearing garter belts and teddies didn't faze me, even though he was taking it to another level than the rest of the guys I knew. Most of the guys were completely normal (well, *somewhat*) once they were away from The Strip and had their "costumes" off. My gay-dar was completely screwed up from dating these glam guys. How was I to know? *Garter belts? Sure, why not?* His fondness of the ballet should've tipped me off, yes. But again, I was in an eccentric, batty scene that was so much like the Mad Hatter's tea party on acid, that I didn't see what was right in front of me. Still, Harmony was one of the nicest, sweetest, and most interesting people I met out there.

In November of 1991, I went to a new underground club called "The Church," which was off Cahuenga or something, toward the Valley. A bunch of girls who worked for Heidi Fleiss were there and so were all the Hollywood usuals. It was a real church if I am not mistaken. Inside it was all glowing with neon gravesites under black lighting. It was really cool; a mix of the Cathouse crowd and the Sunset crowd. That ended up screwing me because someone in Jimmy's crowd saw me walk in with Harmony, and Jimmy dumped me the next day.

Oh, and I forgot to mention that I single-handedly brought down that place. It was a secret "underground" club, which I guess means operating without license and permits. One night, I was speeding around trying to find the damn place, and I couldn't locate it (hence it being an underground club). I had the New York Dolls turned up so loud that I didn't hear the cops behind me with a bullhorn, telling me to slow down and pull over. They thought I was running from them. I finally looked in the rear view mirror and saw flashing lights. I pulled over and played very, very dumb and bimbo-y to the male cops. When I got out of the car, I said I couldn't find where I was going and I needed help. I mindlessly gave them the address and they tried to help me find it. Needless to say, the place was busted that night and was shut down soon thereafter. Guess I wasn't playing dumb. I *was* dumb!

Around that time, Michael decided to get legitimate and join a band as a singer. After all, what the hell were these people doing on The Strip if they weren't promoting a music career? Well, *partying* of course, but there had to be a front. And Michael wasn't about to go learn how to play an instrument; that would be too time consuming and take away from his social life. So he joined a little-known band called Alleycat Scratch. All of them had long black hair, white skin and wore lots of makeup. They wore mostly Lip Service stuff in black or purple. I don't remember if they were talented or they sucked, because I was usually pretty wasted at their shows. I just know they went from zero to sixty in a week because of Michael's popularity; they really lucked out. Michael was one of the most popular guys on The Strip; he knew *everyone*. Alleycat Scratch had a full house at every show and built-in friends to party with every weekend.

Let's see…Alleycat Scratch. Devin Lovelace was the guitarist and he seemed pissed off whenever I saw him. He rarely spoke around me and never smiled- but that could be because he found me annoying. He had shoulder-length hair that appeared to be relaxed or straightened in some way. Boa (formerly Bobby) was the bassist and was a little intimidating because he was quick and witty- clearly intelligent. He had long, stringy black hair and huge features. He wore a Charlie Chaplin hat and was pretty social; people liked him a lot. He appeared to be the brains behind the operation. Robbi Black was their drummer; girls went ballistic for him. He was very cute, with puffy lips, pretty cat eyes, and kind of feminine features. He had very long, dyed black hair, almost to his ass. He got along well with everyone and was generally a nice guy.

With Alleycat Scratch as a front for many, many more parties and much more craziness, we were wasted non-stop. The three other guys in the band were serious about making music, but Michael didn't really care, he just wanted to party. He moved in with them in a building on the corner of Yucca and Whitley, in a very bad area of Hollywood. I forgot his apartment number at first and stupidly asked the security guard, "Have you seen a skinny guy with long black hair?"

He said, "You just described half this building."

***

Jimmy and I still really loved each other, but neither of us would leave our social lives. They were like families we had created for ourselves and they were more powerful than what we were to each other I guess. We both got something from our scenes that fulfilled us. Mostly ego boosts and confidence, I think. I don't even know why I wanted to *have* a boyfriend. It was absurd. I never *saw* Jimmy that year! If he would've just let me hang out with him as I originally wanted to, I would've never ventured off on my own. That really came back and bit him in the ass.

I turned eighteen that September. It wasn't some joyous occasion for me, I barely noticed. I was already living as an adult. An irresponsible, crazy adult maybe, but an adult nonetheless. I came and went as I pleased; I was never home. I didn't have an established family structure because my mother was working two jobs and my sister spent as much time as possible away from the house. I hadn't seen my father around, which was good. I was still working at the beauty supply store and I started to attend the local community college that fall. I was signed up for film and media classes, which were interests of mine before I turned to the dark side and depended solely on my looks for an identity. It cracked open the hard pod that was my soul. Just a tiny crack. I was so interested in the film class that my heart hurt. It was a class that focused on film noir, mainly Hitchcock. Watching Grace Kelly and Jimmy Stewart in *Rear Window* made me forget about my life. I thought the films were so beautifully put together, so gloriously scored, and so perfectly costumed- it was just painfully wonderful. I longed to do storyboards and direct a beautiful movie.

The media class (Social Values in Mass Communication) was so interesting to me that I read the book in my free time, highlighting passages that I liked. My journalism class also compelled me. I felt a stirring in my gut, swishing around with all of the alcohol. It made me feel like more of a person just to be *learning* something. My mind craved it. But there was a crazy party going on, and not everyone was invited. I foolishly told myself that books would be there when the party was over.

There were some hot new faces in town that fall. They wore lots of glittered pale pink, white, and lavender, and had the perfect shade of expensively highlighted hair, which was the color of baby chicks. Despite all of that, they still had beer bottles in their hands and cigarettes hanging out of their mouths. They were always with beautiful, bitchy blond girls. My crowd took them in on the spot; they got the part without having to audition. Their names were Kit Ashley, Freddie Ferrin, Tweety Boyd, and Keri Kelli and they called themselves the Big Bang Babies.

These guys appeared to have more money backing them than the others. I realized not too much later that Kit Ashley somehow had two different Jaguars and lived in a penthouse apartment on the corner of Franklin and La Brea. I believe he also had a job writing for a magazine of some sort, but that couldn't have paid shit. Kit was a Bret Michaels/David Lee Roth knock off with a face like one of the Olsen twins, very cute. Keri was a very serious musician and did not go out partying with the other three as much. He was super beautiful, looked like a model. He had one side of his hair dyed black and the other side bleached white and had it up in puppy-dog ear ponytails a lot of the time. He thought I was ridiculous and ignored me.

All of the guys in my crowd became best buddies with Big Bang Babies, especially Freddie and Tweety. It was the smart thing to do. They would've lost if they would've tried to compete with them. I latched onto Freddie first; he was the most approachable. He seemed surprised I was interested in befriending him and latched right back on to me. Freddie had the same bleached hair, deep blue eyes and a great smile. He amused me for some reason- he was kind of a sad sap, lacking confidence compared to the other three. I hung with him a lot. Tweety was living with an heiress called Tipsy LaFabula in a house in Laurel Canyon. She supported him, naturally. She wore feather boas, huge Audrey Hepburn hats, and elbow length gloves. He was the one who walked up to me before he knew me, asked if I wanted a boyfriend, and then walked away once he found out how little money I made. I love that.

Tweety had huge eyes that were made up like Twiggy, with tons of eyeliner way outside the rim of the eye to create an even bigger eye. He sometimes wore a bandana tied around his head with the knot on the top like Aunt Jemima and always had a cigarette in his hand. He never had an expression on his face whatsoever; he was always very calm and restrained. He was never crazy, yelling, or fighting like the other people in our crowd.

One time I took Tweety to The Strip and I opened my trunk so he could throw his stacks of flyers inside. He saw my school books and looked up at me with a puzzled face. I stood there staring back at him, shivering in my little gold dress, wondering what the problem was.

He said, "You are like...*smart*? You're in *school*?" He took a long drag of his cigarette and blew smoke from his lungs. "How old are you?"

I felt nervous for some reason. Was this going to ruin my image? Was this not a good thing? I was convinced I should have hidden my books and thrown a couple of gallons of Jim Beam in the back with a dead body.

I told him how old I was and he said, "Eigh*teen*? What are you doing hanging around guys like *us*?"

I scrunched up my eyes and said, "Well, how old do you have to *be*?" and slammed the trunk.

I went to a party with all of the popular guys one night. At one point, I was holding court- they were all around me in a circle, sipping drinks and talking. Tweety, Robbi, Freddie and a few others were there. I was flirting and being coquettish and feeling all great. Without realizing it, I backed into a candelabra. I saw a few of their eyes widen and I smelled something burning. My hair was starting to go up in flames. Everyone at the party stopped what they were doing and watched me scream, shriek, and try to stamp out the flames on my head. Michael helped me to slap myself in the head; he enjoyed it far too much. Luckily, the fire was eating up my hair spray before really getting down to business with my actual hair, so the damage was nothing a little teasing couldn't cover.

In the coming winter months, my crowd hit party after party and went to lots of shows. We all seemed to be paying attention only to each other. There was a band we saw all the time called the Shrinky Dinx. They got a record deal and changed their name to Sugar Ray, because Milton Bradley was going to sue them for using the name of one of their toys. We were like "Sugar *who?*" Then there were our buddies that were in a band called Slamhound. We must have partied at their place on Orange five thousand times. They became a band called Buckcherry, and went on to fame and fortune, while we were all chugging beers in the dirt somewhere.

I still hung out with Harmony on some nights. We laid under his covers, giggled, and talked about skiing, Palm Springs and other girly shit. We should've done our toes and watched Molly Ringwald movies. Harmony would have made a great best friend, but I couldn't get past how attractive he was. I kept hoping for more, even though he clearly was not interested in me in that way.

I was also still hanging around Tricia, who didn't mind that I had pounded her face in only six months prior. We took my sister and her Middleton friend Lainie to El Compadre one night. Strange from the Glamour Punks and Michael went with us, and it was raining. Michael and Tricia started making fun of each other and bantering. It started when he looked at her with all seriousness and said, "Nice 'stache." She put her hand to her upper lip and her eyes got big. She called him an asshole and it went on from there. I wrote:

Michael threw a handful of lettuce at Tricia, then all of the sugar packets and then some of the beer cans we smuggled in. Then he threw the salt and the pepper shakers, the tortilla chips, and even a butter knife at her forehead (she moved and it hit the picture on the wall). Stacy Star came in with his bandmate Dazzle and ordered a bunch of food and drinks for us. I thought he was so generous and even started liking him after twelve drinks. Next thing I knew, he jumped up from the table and ran. Dazzle followed. I was like, "Wait...what the-" Before I could get the red straw out of my mouth, I realized, "Oh shit. They just ditched us with the bill." And you know me- I don't even carry any money. So anyway, they jumped into a van, reversed at top speed and slammed into the car parked behind them. Then they slammed into whatever was in front of them. Stacy kept reversing and then accelerating, reversing and accelerating- he was literally smashing his van on both ends, as hard as he could. He finally compacted the car behind him enough to get out of the space. Then he swerved out, reversed into a wall, and smashed yet another car. We were screaming, "Stacy! Stop!" He was making the biggest, loudest scene and everyone from the restaurant was yelling, "Get the police!" El Compadre tried holding us, but we jumped in my car and left because both Michael and Strange have warrants.

It rained a lot that winter. I drove completely drunk in the rain to hang with Harmony and Bobby Berry a few times a week. They seemed to appreciate my style, but neither appeared to be attracted to me otherwise. I was convinced I needed to be just a little more cool, but I was always doing clumsy or dorky things when I was around them. I dropped Harmony off in the street one night and as I was pulling away, he yelled something. *Maybe he wants to kiss me. Finally!* I was so thrilled. *This is it!* I carefully reversed and drove backwards to him and pressed the brake, fluttering my eyelashes and trying to give him sexy eyes. I talked to him for about five minutes, long enough to where I forgot my car was in reverse. There was no kiss. Bummer. We said goodbye to each other and I was going to step on the gas and peel out, to be cool. Thank God he was no longer behind me when I hit the gas- I would have ran that bitch over. I just remember shooting backward really fast and almost slamming into a tree.

Another time I was outside of his apartment in the daytime, looking for a parking space (he lived on Hollywood Boulevard, just past La Brea). There was no one on the streets; they were completely dead. It was very quiet; all I could hear were birds chirping. I was a new driver, so I was a little nervous. A stoplight for one of the little teeny side streets was yellow and instead of going through it, I hit the brakes so hard that I skidded through the light with the loudest screech you ever heard in your life- it brought people out to their balconies to see what the commotion was. That screech was so loud; it was as if I had avoided a semi or a deer or something really crazy. I left black marks in the street.

Journal Entry 1/13/92

I am in a gray sweatshirt and cut off sweat pants. I haven't showered or gotten off my ass all day. Get me out of this rut. Drinking, staying on couches, throwing up. I am stuck on these drag queen guys and I am secretly hoping something will interest me more. I am sick of this lifestyle even though Tricia and I are going for test shoots for bikini modeling on Sunday. I am going to end up backing out of it, but she needs the money.

Tricia went to the shoot without me and the guy tried sleeping with her when she got there. I had been in situations that were similar. Once I called an ad for a "figure modeling" agency called World Models. I didn't know that they started girls like Traci Lords and a slew of other women in porn. They acted as if it was bikini modeling, and I thought it would be the perfect thing for me. They had someone call me for a pre-interview and he asked me how my private parts were shaved. *Whoa Nellie.* I flaked on my appointment. Another time I met with a photographer that said he shot for Ziganne's Bikinis and needed a model. I met him in the Valley and had a margarita with him and he showed me his book. It was the Ziganne's catalog. He said, "I shoot pictures like these." I said, "Wait...'like' these? Did you take these pictures we are looking at?" and the moron said no. He didn't even have any pictures that he took, because he had probably never taken a picture in his life. He was surely too busy raping and killing dumb girls like me and burying their remains in the desert.

Another time, I answered an ad for lingerie modeling (I was pretty dense; it took a lot for me to learn my lesson). I showed up at this office building on Ventura Boulevard in a nice part of Encino. I went up some stairs to an empty office with little dressing rooms in it. It was just some pervy man and me. Here was how his business worked: He had some crappy lingerie line that was a front for prostitution. Clients paid him to see a girl "model" the lingerie. If the girl wanted to take anything off for tips or take it further, well, then that was her prerogative. The man said he needed to see me dance naked before he could think about hiring me. I was like, *Say what?* It was just us two and I was afraid he would rape me or something so I tried to remain cool and just get out of there. I played dumb and said I would come back when I had a bikini to dance in, or something awkward like that. I burned rubber out of that joint. In my car on the way home, I thought about the poor girls that actually had to do such things for a living. I didn't know it at the time, but I would be meeting one very soon.

CHAPTER TWELVE

Dodging Bullets

Tricia introduced me to a dancer named Willa, who had once lived in her apartment building but had since moved to Hollywood. She was fair-skinned with long, wavy, platinum blond hair and bright red lipstick. She had big, sparkly blue eyes and a gorgeous smile. My next 'friend crush' formed instantly. I joined her and Tricia on a few nights out, and then I started going out with Willa on my own. She loved to go to the Rainbow and dance- something I had never done. I was a horrible dancer, so in order to loosen up, I needed twenty-five Long Island iced teas. The dance floor at the Rainbow was sunken down five stairs and was dark, so that made it a little easier. It had a railing that I could hang onto while flipping my hair around, trying not to fall. Willa propped me up half of the time. We always requested the Prince song "Erotic City," and at some point, they started playing it when we walked in the room. I felt all cool. Other than that song, I heard a lot of the Red Hot Chili Peppers' new album *Blood Sugar Sex Magik*; the songs "Give it Away" and "Under the Bridge" were big around this time. I also remember that one night, the bouncers made everyone leave the Rainbow so Guns N' Roses could film a portion of their "November Rain" video in the red booths (it didn't come out until that summer). We were totally irritated to have to cut our night short. We stumbled outside and saw that a portion of Sunset Boulevard was also shut down for the shoot. We had to move the party elsewhere.

Willa taught me some social etiquette: For one, she taught me to tip the cocktail waitresses when they brought my drinks. I had never even heard of such a thing. I knew nothing about tipping, probably because I rarely bought my own drinks, but it was good to know. Willa was also a pro at scamming drinks off strangers, which was part two of her etiquette lesson. One must be able to secure herself a certain amount of cocktails for the pleasure of her company. I watched her work the older men; her face lit up and she looked like she was really interested in them, while they forked over drinks. When she had had enough cocktails, her face dropped and her eyes went dead and she moved on. It was kind of frightening really, like an evil robot or a Stepford Wife. I had never seen a face change so drastically. But that was what was called 'survival mode' in the world of dancers: They will do whatever it takes. If they don't learn that charm, another girl will take their customer, i.e. their *money*. It was the work of a true hustler.

She was blond and paid for everything, two things I required in a friend at that time. She got us cabs to clubs, bought or swindled us drinks and paid for my food if I ever needed any. She originally said she was in public relations, which I knew wasn't true because of Tricia, but I didn't say anything. Who was I to make her uncomfortable? After hanging out with her a bit, she admitted to being a dancer. I had hung out with other girls who had 'danced' so I didn't question it any further. I was a little thrown off by her figure though. If you looked past her beauty, she was not in great shape. She had no chest, a kind of a big, shapeless butt and no waist. She hid it well by wearing a lot of black. I was puzzled as to how she made good money. It didn't add up. There was a lot of competition out there, especially in

Hollywood where the prettiest girls in the world danced.

As we got closer, she confided in me a little bit more, admitting that she made $1,100 in one night by letting some old guy spank her. She said the first thing she did was buy hundreds of dollars' worth of groceries and fill up her cupboards and fridge. She had been living on Top Ramen for months and was so delighted to go and buy beautiful jams and jellies, French pastries, Italian sparkling waters, gorgeous cuts of steak and fresh berries. I didn't judge her. I remembered that some of the other dancers I knew had a "regular" from whom they would make side money. They always painted a picture of something harmless that had nothing to do with sex. *Oh, I just walked over him in high heels* or *he just wanted to be yelled at,* things like that. I figured Willa was just doing the same thing and I didn't ask her any more about it. I never asked *any* of the girls about what they did for money. I knew that would make them uneasy and unable to trust me. I handled Willa in the same way. We were to have fun. We were to laugh, dance, drink, flirt with guys and forget our troubles.

Tricia's French boyfriend, Pierre, hated Willa. We were both over at Tricia's apartment one day and I overheard Pierre threatening Willa with something. My ears perked up. In a low, quiet voice, she turned very vicious toward him and he shut up *real* quick. She threatened to tell Tricia all about him. All *about* him? What did she *know*? I wasn't sure what she had on him, but I was impressed at the way she had him shaking in his boots. I had never seen a woman pull that off in real life. Only on *Dynasty* or *Dallas,* of course.

Willa always seemed to be putting men in their place in a shocking fashion. Once again, her deep blue eyes would be happy and smiley one minute, until someone tried to scam her. Her eyes snapped into this piercing stare and she would say crazy things like, "Do you want to fuck with me? Because I don't think you want to fuck with me, so and so. I will fucking *destroy* you. So you need to shut the fuck up." I thought I had fallen in love! I wanted to be like that! She was beautiful and fun, but would cold fuck you up if you crossed her. I craved protection, so I clung to her. I wished I had known her earlier in my life, so I could have let her loose on my old gynecologist and a half dozen other guys- she would have torn them to shreds and had a cocktail afterwards.

I noticed that a new crowd was starting to spread on The Strip at that time. They were from Seattle. They were still considered glam guys at that point, but they were different. They were...*angry.* And they were into drugs, mainly heroin. They were a dirty crowd. The girls were not blond California girls; they were pasty with black hair. Some of them were still pretty, but they were more Goth or Punk-tinged. I didn't like that crowd; they were not glamorous enough for me. I preferred to keep company with the most beautiful, most popular people I could find, so I avoided those misfits. I had probably spent a year or so glossing them over and not giving them the time of day, because around 1992 I noticed that there was a group of people who knew who I was and didn't like me. They said I was a snob and that I thought I was hot. I was like, "And you are?"

***

A few months passed. My grandmother started dating a new man and she wanted her space. It had been three years that we had lived with her in the tiny Canoga Park house, and she told my mom it was time for us to go. It really *was* time. There were still roaches scattering in the house when you turned on a light. My room was still full of smelly clothes that needed to be laundered, stale pretzels that I had thrown in the ceiling fan to watch them break, stacks of magazines and records and God knows what else. And my sister's feet always smelled like cheese popcorn, so that scent was not helping the ambience in the house when my grandmother was trying to date. Both my sister and I blasted music very loud and I got phone calls at all hours of the night- I would have booted us out too. We moved from my grandmother's house to a house in Northridge. It was a good-sized house and my mother received some sort of a smoking deal. I think she only paid $700 a month and we all got our own rooms. Because I had turned eighteen, I had to start paying my mother rent. I chose the smallest of the rooms, for $200 a month. My mom had her eye on me, letting me stay only as long as I behaved.

I started hanging with Razz again. He was no longer friends with Darren Tyler. Darren had stopped dating the rock star's wife and took up with another dancer. We had never seen him so sprung on anyone- he was totally in love with this chick, a green-eyed brunette. Razz was dating the girl's friend and they had all spent a lot of time together holed up in the house, rolling on Ecstasy. There was some point where Darren's girl and Razz hooked up- Razz blamed the drugs and felt terrible afterward- but Darren never forgave him. (The chick, incidentally, was one of the girls on the inside cover of Poison's *Open Up and Say... Ahh* album). So without Darren, Razz's new partner in crime was his old friend Teddy St. John, who was there at the beach on the night I lost my virginity. I would have not even remembered it was him if he hadn't reminded me. Anyhow, he was really funny and had a very low voice like a DJ. He was Greek, with very wide set eyes; black, spiky hair like Nikki Sixx; very nice, smooth, pale skin and huge lips. He was really tall but I wouldn't say he was thin. He wasn't *fat*, he just looked regular. Oh, okay, sometimes he could get a little chubby if he wasn't watching it. He had known all of the guys I knew since they were teenagers.

Teddy and Razz were a little more upscale than the Glamour Punks or Alleycat Scratch. They had jobs, cars, and nice clothing; they bought me all of my drinks, and made sure the doormen took care of me wherever we went. The Glamour Punks and Alleycat Scratch passed me the community bottle of Jim Beam at trashy parties in random apartment buildings, wearing the same clothes they wore the night before. Cars? Yeah, right. Jobs? *Please.*

Journal Entry 2/13/92

Went to hang with Robbi Black last night. Well, hang with him in a crowd of people, really. Strange lost a $250 contact lens when we were on the way to some girl's house and he was all upset the whole night. When we all got back to Alleycat's apartment four hours later, he got down on his hands and knees in a bunch of debris by the elevator and found the lens! And I don't just mean a few crumbs on the floor, I mean like, broken plaster and rocks- there was a broken wall. How does one find a tiny clear piece of glass? While completely drunk, at that? We were screaming at the miraculous sight. We drank a lot at the apartment and I woke up at four in the morning in a sitting position on their couch. There was a Clint Eastwood movie on. Michael and Strange were sleeping on the other broken couches. I cleared a path through all the beer cans and bailed.

Robbi looked like he would be a dick because he was so attractive, but the truth was that he was a little bit shy. Women were mobbing him all the time and he almost didn't know how to handle it. Tricia came out with me the next night, saw him, and screamed at me in her crow voice with a hint of a British accent from her mother, "He is *gorge*JAS! Oh my *gawd*!"

Jimmy's band's songs started playing on the radio at that time. They started doing photo shoots. Razz and Teddy were impressed, which made me roll my eyes at how easily they were swayed from thinking he was out of style, ugly and uncool. Robbi commented that he liked the band as well. I was doubly annoyed.

One weekend, I went to a party with the Glamour Punks where Dizzy Damage (who would sadly die a few years later) started violently throwing bananas. He then did a flying leap onto a dining room table, sending all of its contents crashing to the ground (alcohol bottles are loud when breaking, so it was a great scene). It was at that party that Michael introduced me to the new dancer he and Strange were living with, a girl named Collette. She was tall and brunette, sort of a Sandra Bullock type. I had heard she was a rival of Missy's through the grapevine; they had dated the same guy at some point and didn't like each other.

I went to visit Razz one night soon thereafter. He had moved back to the condo with Dusty and good old Holly, who spent that particular night puking for hours on end. I stood there with a bowl while he wiped his face and blew his nose. I held back his hair like he was a girl. Later, he started crying really hard; it was horrible. I wanted to hug him and hold him- the guy always seemed so miserable. Razz, not fazed by his friend's sickness and sadness, started looking me up and down and told me I looked really good and that I blew Missy away. He usually critiqued me, telling me I was overweight or I needed some Laminates or something like that. He made me step back, looked me over and said Jimmy had been a lucky guy. I was shocked because he was my friend- it made me uneasy. Where was this coming from? Then he said I was his little sis and he wasn't letting anyone fuck with me, even ten times more than before. Then he handed me a bottle of nail polish and put his thumb out on the table. I laughed inside, and painted his nails.

I partied with Tweety from Big Bang Babies the next week and got more of a peek into his life. I was completely fascinated by him because he seemed to be the only person in all of Hollywood who was in on a big joke. He didn't take himself too seriously, was always calmly dragging on a cigarette and never worried about a thing. He was there to have fun; his life did not depend on being signed to a record label like the rest of them. It was as if he saw an opening to where he could live the good life and he was smart enough to capitalize on it.

Journal Entry 3/22/92

If I ever mention Tweety again, slap me. His blond girlfriend is some rich chick- one of the LaFabula Twins, whoever they are. She looks like an old film star: platinum white Jean Harlow hair, long fake eyelashes, big boobs and hips, plump cheeks, glamorous clothes. I thought her name was Gypsy at first, but it is Tipsy. Tipsy LaFabula. She has a house up in Laurel Canyon. Tweety gets everything he wants, I am sure. I will never have a chance with him. Strange and I climbed the gnarly old stone stairway up the ivy covered hills to their house the other night. We had to duck under rails and step over potted plants, finally coming to a deck that led to the front door. The first thing I saw in the living room were a bunch of blond wigs on Styrofoam heads that were perched on the mantle over the fireplace. There were black rabbits running freely around the room amongst piles of board games and all of the clocks were set to different times. It was like Alice in Wonderland.

"I call this the do room," said Tweety, giving us a tour of the place, "Because I don't know what to do with it." He gave a wave of his hand over the room and inhaled on his cigarette. I peeked into a bathroom that had an old fashioned, footed tub. A winding staircase led down to more rooms, most of which were empty. Once we got back upstairs, Tweety announced that he was going to make the living room into a haunted house, just to freak people out. He pointed to a little bat hanging from the ceiling. "See? I already started."

Tipsy, in bare feet and a long 1930's evening gown, stepped over a low lacquered table and invited us to sit down. We sat on pillows on the black and white checked floor as a bunny hopped by on soft paws. Tweety brought out a deli platter that he had arranged with little sword toothpicks. Tipsy sipped a cocktail and held up the glass to show a straw that changed colors from purple to pink.

*"He buys such **necessary** things when he goes shopping."*

Kit Ashley, Tweety's bandmate from Big Bang Babies, showed up with a petite platinum blond girl with crystal blue eyes. He dropped her hand and came straight to me.

"Strange, is this your action?"

"No, she is my really good friend."

*"Who **are** you?" he said, staring into my eyes. "Oh my **God.**
Marry me. Are those your real eyes?"*

He kept trying to paw me and I removed his hands.

*I was drunk, but I do remember Tweety saying, "Someday, I
would like to eventually learn how to **play** the bass," no matter
that he already played his bass to unsuspecting screaming
crowds on the weekends who thought he was a god.*

*"It is good enough how it is right now. I don't really want to be
a musician. I just want everything that comes with it."*

Journal Entry 3/29/92

*Willa's apartment is a mess and Collette's is thrashed. Spending
all of that time at their places makes me appreciate the clean,
palace of luxury I live in now. Okay, so it is a little house in the
Valley- so what. My mom cleans and there is food in the fridge. I
can **never** move to Hollywood; I would lose it and become like
all of them. They don't have plates. They don't have food to **put**
on plates. They live in pigsties. People come in and out of their
apartments, sleeping on floors or on furniture- if there is any.
Being at these girls' places makes me ill. So trashy and dirty
with bugs and backed up garbage disposals and bathrooms full
of hair.*

I was partying a lot, but I still had something in my life that
made me feel secure, no matter what happened. Jimmy. I still
loved him and still knew in my heart that I would always have
him there. I felt comforted to know he loved me, in the midst of
all of the chaos. We were very on again, off again. We had so
many breakups, I didn't even mention them all here. We always
got back together, until one day in April of 1992.

Willa was old enough to get into the Cathouse. One day she told me that she saw Jimmy there while he was still dating me, ferociously making out with a girl who he had pinned to the wall. I was stunned. I felt a stab in my heart. I was so guilty all of the time about my own flirtations, that I never considered that *he* would do such a thing. I felt like an idiot. It never occurred to me that it would happen to me. I always thought he was so in love with me that he would never look at another woman. I was a fool!

Although I had no business even being mad at him considering all of the guys I hung around and the fact that I did have an affair with Roxy, I was still shattered. I was also very grateful to hear the truth and did not shoot the messenger. Willa told me it wasn't just Jimmy who was a cheater; Pierre had cheated on Tricia. With *her*. She said she had slept with him in the laundry room of the apartments. That made me feel queasy. I thought Pierre was totally in love with Tricia. Was this what all men were like? Just like my dad? I knew that men were wired to want to be with a lot of women, but it still seemed shocking. Was I that naïve? It was at that point that I truly ended my two-year relationship with Jimmy. I was very heart broken, believe it or not. Even though my life was completely different than it was in the beginning of our relationship, I was very sad to hear he cheated while we were together. I confronted him and he admitted to not just cheating that time at the Cathouse, but cheating all along. Even when I was in the psych ward. Something inside me broke at that point- It was such a deep pain to hear that nothing we had was ever real. Even though I had moved on to my own scene and life, I still held him close to my heart. He had given me love when I most needed it, when no one else around me gave a shit about me. I tried my best to not to disrespect him, but I had. I was publicly disrespecting him every night just by being in the company of so many other guys and flirting with them.

Journal Entry 4/11/92

I went over the deep end. I am a lush. I feel like crying every morning when I wake up drunk. It is degrading. Supposedly, I am the major hot item right now. But I can't enjoy it. I found out Jimmy was cheating on me the whole time we were together. I am so humiliated. I have been getting drunk every night and throwing away any money I have. I fooled around with Kit Ashley. Don't worry, I didn't do it. I might as well though.

I was completely game to sleep with Kit, I didn't care. I was so hurt and angry with Jimmy, I was willing to do anything. Earlier that night, I spritzed myself with perfume, threw on a lime green dress and went to a party in the hills where I randomly ate some ice cream out of some stripper's mouth (I know, I know. But I was in Hollywood and that was just a normal occurrence I guess). She was friends with Kit, and asked me what my story was (this was *after* we were already sharing germs, but that was the way it went). I told her I hadn't had sex with a guy other than my boyfriend for two years. She asked me how old I was and I told her I was eighteen. She was concerned, for some reason. Most people in Hollywood had no conscience; I didn't understand why *she* did. She pulled Kit over and sternly told him how old I was and that I had just broken up with someone and not to do anything stupid. I couldn't believe it, but he listened to her! I was annoyed.

Continued...

*I woke up in the morning, called a cab, and ditched Kit. He was like, "Where are you going!? It is seven a.m.!" He called me the next night and told me to be careful. Not sexy. The cab brought me to my car and then I drove to Harmony's and took him to the beach with me. He was so gentlemanly that it made me sick. We made a date for the next night and he stood me up so I went out with Willa and got drunker than ever. I ran into Razz, my loyal friend. We ran off together and told the whole world to fuck off. He looked at Willa with his eyebrows up and a scrunchie on his wrist and said, "Honey? You need to lose weight. You have **no** tits and you have **two** chins." I cringed. She was **furious!** I can't* *believe I did this, but I burst out laughing right in front of her, because I couldn't believe what he was saying. But that is Razz for you. She was so mad at me. She started yelling at me and said she didn't want to meet any more of my friends ever again. Then Razz ran into Missy and told **her** off (and later he started crying because she hurt him so badly. The cab driver told him to be a man). Then we went to the Rainbow, where Razz ran into his best friend Jay-Jay and told **him** to fuck off as well- I was standing there egging him on and I don't even know why. Tricia saw me on a rampage and looked scared, she avoided me. At the end of the night, Razz and I drove up to some house that he was house sitting (a 1970's sitcom star's place), and slept in the guy's huge bed filled with white pillows. I woke up in the morning and started crying. Razz felt bad for me and tried to make light of the whole thing.*

"Oh my God! I told Jay Jay to fuck off! Didn't I? What did we do to Willa?! Didn't I knock a lamp on her head? Oh shit!"

I started laughing through my tears, suddenly remembering how he jumped up and hit a fluorescent light in her apartment building and the plastic cover came down and slammed her in the head when she was already furious.

*"What did we **do**?" I asked.*

"We told everybody to fuck off!" He said in a high-pitched shriek.

*"Well, I am going to be hanging around **you** a lot more, because nobody else **likes** me now," I said, thinking of Tricia and Willa's faces.*

I was really affected by Jimmy; my reactions were extreme and my hurt was very deep. I started to feel an explosion of anger toward men in general, so Willa and her cold persona was just what I needed at that time to make me feel better. I felt solace in being around a woman who was an ice queen and took no prisoners (Razz was immune though; he was a rare bird). I didn't care that she had no soul. She was afraid of no one, which is why she didn't hesitate to tell on Jimmy. No one else who knew about him told, fearing the social repercussions, but she didn't give a fuck and I admired that. I wanted to try out her persona, to see if I liked it better than being all sunshine, glitter, and smiles. Besides, I didn't think I could smile even if I tried, at that point. I was too heartbroken. I clung to Willa to the point of obsession on some days; I didn't want to be away from her, I didn't want to lose my strength.

A bunch of guys tried getting me to be their girlfriend when the word hit the street that I was no longer connected to Jimmy. And even more tried sleeping with me. I had to choose someone to date...who would it be? I went into public relations mode and picked Robbi from Alleycat Scratch. He was safe in my mind because I didn't feel he could break my heart. I didn't have a true connection with him, I never got to that place with him. He was sweet, considerate and had been my friend for a while; not to mention he was physically one of the best looking guys in town.

I hooked up with Robbi eventually and I felt empty and miserable afterwards. I was cursing myself. I knew if I started fooling around with these guys, I would go down the tubes, fast. We had a talk a few weeks later. I told him I regretted hooking up with him and thought it ruined our friendship. We couldn't even *look* at each other anymore. And I felt even more foolish because he had acted as if we would be a couple, but then started to avoid me afterwards. I was so mad at myself for being such a chump. I hadn't really even clicked with him and thought his personality was too nice for me. We ended up hooking up maybe two or three times after that, but nothing came of it.

I started hanging with one of the Seattle guys named Lesli Sanders. He was tall, lanky, and pale with long pink hair and green eyes. Though I normally avoided his crowd at all costs, something struck me about him. He seemed awkward- even shy sometimes. His look was cool; he was very fashionable in the way he presented himself. My crowd avoided his, even when they were at the same party. I thought if I hung out with him, it would go undetected. It did, for the most part. I was so hurt and damaged by Jimmy's betrayal that I tried to take it out on Lesli by humiliating him every chance I got. I guess he was just in the wrong place at the wrong time. I slammed doors in his face while he was talking to me, I ate in front of him and didn't ask if he was hungry. I ditched him and left him places. I slapped him across the face when I felt like it. He kept *letting* me. He *really* liked me and I didn't care. If he dared say something about the way I was behaving, I would say, "Are you being a jerk?" and he quickly said no. I felt like shit inside, but kept torturing him.

So anyway, I didn't know what to do with myself around all these guys. I was in such a bad state, that things could have gotten out of control very easily. Not only that, but I couldn't be away from Willa for even a day or I would fall into a crying heap. I decided to move in with her. No matter that she lived in an apartment in a dangerous part of Hollywood, with no food or furniture in it. It was on Cherokee, about a block from the Alleycat Scratch apartment, off Yucca Street. I don't know what the hell was so irresistible about the situation. Most nights I heard gunshots and saw police helicopter spotlights shining right on our building. One time we weren't allowed to leave the building, because a criminal was on the loose inside. Those were the first times I ever heard real gunshots. 18th Street gang ran the neighborhood- and they were no joke. One day Willa and I were walking to the store and had to fall to the ground and cover our heads because someone was firing shots at an armored bank truck. The sun was out, birds were chirping, and *bullets* were flying. It was so crazy.

Another day, while I was walking to my car, I saw a dead body covered in a white sheet on the sidewalk. But the scariest thing happened one particular night when I was driving back to the apartment after a night of partying with Willa. We were only half a block from the parking garage, when a car suddenly got right on our tail and started shooting. I couldn't believe it. I thought, *This can't be happening. I was having fun, going to shows and writing for the school paper...now I am being shot at- what the fuck?* I started screaming and ducked down in the car. I couldn't stop driving or the guy would crash into me. I started crying and was driving with my seat reclined all the way back. I couldn't even see where I was going! I didn't crash into anything, luckily. Glass never shattered in my car, so we realized he wasn't shooting at us. It appeared he was hiding behind us. We heard people yelling on the street corners. He was shooting at the drug dealers! Maybe they were on his turf. I got us into the parking garage and we both sat there in my car, crying and scared. She told me not to look at him if we saw him outside because he would kill us if we could identify him. I started to think that maybe I was in over my head.

I was quickly seeing that Hollywood was not at all glamorous, but I pushed that to the back of my mind and trudged forward. Things started to take an awkward turn once I moved in with Willa- I got the feeling I was going to have to pay the piper. She began to try to pressure me into having a relationship with her. *Ha ha, sure, let's be girlfriends!* I said, trying to keep it light and cute. No, she wasn't talking light and cute, or little pecks on the lips. She was talking the real deal: doing it. She started dropping hints, walking around naked. It probably seemed like I was game for it, the way I was clinging to her. My problem was that I didn't know how to let someone down and still remain friends with them. I thought, *Okay, I do hate guys right now and want to destroy every male I see. But do I like **women** in their place?* It would have been totally acceptable in Hollywood. But the answer was no. I didn't like chicks. She became offended when I finally rebuffed her and things started to change between us.

We went to a party that spring with a guy named Bang, who was friends with the Glamour Punks. He was super-duper tall, incredibly thin, and had a dark green Mohawk that wasn't styled- it hung down on one side, showing the shaved sides of his head. He wore purple striped tights under his baggy shorts, big T-shirts, purple Doc Marten boots and a Sid Vicious bondage chain around his neck. He was always yelling in a New York accent and everyone was too scared to tell him to shut the fuck up. I felt like clocking him in the head with a shovel. Anyway, that particular night in April of 1992, I drove Bang and some other guys to Rock n' Roll Ralphs on Sunset to buy some Jim Beam. Some crack whore tried to solicit him in the parking lot and he started yelling at her and calling her Toothy McSnuggle, which we found hilarious because it made no sense. She got really pissed at him and decided to kick a huge dent in my car. I was in mid-swig of the bottle of whiskey and my eyes bugged out when I saw the commotion. The whole night was violent, even at the party we went to afterwards. Everyone was pushing each other, socking each other, and being rowdy- the mood of the crowd was really shifting from the bubblegum nights that Michael and I shared a year or two prior. The guys were being far too rough around me and I saw that Strange was the one egging them on. I dove for him and we got in a huge fight, rolling around, and wrestling. He pushed me into a stove and tore a huge hole in my daisy print hot pants.

Bang started to take over as the new party leader, introducing his musical tastes to us outdated folk. He brought a Cypress Hill cassette tape to play in my car, rewinding the song "Hand on the Pump" repeatedly, and screaming the "Duke of Earl" sampling portions loud enough to break the glass on the goddamn Empire State Building back in New York. The rest of the guys got into the music too, seeming to like the new sound. The glam scene was dying before my eyes, but I was determined to continue on in Hollywood. What would become of us? Where were we headed?

I saw Tweety a few days later and he said, "I'll *be* your boyfriend," as if I had been begging him. I replied that I couldn't afford him, remembering he said he needed at least $200 a week from a girlfriend. He said we could work on it and then suggested I start dancing. I told him I didn't want to do something slutty like that, and he said it wouldn't be slutty, because I would be coming home to *him*. My heart sped up at the thought of coming home to him. But I couldn't be a stripper. No way. It would be too embarrassing to be naked in front of a crowd of people. Knowing me, I would trip and fall off the stage or break the damn pole off the ceiling with my fat ass. He came up to me a few days later and lowered his price while dragging on a cigarette. He didn't take his eyes off me.

"One hundred dollars a week- final offer."

I looked at him and just walked away. But inside I thought, *Shit, I would do it if I had that money to spare.*

CHAPTER THIRTEEN

Will She be Chopped to Bits in There?

The spring continued. Willa was still supporting me by providing a place to live and booze, the only two things I was convinced I needed in life. She left her apartment on Cherokee and got new a place down the street in Alleycat Scratch's building on Yucca and Whitley. I was only working a few days a week at the beauty supply store back in the Valley- my meager paychecks went straight to my mother for rent. Even though I only came back to her house to do laundry, pluck my eyebrows, and Nair my upper lip, I still had a room full of stuff there. I saw how quick she could be with the garbage bags and I knew my things would be straight out on the street if I didn't pay up. Basically, I had a job, but not a cent to spare. Being the total user that I was, I fully expected Willa to pay for me like my past dancer friends did. The fact that I was not contributing a penny was unfair, but I thought nothing of it. I know, I was so rude.

A year prior, a black dude on drugs named Rodney King was running from the cops. As you probably recall, some cops caught him and beat the shit out of him. Someone videotaped it and showed it to the media, and it sparked a huge controversy that implied the cops were abusing their power by using excessive force. People assumed it was due to racism because most of the cops were white. The cops went on trial during 1992 and at the end of April, the verdict was going to be announced as to whether or not the cops were guilty. The night before the announcement, Willa and I saw that cops were staked out around the area. We asked two of them why they were all out and they said that the verdict was being announced in the morning and they were all called out in case some shit went down. We were like, *Huh? Like what could go down?* They were cool cops and started chatting about it- they didn't think anything was going to happen, they were just following orders, bored and eating fast food in the car.

Lo and behold, when the verdict was announced that the accused cops were acquitted, much of the black population went ballistic in South Central Los Angeles and called it racism. Huge riots started to occur by the next evening, the largest at the intersection of Florence and Normandie. There were so many people that they outnumbered the cops. They started burning buildings, attacking storeowners, throwing bricks through windows, and torching cars. There was plenty of looting and fires going on in Hollywood as well. We all took that opportunity to watch from the apartment roofs, which overlooked Hollywood Boulevard. We barbecued from the rooftop and watched people roll huge TV's out of an electronic store. Michael and Strange went and looted Melrose and got some clothes from The Gap, of all places.

There was a curfew put in place by the police department, so I drove back to my mother's house in the Valley, a place I hadn't seen in weeks or maybe months. Jimmy called to check on me. I screamed, "If you were so *concerned* about me, you wouldn't have *screwed* a bunch of chicks without *protection* and then come back to *me*!" and slammed the phone down. I went to Tricia's and watched downtown L.A. on the news. It was in flames. We were stunned that the verdict of the police beating caused such an uproar in the community. But things were contained after a week or so and I drove back out to Hollywood to continue torturing myself.

Willa needed to make some money so we could continue partying, so I took her to the Holiday Inn on Highland, where she was to "dance" for some guy. She told me to come with her to knock on the door and collect the cash. She was annoyed and wanted to get it over with. I shuddered at being so close to the transaction. I knocked at the guy's door, carrying a portable stereo with one of my cassette tapes inside. It was stuff I had recorded off the radio, and it was all cued up and ready to go. We stepped in and saw an old fat guy in his underwear. I tried to act cool and not look down at his tighty whities and fat gut. He said, "Which one of you is it?" She piped up and said it was she, and that I was there to collect the money. I took his cash, a few hundred dollars, and went back to the car in the underground parking garage and waited. Before I left, she whispered to me that if she didn't come out in a half an hour exactly, I was to come back up and knock on the door and get her. *Whoa*...what if she didn't come out? Was it possible he would like...*kill* her in there? And what the hell could *I* do to save her? Wouldn't he just...pull me in the door and kill me too? I realized that I was playing the role of the "muscle" and I didn't feel I could do an adequate job in providing her protection.

I waited, listening to Right Said Fred in the car. I was nervous, hoping she would be okay and come out of the room on her own. Thirty minutes passed. She didn't come out. My heart was beating like a loud bass drum. How did I get tangled up in some shit like this? Now I have to go and try to save a strangled dancer from some fat guy's hotel room? What was I going to *do,* exactly? Beat him with my brush?

I went back up and knocked on the door. She answered the door and looked fine, but she was no longer wearing her red lipstick. She quickly pushed her way out the door and closed it behind her. We walked down the halls to the elevator in silence for a few minutes, and then she said she wanted to go out that night for some drinks. When I listened to the tape later, it had not been played. It was still cued up. I knew at that moment she had not danced at all. My friend was not a stripper. She was a hooker.

I guess I kind of knew inside, because she wasn't a dancer at a club and didn't even do bachelor parties (which can get pretty sketchy in and of themselves). When I actually let myself think about it, I was taken aback at how ugly and dirty it was. That was her reality. She had no family and no friends other than Tricia and me. She had no skills and she didn't have enough money to pay rent on an apartment by herself. She sold her body. My glamorous picture of her had disappeared. It was not dazzling. It was not powerful or glamorous. It was nothing to look up to. She had to sleep with a big fat man for money. She lived a life of shame and degradation.

Willa told me that she was from Georgia, or somewhere in the South, and she used to get beat up every single day at school. She was incredibly angry; very, very angry and just trying to survive. And there I was, mooching off her! I could've lived with my *mother* and I was mooching off this poor girl who had to do *that* for money. She was so lonely that she gladly supported me along with her.

Most of the time she tried to scam things for free. There was a liquor store on the corner of Hollywood Boulevard and Cherokee. We walked over there, took Ramen noodles and other food, and she sweet talked and made promises to the poor little Hindu guy who owned the store. He let us have the food without paying. Some nights Willa and I ditched our cab without paying. We would take a cab home from the Rainbow, tell the driver to hold on and that we would be right back. Willa would let the cab driver hold her purse (that had nothing of value in it) and we would get out, go inside, and never return. We did that a few times, until the cab companies would no longer even come to pick us up because they were warned of our address.

She stopped paying the rent at the apartment, and they couldn't legally evict her for thirty days or something. So we stayed that thirty days, living it up and having parties. If the parties got too big, we left and let everyone stay and party without us. She didn't care, because she only had a mattress and a broken down TV. There wasn't even any toilet paper. Her room had condoms all over the floor and old dried up slices of pizza in open pizza boxes. It was sickening.

The night before they changed the locks on the doors, we packed up the few items she did have into my car. She then set up shop at the Howard Hotel, which was about two blocks away, in the same neighborhood. We both had fun at first- we jumped on the beds and played the radio (I remember hearing "Tennessee" by Arrested Development specifically while jumping on the bed). We partied and brought back whoever wanted to hang out. Lesli and Pepper (who had left their previous bands and started a new band together called Queeny Blast Pop) came over once and we robbed them and then threw them out. We took their toothpaste and other belongings from their fanny -yes, fanny- packs.

In the bright blue mornings, Willa walked outside of the grimy hotel in her white robe and picked up an L.A. Xpress. It was a sex industry newspaper that advertised porn stores and strip clubs, but was most known for escort services. She opened its inky pages and called a random service to pick her up on the spot and send her straight out on call. It literally kept her off the street corner. One day she called a service and a black guy pulled up to the hotel in an old, crappy brown car. I'm not shitting you, he looked exactly like J.J. Walker from *Good Times*- clothes and all. She told me to come with her and I was scared inside, but I went. Soon we were on a freeway going to Culver City. I looked over at Willa's blond head looking out the window. Surely, she would have some plan if he tried to kill us. She would protect me, wouldn't she?

The guy soon pulled off into some run down area, toward a dingy motel. She told him, "Thirty minutes," and off she went, in a black velvet top and black pants. I then had to sit and wait in the car with him. I felt like I was going to shit my pants. He said he needed to get gas. *Wait...I can't let this guy drive away with me! No one but Willa knows where I am and neither of us know who **he** is.* I was terrified that it was the end of my life. He drove to a gas station and as he pumped gas, I considered getting out of the car and running...but I didn't. What if he were really only going to get gas, and I hastily jumped out like a maniac, stranding myself in Culver City? I pictured him driving back to get Willa and telling her I was gone. *Shit. I guess I will stay in this car and take my chances...* I tried to hold in my diarrhea. Luckily, he drove back to the motel parking lot after getting gas. I exhaled in the backseat, counting the seconds until she would walk back out of the motel. J.J. had a beeper or two, and she was supposed to page him if there was a problem. I thought, *How is she going to page you if she is being cut to bits in there?* But lo and behold, she came out twenty minutes later. It was the longest twenty minutes of my damn life. She got in the car without making eye contact with either of us, blond hair falling over her shoulders. She had cash in her hand and started counting it, her bright red fingernails flipping the bills. I tried not to stare. She kept a portion of the money and then gave J.J. his cut for driving. Drivers always got a cut because they also counted as the muscle- they were insurance. They were the one who would go and save the girl if she didn't come out within the allotted time slot; the person who could save the girl from danger, maybe even death. It was worth it to the girls to have this back up and they gladly paid their drivers. Willa then counted out a separate cut that was to be paid to the actual escort service for bringing her the "client." After receiving payment, J.J. brought us back home. As we were driving back past palm trees and spray-painted buildings, I thought about Willa. I couldn't believe that was her life. She was only a few years older than I was, maybe twenty-two. It was no way for a young woman to live.

Willa took some of her money to pay the rent on the next week of the hotel, and the rest I believe she was using for pills. She bought them from some European dude with poufy hair that she used to hook up with in the Yucca building. She got in terrible moods on those pills. She also took diet pills, which made her a cold bitch, as well. One night she was screwing some guy in the bed we slept in, so I went and slept in the bathroom. I got into the empty bathtub with my clothes on and curled up as best I could. The guy's friend was there waiting for him and had nowhere to go, so he tried to sleep in the bathroom as well. He got into the bathtub with me. I was so tired and he looked like such a wimp, that I thought, *Ah, who cares. I could probably beat him up if I really tried.* But when I tried to sleep, he kept putting his hands on me. He wouldn't stop, no matter how many times I yelled at him. For a minute I thought, *Am I going to get raped?* But then I got so mad that I wasn't scared any more. I got up, kicked open the bathroom door as hard as I could, grabbed my keys, walked out the front door, and drove to my mother's.

Another morning I woke up at the Howard Hotel and I was sleeping outside of the door on the dirty floor in the hallway. I remember thinking that I had to stop going to Hollywood. I had to stop *drinking* so much. I was ashamed of myself for not putting that energy into college. I never wanted to drive back to the Valley, so I rarely showed up to any of my classes. I didn't turn in assignments, I had dropped off the college newspaper staff and I was usually either drunk, getting drunk, or hung over. I felt myself kind of tipping. Tipping over to a place that I didn't want to be. I went from having this social circle on the weekends, to entering this actual lifestyle, day to day.

I went to a party with Willa a few days later and some homely fat guy in glasses offered me a sip from his bottle of wine. I remember drinking from it and then just total blackness. I had been roofied.

I could hear, but couldn't move my body. I heard Willa laughing at me and talking behind my back, making fun of me. Someone brought out a snake and was letting it crawl all over me. I couldn't get it off me, let alone move at all. I was paralyzed. I couldn't even open my eyes because I was completely shut down except for my hearing. It was so scary. Then I woke up in a room on a bed. The weird fat guy was sitting in the corner, staring straight ahead. I rubbed my eyes and immediately looked down to see if I were naked- I wasn't. I was fully clothed and so was he. But what if he had raped me and put everything back on me? I didn't know. I had no recollection of anything. Nothing hurt, so I didn't think I had been raped, but I wondered if he peeked at me, lifted up my shirt or something, felt me up maybe. I asked him where I was and he said I was in the Yucca building. I got the fuck out of there, running a block or so to Willa's hotel room without shoes. I jumped over glass on the sidewalks, crying and sweating.

I remember the very last day I ever saw Willa. We went to visit Michael at some girl's apartment on La Brea and Franklin. Beautiful, young Birdie Montgomery was also there in a sheer floral baby-doll dress and cherry lip gloss. Willa despised Birdie, but found her stunning. She randomly took Birdie into the bathroom and made out with her (again, things like that were kind of just normal behavior in that town). Not too long after that, the keys to my car were missing. We all started looking for them in the apartment. While everyone was searching, Birdie took me aside and whispered that she saw Willa hide my keys. She was sure Willa was planning to steal my car, but was afraid to tell me because Willa had threatened her. I was like, *Was that before or after you guys made out?* Then it dawned on me that Willa *was* planning to steal my car. She had asked me earlier in the week to show her how to drive it (the transmission skipped, so I had to skip over third gear, even though it was automatic). Does that mean she would steal a car? Probably. The bitch wasn't scared of much. She ended up living with the little Hindu man who owned the liquor store, and driving *his* car. His store was robbed not too long afterwards, and he was shot in the private parts. He lived.

I never saw Willa again.

***

Okay, so there I was, in the thick of things. I didn't seem to notice that the crowds on Sunset were no longer large. Things were very slowly dying out because there was a new sound trickling through radio and MTV and it was as sure as shit not glam. It started with a band named Nirvana. They looked dirty, angry, styleless and colorless -quite the opposite of what the Sunset Strip stood for. Nirvana was from Seattle, so the record companies began to look to the North for bands and less to the Hollywood scene. My friends and I were so drunk that we didn't even pay attention. It wouldn't be long until we would be forced to take notice, but at that time, things were still a party to us.

Journal Entry 5/27/1992

Birdie Montgomery asked for my number the other night and I gave it to her. She has been calling me. She is actually my rival-a threat to me. She appears to be dumb, but she is actually quite sneaky. She is very sweet and smiley to girls while insulting them and/or stealing their boyfriends. It doesn't matter that they all talk about her when her back is turned. She has the code cracked and it would be too much trouble to compete. And the girl is beautiful, more so than me. The thing that sucks is that she wouldn't think twice about doing anything she could do to win popularity over me or bag a guy I liked- we aren't close enough at this point to where she would have loyalty toward me. I have to be very careful not to give anything away in our fake phone conversations. I have the upper hand for being admired and fawned over without having slept around as she already has. I played my card better than she did already. I will win in the end because her age shows and she can't be subtle.

Regardless of the fact that she annoyed me, I started to hang out with Birdie. She was *so* pretty and had *such* great clothes and *such* expensive cosmetics that, being the user I was, I was like, *Where do I sign up*? I liked that she lived with her parents, so we wouldn't have to worry about our safety. It was like another Cristabelle. She was really fun, girly, and enthusiastic. Bright-eyed and bushy-tailed and all that shit. Birdie felt that we needed to stick to our kind: pretty girls, and she was peeved if I talked to anyone who wasn't good looking. She gave me a lot of crap for that. She loved to talk about the 'less fortunate,' which made me uneasy.

One night, I was with Michael and one of his female acquaintances, who was rather average looking but harmless. Birdie showed up and saw her, thinking I had brought the girl along. She scrunched up her face and asked me right in front of the girl, "Is *this* another one of the girls you've picked up as a *friend*? I swear, you pick up all these unwanted *friends.*" Without missing a beat, I said, "And you're *one* of them, honey." Michael started cracking up.

Birdie and I had a crazy night about a week later. We were driving back to her parents' townhouse at about three in the morning. We were at a stoplight and looked over to see two guys who we knew from around Hollywood. One of them was pretty well known- he was the singer of a popular band who I had seen on MTV. The other guy was named Sparkle- he was blond, swishy and feminine with tons of makeup and glitter all over him. We thought he was amusing. They yelled stuff to us, we yelled stuff to them. They followed us to the townhouse parking lot, got out of the car, and came to our window. Birdie had her camera out, so Sparkle grabbed it and put it down his pants to take pictures of his thing. We were all laughing and making jokes. Hardy har har. Then we were getting tired so we started to say goodbye to the guys; we were going to be on our way.

Sparkle said in his sassy girl voice, "I need you to give me thawt roll of film." Back then, you couldn't erase a picture on your camera. Whatever pictures you took were on the roll of film, period. Birdie said in her bitchiest of voices, "Give you the *film?* Uhhhhh, *No"* (But she said it like "*No*-wh").

Sparkle's eyes got a little mad, and he sighed like a thirteen-year-old. "I *said*, give me thawt roll of film! There is a picture of my *dick* on your camera." We stared at them in the dimly lit parking lot. Birdie then put the camera in her inside coat pocket and lifted her eyebrows. She always had to be totally dramatic. I looked at the two of them and thought, as I had in similar instances, *Shit, what could happen with these two wimps? I could probably take on both of them and kick their asses myself.* I wasn't worried- I was kind of a bad ass. I yawned and hoped she would hurry up. I was tired.

Suddenly, something changed in Sparkle. I watched his soft powdered face go from lisping Valley Girl to something entirely different. His eyes turned red. His whole expression and his body language suddenly morphed into some Satanic fucking demon. He tilted his chin downwards, looked up at her with evil eyes and said in this slow, deep, possessed voice that sounded like *The Exorcist*, "I said, *give me the film.*"

Birdie and I screamed at the same time. He reached through the window, grabbed her by the neck, and started choking her. I panicked, jumped out of the car, and went around to try to pull him off her but the other guy grabbed me. *Oh shit- these guys are going to beat us up! And Sparkle looks like he will sacrifice us to the devil afterward!* We were flying all over the place. Sparkle started punching Birdie and she was screaming bloody murder, but no one came outside to help. I was shitting my G-string.

"Give him the film! Give him the film!" I yelled to her as my arm was twisted back and nearly ripped off my body. Sparkle stopped punching her and she fumbled with her leopard skin coat to get the camera. She was visibly shaking. She had black mascara running down her face and her nose was running. She handed him the camera and he opened it and yanked out the film. The other guy let me go. I got back in the car and locked the doors and we looked at each other with our eyes bugged out.

"What the fuck just happened?" I asked her.

"Drive!" she said

Journal Entry 5/17/92

*I am lonely, sick, and unhealthy. Girls are calling me asking for advice on what they should do to land my guy friends. I don't even know who some of them are or how they have my number. Some stranger came up to me and said that people used to drive by my grandma's house like it was a tour. What the hell? He said he knew Fritz and Andy and they talked about me all the time. I put on an ultra-bitchy face and said, "I am sure they do," and flipped my hair and walked away. Yuck. They **wish** they still knew me. Please. It must have subliminally affected me though, because I told off the financial aid woman at school today and gave two weeks' notice at my job.*

I don't know why a) I thought I was so great: I wasn't, and b) I thought quitting school and my job was a good idea. I guess they were getting in the way of my partying. I thought that maybe I could try to be a dancer. I stayed up eating tacos with Michael one night and he warned me not to do it. It wasn't every day that I agreed with a guy wearing lipstick, but I somehow knew he was right.

Okay, so, I was still feeling all cool, popular, and untouchable. What a feeling that is- it is a real high to get to feel like that. Maybe I was getting too big for my britches, or maybe it was flat out karma for all of my conceit, but out of nowhere I was blindsided by something I thought would never happen.

Jimmy was still garnering attention with his new band and Razz, of all people, was convinced they were going to make it big. The next thing I knew, Razz, the one who told me how *out* Jimmy was, the one who told me to dump him *countless* times, the one who told me to go out with someone *cooler,* got so into Jimmy that he ditched *me* for *him*! (slams fist on table) I felt so betrayed. The hypocrisy! If that wasn't bad enough, Jimmy moved into the same apartment building as Michael and Strange and they started to hang out with him too- (screams) and they didn't *invite me*! They didn't want me around! They all stopped calling me. I couldn't believe Jimmy had the audacity to weasel into my crowd. He had hated them so much! And they thought he was a huge dork! *What had happened?!* I had to put a stop to it. I couldn't let that shit fly.

Journal Entry 6/11/1992

*I don't want to talk about it. Everyone is making friends with Jimmy and starting to ditch me. I never thought it would happen to me. Even **Strange** is ditching me and he has no brain in his head. Oh wait...that is surely why. Anyway, I talked to Razz for a few hours. He said, "Honey, I can't even count my real friends on my five fingers and you are one of them. The only chick, too." He kept saying it wasn't what I thought, no one was ditching me, and that Jimmy and I should just get back together. Never! I would never, ever in my life be that dumb. Aside from that, isn't Razz the person who tried to break us up for two years straight?*

I went over to Teddy St. John's that weekend and laid by his father's pool. He made me a chicken patty sandwich, poured me a drink in a fat glass, and stayed very quiet.

"What's wrong with *you?* You're supposed to be obnoxious," I said, eyeballing his soft skin and full lips.

"So. What's up with Jimmy?" he said in his deep voice, locking his big dark eyes on mine.

"Nothing. He just wants to kill every guy that speaks to me."

"Well, the guy has your name tattooed on his back and says he wants to fucking marry you."

"So? So what! SO WHAT." I asked for some suntan oil and spent the rest of the day on a raft in his pool, ignoring him.

Journal Entry 6/19/92

*Fuck Razz, fuck Teddy, and fuck Michael. Those three are the
biggest traitors on earth. They ditched me and left with Jimmy
the other night! Fuck Robbi too! He was hanging out with Jimmy
as well! They all try to screw me behind his back and when they
see Jimmy, suddenly they cling to him! I can't believe people
actually don't want to be around me! I was popular for so long
and it never crossed my mind that I would ever be on the other
end.*

Journal Entry 7/4/92

*I went to a party and ended up throwing an open beer at Strange
and it nailed him. He tackled me in front of everybody and put
me in a headlock. I pulled a phone out of the wall by tripping
over the wire. Michael and Strange moved and are now living
with a dancer named Gypsy who lives in a dreadful part of town.
She has spiky, honey-colored hair; pale skin and a friendly
demeanor. She wears really crazy hooker clothes, like, things
she should not be wearing in public. Especially in the daytime!
But she seems like a nice girl. When we got back to her place
after partying the other night, Michael was passed out in my car
and I couldn't lift him out of it. The neighborhood was so bad
that I was getting scared. But then I saw a gay hustler on the
corner wearing a neon pink spandex bodybuilding suit that went
straight up his ass and showed both buns. When car headlights
hit the corner, he turned his ass toward the car, advertising.
That was amusing. Michael finally woke up when I was dragging
his lifeless girl body out of my car. His Cover Girl powder
compact fell and broke in the street. Razz would've looked down
on that shit because he wears Shiseido. We got upstairs and
opened the door and Gypsy's beloved Dalmatians ran out of the
apartment. We were so tired and they wanted to play with us.
Michael just slammed the door and left the poor things out there.*

Journal Entry 7/8/92

*It is 8:15 at night and I am **still** not over my hangover. I got so wasted that I blacked out. Apparently, I went to a party at Chris Holmes of WASP's house- but I don't remember going there or anything about the party. In the beginning of the night, I went over to Gypsy's to get Michael and Strange to go to Red Light District. We scrounged up some change and bought a bottle of Night Train and it got me drunk within five minutes. Gypsy is one of the sequined bikini dancers on the pole at Red Light. She kept bringing me drinks between songs. I saw one of the most handsome guys I ever saw in my life that night. His name is Joey and Michael just happens to know him. I started talking to him by the bar and out of nowhere, Jimmy flew up and grabbed my arm and yanked me away! Then he got in the guy's face and said, "Do you have a **death wish?**" The guy got scared and took off and Jimmy was thrown out of the club shortly thereafter. I got even drunker. I couldn't stand, let alone drive. The next thing I remember, I was in the backseat of my own car making out with Andre, Jimmy's egotistical asshole drummer who is very hot, but who I have always hated. He is always such a dick around me. I don't even know how we got to that point because I just remember we were talking shit to each other at the beginning of the night. I guess we just started making out. Don't get me wrong- I really do still hate him, I can't stand him. He is so arrogant. He asked me about hooking up with Robbi earlier in the year and I admitted to it. I blacked out after making out with him in my car. I think it was that Night Train. That shit is evil. I just remember sleeping on the floor with Strange and those Dalmatians, after puking my guts up.*

Andre panicked the next day and tried calling me with a very rehearsed speech to do some damage control, but his idea of damage control was to piss me off, I guess. In a nutshell, he told me a) I was a slut, b) I was all over **him** and he didn't even find me attractive in the least, c) he was innocent; he had only made out with me because he was drunk, and d) Jimmy would *kill* me, and would only be mad at him.

I didn't fall for that shit. I knew he would be thrown out of his band immediately. He had a lot more to lose than I did. But I did nothing. We both kept quiet and tried to forget the whole thing.

Journal Entry 7/9/1992

My sister was saying that Hollywood is such a hard place to be a part of because it is all based on looks and image. She says she feels like shit for weeks every time she gets back from there. It is true. A lot of people come from all over the country to try to be in this scene; to make it in Hollywood. Most fail. As for me, I guess I am kind of a fly on the wall, a spy almost. I am in the middle of it, but I also see it from an outside point of view. My friends in bands have sort of a cult-like following, so the same crowds of people show up at their shows. The "usuals," such as me, arrive late- just in time for the headliner, with whom they are usually buddies. Some of us go there to party, some go to see someone they have a crush on (not a good idea) and some actually go to see the band. The actual performance is very loud and it gets very hot in the club and sometimes too smoky. You can't hear anyone talk and sometimes you can hardly move. The sluttier bands have the biggest audiences, filled with girls. The girls won't smile at anyone except the two friends they brought along. Slutty bands know that the girls they bang will show up and bring friends, so they bang away. They also flirt with every single girl who they pass out flyers to. Very average girls get all excited and feel pretty and come to the show to see the guy on the stage who was talking to them. The band hopes that on the night of the show there will be someone from a record company or someone from one of the magazines writing a good review and taking pictures of how many people were there. All of the unknown miscellaneous guys just stand around hoping some of the girls will sleep with them.

Half of us usually get thrown out of a club on a regular weekend night. Someone will steal a bottle from the bar, smash a fire extinguisher's glass, won't pay for something, or the most common, get into a fight. Sometimes we are thrown out just for being too drunk (like I was at The Roxy one night- they threw me out on my ass). The people who are not our friends usually stare at us because the girls are so pretty and the guys are so weird or maybe because of how loaded everybody is. We will hardly speak to anyone we don't know (except when the guys are "promoting," then they try to be friendly). After the shows, there is either a party somewhere (from which we will all be thrown out by cops with flashlights) or we make our own party up at Errol Flynn's burned down and haunted estate at the top of Fuller (in which we will also be thrown out by cops with flashlights). We migrate a lot in a typical night. For a few years now, it has been the same thing. Go to show. Go to Rock n' Roll Ralphs and get Jim Beam and see all of our friends buying the same thing. Go to parties and leave because of cops; go to Errol Flynn's and leave because of cops; go pass out, anywhere. Wake up and be miserable.

At the parties, something pathetic will usually happen. Someone will fall into a glass table. Strange will try to do a beer bong and it will come out his nose. Michael will go outside and try to reason with the cops while staggering drunk. Bang will go around trying to bite people. Boy Mandie will grab you by the hair. We leave the clubs with glasses still in our hands. I've been burned by countless cigarettes, thrown up in every place known to man, had beer cans thrown at me, drinks dumped on me by strangers, and have been left places, stranded. Guys ask you to marry them in a slur, you hear rumors about yourself, you try to walk straight in front of the cops so they don't notice you getting into your car and driving off. You help your wasted friends off the lawn or out of the hallway; you go looking for toilet paper after pissing in a bush and use a leaf instead. We have all come across the very rich and the very poor. We have partied in Malibu amongst stars and in parking lots alongside homeless people and junkies.

That, my friends, is what I had worked so hard to accomplish. To be a part of that ritual of totally reckless behavior. I don't know why it felt so much like home to me, but it did. That is all

I knew and it's all I wanted to know. I didn't want to be different. I only knew how to deal with my friends when drunk, and that was fine by me. I rarely saw them in the day, and I never saw them when I was sober. Their life became my life. They were my family, people who accepted me. They didn't care how I lived my life. They didn't ask each other what they did for a living. They didn't want to know your background. You could have killed someone (one of the guys actually did) and you wouldn't be judged for it (but having brown hair would get you tossed out of the crowd. Priorities!). They never called girls 'sluts' or 'whores', because many of them really *were*. While there were several things one needed to do to cement status there, the people were non-judgmental when it came to morals and ethics. Nobody had any and they held you to no standard.

Okay, so there I was, trying to figure out how to get my status back. Jimmy had made a bold social move and started hanging out with my friends, the ones who had made fun of him the year prior. They started to turn away from me, and I was not going to take it lying down. Just when I was running out of ideas, some good luck came my way.

CHAPTER FOURTEEN

The Embarrassingly Drunken Spectacle

I had been cruising along with the 'in' crowd for a year or so, when I ran into a snaggle. Snaggle? I mean snafu. I had let my guard down, thinking that I would always have that spot with the cool kids. But as anyone who has attended junior high knows, the kids at the top of the ladder are on a very *shaky* ladder, and in this particular instance, a stroke of luck saved me from losing all of my friends to my ex-boyfriend of another scene.

Out of nowhere, I heard that Sunny from Swingin' Thing was interested in me. I started jumping around my house in my old shredded up Maui and Sons T-shirt and men's boxers. I'm pretty sure I did the Maniac dance from *Flashdance,* and possibly The Robot. I was happy for two reasons. One, his band was the most popular of our crowd and his social standing would improve *my* social status. I thought, *Try going against me now, bitches!* Two, Sunny was another one of the guys I had drooled over in magazines before I got to Hollywood. By that time, I was partying alongside him nearly every weekend, but I never let on to anyone that I had a huge crush on him. I had to keep it cool, not be a groupie and shit. Those girls weren't invited into the inner circle and that is where I was determined to stay.

Sunny had blue eyes; long, dyed black hair and sometimes wore a red hat. He was of average height and build, but on the skinny side, of course. We started talking on the phone and he was actually a genuinely nice guy; upbeat and happy, no attitude or ego whatsoever. He was always laughing and joking around, no game playing, no sneakiness, just a solid guy. We dated a little bit and started getting to know each other. I was like, *Shoot...this guy is actually really cool.* Things were going great and I was stunned at my good luck. I would have dated him even if he was a jerk, but he was awesome.

There was a big-ass party going on one night, and I brought my sister and her friend Lainie. The whole Hollywood crowd was there around a big, lit-up, blue pool. Toward the end of the party, Razz showed up with Jimmy. I rolled my eyes and wanted to get the hell out of there. When I was leaving, I went to hug Sunny goodbye and the following events occurred:

Journal Entry 7/12/92

I hugged Sunny goodbye at the party this past weekend and all hell broke loose. Jimmy tried to swing at him! Sunny dropped his beer, put out his hands, and said, "Let's go!" (which was hot, because half the guys in that crowd are wimps). Swingin' Thing has a roadie named Ronnie who kind of doubles as their bodyguard. He is a total badass. He could easily take on two or three guys, no problem. He removed Sunny from the situation, stepped in himself, and beat the living shit out of Jimmy. It was terrible. I didn't know what to do- I couldn't watch. I didn't try to stop him; maybe I should have. I grabbed my sister and her friend and told them we had to leave right away. On the way out, I heard someone say, "Someone tried to fuck with Sunny!" and a bunch of guys started to run toward him. Jimmy got jumped by at least ten guys. It was horrible! It was just a big mess of bodies in the dark.

Cops arrived shortly thereafter with lights flashing, trying to find out what was going on, talking to the wrong people. There were probably two hundred people at that party- it was crazy. It was pitch black and a warm breeze was blowing. I saw Johnny Valentine from the Brats holding Jimmy's neck. He had him pinned against a car. He wasn't hitting him, he was just talking to him and trying to calm him down and he kept pushing Jimmy's head back down to the car each time he got loud. There were people yelling and running back to their cars in front of the blue and red flashes of lights.

I turned to my sister and said, "Did all of that happen because of me?"

"Yep."

I heard Razz's voice in the dark. He told me to come over to his car. When I did, he started scolding me.

"If you wouldn't have talked to Sunny, none of that would've happened. You were egging Jimmy on."

*"Are you kidding me? That was not my fault! And by the way, I have known you WAY longer than Jimmy and I can't believe you're defending him! I was just **hugging** the guy-"*

"So what. You know how he is. You didn't have to throw it in his face."

*Then Jimmy yelled my name. I turned around and saw that his face was dripping with blood. He said, "Are you **happy** now?" and started screaming at me and telling me he would kill those guys. He said he had a gun and he would use it, blah blah blah.*

After he got beat up in front of everybody who was anybody, things started happening just as I thought they would. I sat back like J.R. Ewing and put my feet up on a proverbial desk, filed my nails and drank a scotch. All the guys started making fun of

Michael for hanging out with Jimmy. They were like, "This Jimmy guy, he's **your** friend, isn't he?" and Michael started to make excuses. He knew better than to risk his social standing. He said, "Jimmy's my friend and everything, but bros are bros and I am down with them." I was not surprised. Michael only cared about popularity and dropped Jimmy quickly.

I laid down on my bed under my Marilyn Monroe poster at my mother's and knew that Razz would be calling. *Three, two, one...* and the phone rang just as I thought it would. Razz was on the other end, telling me that I took it wrong when he was defending Jimmy and that he was just drunk. I let him talk for a minute and painted my nails with gold glitter. When he was done, I started yelling at him and told him I was never going to speak to him again and that he was lucky he had called. He said it was a misunderstanding. I thought he was full of shit, but I let it go. I slammed down the phone, put on a 1940's kimono and some marabou slippers, and made my way into the kitchen to eat some Fruity Pebbles.

It was about that time that I started hanging around another dancer named Natalie, who was a co-worker of Collette's. They both worked at a strip club called Fritz. Natalie hung out with our crowd from time to time, and after seeing each other around for a few years, we became friends. Natalie was impressed I was dating Sunny. I wasn't sure if that was why she was hanging around me more than before, but I didn't care. I needed her place to crash when I was in Hollywood- she lived on Poinsettia, near rock n' roll Ralphs. She could use me if she wanted. I considered the trade a fair one. She very often pumped my ego when I was with her, by saying things like "Sunny *calls* you? You are on his personal *guest list*?" I could tell she liked him herself; she didn't hide it very well.

She was originally from Indiana and had shoulder length blond hair. I could tell she was a brunette underneath, because she always had roots. She was one of the most unlikely candidates for a dancer that I had ever seen. Her clothes were pretty conservative; she was not at all flashy. She was also really self-conscious, and sometimes a little shy. She was always worried about something, or complaining. Dancers never worried about shit, in my experience, so this was a first. Regardless, I liked her and she amused me. One night, Swingin' Thing played a show with Big Bang Babies. I wrote the following:

Journal Entry 7/18/92

They stamped my hand to go inside the club and Natalie said, "There must be some mistake, I must be on the list too," but she wasn't. Then some backer for Big Bang Babies named Jennifer paid for every single person outside to get in. Birdie Montgomery was in the bathroom sobbing because a bunch of the Seattle girls jumped her. I knew that would happen eventually. I saw Lesli and I let him drive my car to a party. He was running red lights so I punched him in the mouth. Everyone was smashing the windows out of the house at the party.

Journal Entry 7/19/92

Natalie is a closet speed addict, and suspects everyone walking the streets of doing it too. I went to a party with her last night and all the new Grunge bands were there- Primus, Pearl Jam, and Soundgarden. I am ignorant to all of them, even though they are the new thing and are doing well. We were chuckling about how out of touch we were, not even knowing who these people were and how we only hung out with outdated scumbags wearing tons of makeup. These people were talking about flying private jets to places to do their next videos and our friends were playing the Coconut Teaszer. We thanked our stars that we didn't bring Michael and Strange with us because they would've embarrassed us. Actually- the guys there were pretty juvenile, believe it or not. They were not very mature- my wacky friends have better manners than those dudes did.

Journal Entry 7/26/92

Okay. Are you ready for this? Sunny managed to make us a couple in a total of 24 hours. Word must've gotten out because Jimmy just called here and asked me to marry him. He said he'll get a job and quit partying. Lesli called ten minutes before that. He said he couldn't talk to me anymore because he really likes me and I don't even care about it and I never invite him anywhere and he wants to be with me all the time. He says he is going to stop talking to me completely so he won't feel hurt anymore. What do you say to something like that?

*I went to Newport Beach with Sunny in the day, and at night, we went to a party in Hollywood. When I got there, he introduced me to his entire band and the singer said, "So **you're** the one he has been talking about." Sunny said he didn't want me hitting on any guys and he wanted to let me know where he stood. I couldn't believe it. None of these guys have made any serious move like that with me. Especially not someone as popular as him. One of his friends said, "He never goes out with anybody. You are really special." He called me his woman and all this stuff. He totally made me his property by the end of the night. I was on top. I got where I wanted to be. In high school, I dreamed of this guy, looked at his face in my classes, dreamt of going to Hollywood just to see him from afar. And there I was, his girlfriend.*

For all of one hour.

It was going so fast that I got nervous. Really nervous. I started drinking very heavily. I went into the bathroom with one of the beach bunny Barbies they hang out with. I don't know what I said to her, I just remember her backing up against the wall with her eyeballs popping out and then she got out of the bathroom and ran. Did I say I was going to hack her to pieces? I still don't know what I said! If that wasn't enough, I proceeded to do cartwheels in the street in front of everybody. There were tons of cool people standing around watching another girl who was all graceful, doing cool walkovers and slinky moves. I stumbled over, all clunky and belligerent. I tried to do a straddle roll on the front lawn, and I got stuck with my legs over my head in front of all of Swingin' Thing. I was a total spectacle. I can't believe I did that only hours after Sunny said I was his woman! And it didn't stop there. I had to cement the deal. In front of everyone, I proceeded to fall backwards over a counter, crash into a sliding glass door, land on the ground and pass out. I woke up with a swollen eye, a fat lip, two skinned knees, a cigarette burn, and one of my legs popped out of my hipbone. I had to jerk my leg really hard to get it to pop back into place. I looked down at a huge crooked tooth mark on my boob and remembered that Strange bit me. I remembered slapping him across the face. He tackled me and tried to beat the crap out of me and Michael pleaded with him, "What are you doing!? She is our little sister, bro!" I pointed to the bathroom and made him go in. I lectured him in there and he apologized.

Anyway, I can't believe I screwed up my chance at being Hollywood royalty. I am so embarrassed for acting like such a fool. I cried about it to Michael the next night while we sat on the curb swigging beer. He said in a nasal, Valley Girl voice, "I know you're on Heartbreak Boulevard and everything, but at least they're talking, you know what I mean? If they don't talk about you, then you're nobody. At least you got people talking."

Michael may have been a drunken glam rocker wearing leggings and eyeliner, but he had the sense to quote friggin' Oscar Wilde. It made me feel a teensy bit better. I tried to tell myself it was true. Yeah. I was a big name. If people were talking about me, it was because I was interesting and cool and gossip-worthy! Then I had a little flashback of seeing the room upside down when I flipped over that counter backwards in front of the whole party and I winced. I really liked Sunny. I thought he was funny, cool, and respectful, and it didn't hurt that he had status in my crowd. He was a nice, genuine guy. Except for when he told me my perfume smelled like carpet freshener- that was sort of messed up. And that time at the beach he told me I had sand in my nostrils in front of everyone... Other than that, he was honestly a nice guy! I was so upset with myself for behaving so poorly, that

I cried and cried. I listened to a tape that he and I listened to together (*Mother's Milk* by the Red Hot Chili Peppers) repeatedly in my car. It pained my heart to hear "Subway to Venus." I took it out of my stereo while I was driving and threw it out the window on Ventura Boulevard. It was all quite dramatic (laughs).

Sunny backed off from me after that night. He stopped calling. I was a wreck. A very long week passed, where I cried in my blankies and blew my nose on my Hanoi Rocks T-shirt sleeve. Then he called again. He wanted to know what I was doing that night. I launched out of my bed and jumped straight into the shower. We agreed to hang out over at Natalie's, which was down the street from him. Do you think I rectified everything? Of course not! This is *me* we are talking about. I got really nervous and (long drum roll) started drinking.

Journal Entry 8/1/92

*Natalie said I told Sunny off at the top of my lungs for a half hour last night. I was over there drinking a bottle of Night Train and I **completely** blacked out. Again! I remember none of it! She said I kept going into the bathroom and she was **sure** I did a line of speed! I said, "No! I **couldn't** have! I have never done any drugs!" I still don't know if I did it, if she gave it to me to sober me up from the Night Train or if nothing happened at all.*

Sunny told me later that I was talking about my father! And my family! I wonder what I said? Why did my mind go there? Worse than that, I do feel like I am on something! I have never done drugs so I don't know what to compare it to, but when I wet my face to wash it this morning, it felt like someone punched me in the nose. I haven't eaten or slept and I couldn't drink last night, but felt buzzed on something anyway. And I was as paranoid as Natalie, who IS on it. We went to Denny's at 9:00 in the morning and she doesn't even remember it. We went to the store later on and the only things in our basket were milk, gum, and Jim Beam. Neither of us wanted to hold the basket! We were trying to make each other hold it.

Natalie had to drink half the bottle of whiskey and do a line just to go on a date the next night. She kept saying things like, "Am I talking too much? I need a drink to get a little mellower" or "Am I acting drunk? Am I babbling? I need to do a line to be more normal" or "Do you think I am acting paranoid? Should I have a drink?" Sometimes she gets paranoid that something else is in the drugs: "I hope there wasn't any heroin in that stuff, because I am allergic to it."

Natalie says she is studying medicine. She says she wants to go back to college for it, but all she really does is sit around and look up pills in her pill book, which I have seen at Sav-On right next to the romance novels. She is always sick, bruised up, depressed, and whining. I have stayed there for days at a time, drunk, and just laying on her floor. Never anything in that fridge but butter and wine. She is so paranoid about her health that she is on antibiotics for her ears being plugged, painkillers for her hurting back and Valium to sleep, amongst all the other shit. She is always making doctors' appointments and claims everyone from her landlord to the clerk at the music store is on drugs.

"Look at that guy banging the soda machine! He is on drugs! Look at him!" Today she called and said she had been up for twelve hours throwing up from bad tuna salad. She exaggerates like crazy (twelve hours?) and really cares what everyone else thinks of her, which is not common for most dancers I know. I can't picture her in her sequined neon green bikini (or not in it) on a stage, stripping. I can't picture her giving table dances and asking for tips, but she does. She is the only stripper I know without a bubbly, confident nature. She is pale and wears red lipstick- looks very different from the other girls. Guess it's proof that guys like all different types.

You know what? This might sound naïve, but...I didn't realize that many of the people I have been hanging out with have turned into drug addicts. I thought we were all just drinking.

Now it is hitting me. They don't eat, but they always make conversation about some big meal they just had. They have all been cutting back on the booze and are just holding the same drink all night. That is why Michael, Strange, and I stand out as being belligerent. We are probably the only ones not on drugs right now! Natalie couldn't sleep because of the speed and had to do shots of Jim Beam. And I just found out Collette is a heroin addict. I didn't even put two and two together when she was falling asleep in mid-conversation. I remember one night she was trying to show me how to get to a party and she kept falling asleep and I passed the place. She woke up and said, "Oh, sorry! Make a U-turn. It was right back there." I turned around, started driving, and then looked over at her, asleep again! I must have passed the place three different times.

I guess I should tell you how I was picked out of the crowd at Bar One the second I walked up, and how I immediately bypassed all of the people who were not good-looking enough to get in. Then when I got up to the front, I was on a guest list, waltzed right in, and sat with some big shot named Rich Ross. He gave my friend Sarah (a girl I met in summer school a few years ago) and me free drinks. I danced with Brian Austin Green from 90210. Sarah was feeling left out because Rich was telling me what an asset I was, and that I should come every week. She felt better when she met Rick James later that night. She was flirting with him and gave him her number- I don't know what's wrong with her. Anyway, none of it matters because I was an idiot and spoiled my chance with Sunny.

Journal Entry 8/5/92

I am coming off whatever I did. Feeling all psycho over Sunny. Can't stop crying; depressed and obsessive. Can't get out of bed. I lost five pounds from not eating for five days (note to self: don't eat for ten more days). I don't even know what to say. I have been lying in this bed since I woke up and it is ten at night now. I tried eating dinner with my mother and sister but I started crying when I saw my potato. It got so bad that I had to excuse myself. They just kept eating and ignored me. He hasn't called and it is entirely my fault for acting so idiotic around him. And to top it off, I saw Jimmy and Robbi hanging out at a Cathouse party! I don't even care. Tweety and I got into an argument about who was more stuck up than who (I act like I should be playing polo in The Hamptons, apparently). But I didn't care about that either. I just want Sunny to call. I can't believe I blew it.

Journal Entry 8/10/92

Was supposed to hang out with Sunny the other night, but he flaked. He ended up leaving a message on my mom's answering machine at 4 a.m., which is of course too late to be answering a call from a guy. I saw him out the next night and did a great job of hiding my obsession. He asked what happened the other night and I coolly said, "Well, I went my way and you went your way and we lost each other," and smiled. We were all sitting in the dark, by the empty swimming pool of Errol Flynn's burned down estate in Runyon Canyon, passing around the usual bottle of Jim Beam (I don't even know why we call it Errol Flynn's- I think Errol Flynn only stayed in the pool house at the damn place). Jamie Scrap, Mandie, Boa, and a bunch of others were there. I looked over toward the gate at the top of Fuller Street and a bunch of girls I knew were climbing up over the fence via a winding tree (that I can expertly climb in tiny outfits)- Chrissy, Dina, Amy, Emi, Stephanie, Sandy, Nicole and Chantelle. Some gang showed up, said that we were on their turf, and told us to leave. None of us wanted to get shot, so we took off, stumbling over elderberry bushes. As we were leaving, the cops showed up and busted Natalie for carrying a bottle of booze. They eventually let her go, then she and I went back to her place and danced to the Geto Boys in our underwear. She said, "You had Sunny hooked, before you started yelling at him."

I haven't been with a guy this entire summer. I have to be careful who I let near me because everyone knows each other. I really have to watch out and play this thing right.

Journal Entry 8/16/92

I shouldn't have written that shit! Bang raped me last night! Yes, raped me! I woke up in the middle of the act. He was on top of me. We were on the floor of some room, next to a pile of dirty laundry. He is not someone who I am attracted to, so I don't see how I could have even been in that situation. I was clearly too drunk to make any decisions and he was fine with that. I was puking up blood on the way home, from drinking too much. In the beginning of the night he was kind of forcefully pulling me around with him, and I just let him- not good. Then I remember he wanted to drive in my car with me- I felt cool that he singled me out, so I let him. The rest? My own fault for being so dumb. I have to wipe it out of my mind. I am not gonna think about it.

The Next Day

Bang called here today. He apologized. Instead of just accepting it, or maybe even telling him off, I said I shouldn't have been that drunk around him. I added that I didn't sleep with the guys in Hollywood. He said, "I know. That's why I'm calling." He didn't try to blame me or anything, like I thought he would. He was all quiet and said he wasn't drinking the rest of the week. Oh wow, a whole week. I was happy not to have been roughed up, though. He has knocked out two girls I know personally. Knocked them out cold, just for being annoying. I am glad he feels like shit.

There is nothing I can do now, except move on.

I woke up at about 2:30 or three this afternoon. I was dreaming about tripping on stairs, being in a nightclub, and stealing a big box of bright pink Hubba Bubba gum. I was in some spacey store with my dad and he was borrowing all of my money and then buying me all of this fun stuff with it, like cherry Slurpees. He was buying other people presents with my money. One time he did do something similar. He took my sister and me on a huge shopping spree at like, Sears, or somewhere where the stuff basically sucked, but we were allowed to buy whatever we wanted. I remember buying a red bra, some perfume, and a few other things. We thought it was strange, but who were we to question a free shopping trip? Well, it turned out that he stole the card from someone he knew, charged all of that shit on it, and left them with the bill!

Another time he brought Karen and me to this huge mansion and said we could stay there and do whatever we wanted: eat the stuff in the fridge, watch TV, whatever. So we made ourselves at home. We turned on Yo! MTV Raps, started baking something in the oven, and basically trashed the place. Then we heard a key in the door and some women's voices. We looked at each other, jumped up, and ran. Karen hid in a closet or something and I ran into a bathroom and locked the door. I stripped off all my clothes in a panic. Don't ask me why I thought that would be a good idea. I think I was going to pretend I was taking a shower, but then I decided to wrap myself in a towel (I know, I was an idiot) and face the music. Karen and I eventually came out because they were about to call the cops. A nicely dressed woman and her adult daughter were standing there staring at us and had no idea who we were. I think one of them knew my dad in some way, she may have been sleeping with him or something. Regardless, they sure as hell didn't know who we were. And worse, they did not authorize us to stay in their house.

I probably had that dream because I visited my dad last night. I asked for some money for school and he gave me a dollar and six quarters. He owes a few years of child support for my sister and me and the law is after him for various other reasons like tax evasion and some warrants. He is living with a lady named Debra who is a former disc jockey for KHJ.

Journal Entry 8/19/92

I visited Natalie last night. She had all of her medical books spread around her. It looked like she set them up as props. We watched a little bit of Miss Nude USA and she commented on each girl. "This can't be in L.A. The stage is way too nice. These girls can't be from Hollywood...Oh...*this* girl could. She has got the L.A. attitude and stuff, the way she dances and her face." She laughed and talked about how quiet she was and how no one wanted her because of it. Then the building caught fire and we had to go.

In a half an hour, I have to get ready to go to Bar One. A lot of stars hang out there when they are in L.A. This company called W.C. Productions always puts me on a guest list and asks me to bring really pretty girls. Once I am there, I usually go sit with that guy Rich Ross, who owns the company or something. He looks like Andy Gibb in running shorts and a tank top, no matter the weather. That is an L.A. thing. He examines the girls I bring, nods, and then tells us to order whatever we want. His secretary calls me sometimes and puts him through. He says things like "You are fanTABulous" or "You are a **bomb**shell."

Tonight I am bringing Birdie, even though she is only newly sixteen. They will let her in because of her looks. Her age won't matter. She has been wearing fake eyelashes like me and the same type of clothes. She is stealing my look, but oh well. The only thing I can do is go with it. She looks very exotic and smells like some sort of spice or cinnamon. It is some Chanel perfume that she spritzes all over herself until we are both choking. She is super spoiled and has a ton of nice clothes and calls her dad "Daddy." To watch her is kind of like looking at a rare species of some sort of animal. She is so pretty that people drop things when she walks by.

The other night we went to the Rainbow to eat mozzarella sticks and pizza. That is one thing I really like about Birdie- she loves to eat. She orders extra cheese on everything! Anyway, Axl Rose was there eating by himself in the booth next to us with two huge body guards standing in front of him. No one was even trying to talk to him; he was a little over-zealous with those guards.

Journal Entry 8/22/92

*I bleached Natalie's roots at two in the morning while we
watched Goodfellas. She made me turn it off because the
violence was giving her an anxiety attack. She now works at
some place called Venus Faire, off Lankershim. She dances in
this booth while guys put money through slots. She says there is
a lot of flashing lights and mirrors so she doesn't even know
who is looking at her. She can't see them, they can only see her.
Speaking of jobs, I got a job on Melrose today. I met some old
guy at Bar One and he wanted me to work at his clothing store.
School starts tomorrow, it is two in the morning, and I
can't sleep.*

*Now it is three in the morning. I am laying here listening to Van
Halen. My boobs are swollen and they hurt. It is hard to be
around the people and places I am. I am starting to sweat. I need
to have a normal life. I need to try to be normal: study, do
homework, go on diets, go to keg parties, tan at Zuma 6, dance
at Florentine Gardens... I need to try to be normal so I can live
in this society. I am starting to get obsessed with the past. All
night I have been listening to these tapes we recorded as kids;
tapes of Karen, Becky and me messing around. They're kind of
like time capsules. I used to hold my tape recorder up to the TV
and record commercials, and theme songs from TV shows like
The Cosby Show. I recorded music off the radio, complete with
the DJ, Rick Dees, talking over the beginning of the songs. I
recorded a lot of shit. I wish it were more. I am so glad I have
all the music from those days on these tapes, but they are making
me obsessed. Was that really me? I feel like I am a completely
different person from that girl. Where did she go? I want to be
normal. I want to fall asleep at night, I don't want to be afraid to
die, and I want to hang around regular people. I don't want to
be so calculated and always try to be in the right place at the
right time. I don't want to be so attracted to such losers.*

Journal Entry 8/27/92

I haven't been to sleep yet and I have class at 9:00. I am going to have to go straight to school without sleeping. Jimmy tried to hang himself from his chandelier last night and it smashed to the ground. Then he tried to hang himself with a phone cord and it broke, dropping him into the smashed glass. I haven't slept since Tuesday night and now it is Thursday evening. I am not tired. You would think I was on drugs, but no. My sister is, though. She is doing speed. I heard her whispering about it to her druggie friend last night. I heard the whole thing. I was steaming mad. She is a closet case. I heard her say how cool it was and that she was putting money aside for it every week, and that she liked the fact that you didn't come off it hard. Natalie is right. Everyone IS on drugs.

Journal Entry 8/30/92

My job at the clothing store is really cool. It is next door to Johnny Rockets and Warbabies and across from Bleeker Bob's. Melrose is hot right now- there is even a new show after 90210 called Melrose Place. Yesterday I sold jeans to one of the girls from Wilson Phillips (daughter of Beach Boy Brian Wilson, more importantly) and she was wearing this loose crocheted top with no bra and her tit fell out! Everyone was looking and I couldn't keep talking to her with her entire nipple showing so I told her. It was so embarrassing. The manager, Rico, is a female impersonator who impersonates Cher on the weekends. He is always checking out guys and is really funny. He sits on my lap and plays with my hair. He saw these mannequins across the street that he wanted and he wiggled over there to try to get one to 'bring home and screw.' What is he gonna do? Drill a hole in the thing? The guy next door likes him and Rico isn't interested because the guy 'doesn't know how to dress and is clumsy.'

Last night, Birdie and I went to see The Zeros. We showed up in platform shoes, pale pink lipstick, little clothes, and long straight hair. Right when Birdie got to the very top of the stairs at the Coconut Teaszer, the top of her shoe (strapped to her ankle) separated from the bottom of its four-inch platform. She rolled

*down the stairs screaming and everything flew out of her purse
and all over the place. After the show, everyone went to party at
the Hyatt on Sunset (Led Zeppelin used to party there) that was
being thrown by a rich, fat girl. It lasted about ten minutes. I
managed to have one screwdriver with Strange and we all were
thrown out. So we ended up crowded around the outside of the
Hyatt. Someone was trying to dance with me, Strange spilled his
drink on me, and we tried jaywalking across Sunset in platform
shoes. Some guy I never met from the Seattle crowd tried to grab
my bottle of Jim Beam and I clamped onto it. I actually paid for
the bottle myself for once, so I told him to ask first. He nearly
threw me halfway across the road. Some girl said, "Watch out-
he is really mean, he'll hit you." I let go of the bottle after my
finger started bleeding because he pinched it so hard. He said in
an angry voice: "How does it feel to know everyone wants to
fuck you?" I just looked at him and said, "I don't know."*

*Someone else in the Seattle crowd told me my nose was so far in
the air, they could ski down it. Then Strange started jumping on
these chain link fences laid over huge ditches in the ground and
he nearly fell in. I went over there to stop him and we ended up
wrestling on the hood of a car. Then we got in Birdie's car. She
had just learned to drive and was swerving everywhere. She has
a major crush on this guy named Frankie from Boston, and she
got him into her car to bring him to go hang out with her at her
parents' place, even though he insisted he just wanted to go
home. "You don't **have** a home, Frankie!" she reminded him. He
kept trying to open the car doors and jump out. She was yelling,
"You should be happy that you are in the car with us!"*

(Sighs.) Okay. As far as the drugs I may or may not have done
while blacked out on Night Train. I am not trying to be a goody-
goody here. I did plenty of drugs later on in my life, but at that
time, I had not willingly ingested any. Things were getting very
dark in Hollywood at that point, darker than before. Heroin was
becoming more prominent, creeping in and seducing people who
were depressed about their lives for one reason or another. The
party was pretty much over- we all knew it. Even my days were

numbered. The countdown was on.

CHAPTER FIFTEEN

Enter Heroin,

Stage Left

Journal Entry 9/4/92

Went over to Razz's place. I know, I know, he is a traitor. But I was bored and needed a break from the others. He started a band with Teddy St. John, Frankie (Birdie's crush), Dusty, and this new stuck-up blond guy named Bradley who is dating Sabrina. Sabrina looks like a completely different person- she got her boobs, nose, and lips done. She even changed her eye color- now they are green. Her hair is much longer and even lighter blond, almost white. She told me that she and Bradley were secretly married. Who knows why that has to be a secret, probably for his "image."

When I walked through the front door, Razz led me by the shoulders to meet Bradley, who said he was happy to meet me, and that they all talked about me all the time (great). We all got hammered and went to the shithole that is FM Station, where Razz and I started pissing everyone off again. We were girl-hitting each other, snorting with laughter, and rolling around the booth. Teddy was mad and calling us pricks and assholes. Razz started calling him Damone (from Fast Times at Ridgemont High) and I think we were calling him fat and making fun of his toes for some reason. Whenever Razz and I hang around each other too long, everyone hates us and we end up with no friends. This night was no exception.

Journal Entry 9/5/92

*I sprained my foot last night on Sunset and I can't walk. I heard my name being called from the cars in the traffic jam and when I turned back to look, I tripped right in front of Gazzarri's. I was loaded, but I think I would've tripped anyway. Naturally, it had to be Sunny in the car yelling my name. And I just **had** to trip and fall on my face in front of him! My sister had to take me to the hospital later that night and they were pushing me around in a wheelchair.*

Before that, I went over to Razz's and Teddy was over there. They were bored and stretching their faces in the mirror and trying to chase me with fireplace tools. We finally got up and drank a fifth of Jim Beam between the three of us. Teddy and I were singing the Beastie Boys all loud ("So What'cha Want?") and he was going to pour me another shot. I didn't see him and I pulled my glass off the table to drink it and he dumped the shot on the table. We went to Sunset really late and Teddy was picking me up and swinging me in circles and we were falling all over the place. Right after that was when I fell down and hurt my foot. Teddy called me a training-wheel-needin', limpin' motherfucker. We went to a party after that. Razz and Teddy were being overprotective and it was pissing off Lesli, who thought he was with me, I guess. On the way to the party, Razz and Teddy were singing Dramarama's "Tiny Candles" at the top of their lungs and banging the dashboard of Teddy's Jeep to play the air drums. Teddy tried to slam the windshield for effect, no big deal. Then Razz tried to do it and the whole windshield cracked! We went to Jack in the Box and Teddy laid all of his food out on the hood and stood there eating in the dark; he wouldn't speak to either of us, he was so mad.

Razz showed me a bunch of pictures of himself at fifteen and sixteen. He was shirtless, tan, and lanky, wearing this frosty pink/violet lipstick. He was pouting and striking a feminine pose. In the background were all these pink blankets, a hot pink comforter, and Poison posters on the wall. I asked him what his mother did when he started wearing lipstick and all that. He said she just had to deal with it.

A woman named Shandy Becker started supplying Teddy with drugs. And I'm not talking some pot or a few pills, I am talking straight-up heroin. He started spending a lot of time with her. Razz and I were concerned. He was no longer funny or cool when he was under the influence. Teddy was another person who I actually liked, because he was smart and very witty. I clicked with him and had chemistry with him, although nothing ever happened between us. For some reason, I saved the process of hooking up for people I didn't really like, but who were sought after by others. I couldn't get hurt that way.

Journal Entry 9/7/92

*I drank another bottle with Teddy and Razz last night and it was no fun because Teddy was insulting me and Razz was crying and depressed over Missy, who he is in love with. Teddy came up with this bright idea to call Shandy Becker; he said it was because she would take us all out and buy us drinks. Razz and I just looked at each other. We knew he shouldn't be around her. She is always stocked with coke and heroin and Teddy is highly addicted to it all. She is completely fatal for him- she tattooed a picture of his face on her back! It seems as if she uses the drugs to keep him around, and it always works. There is not a time when he will go out with her and come back sober. We told him we didn't think it was a good idea and he said, "Fuck **you** guys! Do you have anything **better** planned? Becker will treat all **three** of us! I was just making a suggestion! I'm not gonna touch **shit**."*

266

So what happens? We find Shandy Becker at FM Station, go back to her place, and Teddy goes and does lines. We try to leave for hours and he keeps saying, "Just one more shot," and trying to get her into the bedroom or bathroom for more drugs. She came over to Razz and me with a sad look on her weathered face. "I want to go to sleep," she said. She wanted him out.

I always thought she was the one who was cornering him and trying to keep him around. But we saw what was really going on. I found his car keys and stood up with Razz.

"Teddy, we're leaving. Are you coming?"

His back was to us and Shandy's profile was staring at his face.

He looked at her and said, "We're having a barbecue tomorrow. A barbecue...are you coming? They'll be food there, and..."

"Sure," she said.

*"Well, then I'll just sleep **here**. It doesn't matter where I **sleep**, does it?"*

She looked at him and shook her head 'no,' even though it was clear she wanted him to stay with her.

"I'm not partying tonight, Teddy," she said softly. I looked at her messy, damaged, wild blond hair and bulbous nose. He wouldn't turn toward her; we still only saw the back of him.

"So, I'll just sleep here," he said.

Razz had enough. He isn't one to stand around and wait for someone or put up with much bullshit, unless of course it is being doled out by Missy.

"LATER," he said in a loud voice. We walked out and left Teddy there.

267

Later that day

The barbecue was cancelled. Dusty said he didn't want a bunch of drug addicts at his house. Teddy is still at Shandy Becker's and will be for days, as usual. Razz is depressed to tears about Missy, again. He is so in love with her that he is going to get an ulcer. He showed up to her place unannounced and thought it would be a good idea to try to crawl through her bedroom window to leave her a "message." She happened to be home as he was trying to get in and she threw a full Coke can at his head. I told him not to ever invade a girl's privacy and that I would've done the same thing.

"But I love her. I just want to be with her. How can one person turn my life into a living hell? She is probably not even thinking about me right now."

Michael used to be like that over some chick. I remember he begged me to call her up and pretend I found him dead on the floor next to a bottle of pills.

Journal Entry 9/12/92

Razz and I went to FM Station on Thursday night and got into a huge fight. I told him to get the FUCK out of my car. He was stunned. He couldn't believe it. I wasn't fucking around though and he knew it. I pulled over and said, "Get the fuck out." He said, "But we are in the middle of nowhere!" and I said, "I don't give a fuck." He shut his mouth pretty quickly.

Word on the street is that Teddy started smoking heroin one of those nights that he was with Shandy Becker. I don't see how smoking it can be worse than injecting it, but it is a definite indicator to the people in this crowd that you're going street- hard core street- when you start smoking a drug. I feel like these people party because they are sick and hurting.

Journal Entry 9/13/92

Last night I hung out with Lesli. He is living with some girl who wasn't home. He said he went to buy her tampons the other day in a full face of makeup and people were staring at him. While I have a soft spot for Lesli, he is in no way smooth. He kept grabbing my arms and pulling me roughly, saying, "Come 'ere," and tugging at me and poking me and stuff. I am getting sick and tired of all this rough shit with these guys. I said, "Be a gentleman! You are throwing me all over the place!" He said he knew, but he just wanted to hang out with me. As he gripped one of my wrists, the door of the apartment swung open and a guy named Spider walked in with two girls, one of whom was really into Lesli from what I recall at a No Bozo Jam show a few weeks back. She couldn't wipe the scowl off her Seattle face. I had a strong feeling it was because I was there and Lesli verified that once she was gone. She couldn't even look at me. I even asked her what was wrong. She was lying on the floor (the theme of the evening) with long, stringy red hair, a pale delicate face, wine-colored lips, and dark eyes. She wore a navy blue vintage sailor dress, white fishnet stockings, and white go-go boots. What a poor sport. Lesli tried making out with me but I said no because he was wearing black lipstick and I didn't want it getting all over me. He said, "Most girls only like me because I am in some band. I don't like that. It is convenient when I want to screw someone…I can always find a girl who will, ugly or not. I just hate hearing girls talk about all the other guys in bands they know. You don't do that."

Not only was it totally uncomfortable over there, but there was a ferret locked in the bathroom. I had to pee and Lesli had to wrangle the damn thing and remove him so I could go in. We drove to The Strip after that fiasco and I parked in some remote spot and was trying to be discreet about being seen with him. That was pretty hard, because he is so tall and has bright pink hair.

He noticed that I was trying to hide him and said, "You're ashamed of me! Aren't you?!"

"No," I lied, looking into his apple-green eyes. "But I can't have people thinking I'm running around with too many guys. Besides, how do they know that I really love you?" I said, smiling.

"You DO love me, don't you?"

"Sure I do."

Three Middle Eastern men walked around the corner as we were getting out of the car, and started yelling stuff to us. Lesli was scared and said, "Come on, let's go! What if they have guns or something?" I said, "I'm not going anywhere," and took out my compact and checked my makeup, completely ignoring them.

*I saw a bunch of my friends on The Strip. Lesli ran into his friends and told them about the Middle Eastern men and his story was completely different from what really happened. He was saying he got loud with them. I stepped right in front of him, cut him off mid-sentence, and called him a huge liar, telling his friends that he was scared and wanted to leave because he thought they had guns. His friend Dexter (who is wanted for manslaughter by the way), just looked at Lesli and walked away. Pepper looked at Lesli a second longer and then walked away too. Lesli said, "Why did you have to embarrass me!?" I said, "Why did you have to **lie**?!"*

I went to a party and saw all of my drunken friends. Some Asian girl proceeded to take off her clothes and show everyone her crotch piercings. I felt guilty because it was completely my fault—I said, "Let us see" when she talked about having them. I didn't think she'd be whipping it all out. She was so drunk she didn't know what she was doing. Strange was really loaded, lying on a big white stuffed bear. He tried to kick me when I called him a drunken lug. I hit him with a big Sparkletts bottle and then he got my head under one arm and Chantelle's under the other and

*rammed our heads together, which hurt. Pepper cuddled up with
the Asian girl and they fell asleep. Boy, is she going to freak out
when she rolls over and sees him in the morning with his neon
greenish-yellow hair the color of lemon-lime Gatorade, tons of
makeup and an "X" over his lip in place of a beauty spot. [By
the way? That girl became a porn star.]*

Journal Entry 9/19/92

*I am now nineteen, which, so far, has been uneventful. Birdie
and I went to a Faster Pussycat concert in Ventura County. The
night was awful. I had a bad cold and was rubbing my makeup
off and blowing my nose the whole way there. Birdie was driving
us in her parent's car. She only learned to drive a month or so
ago, and had never been on the freeway before. I didn't take that
into consideration and was pressuring her to drive faster and to
get into the fast lane. She started swerving all over the freeway,
losing control of the car. We smashed into the center divider of
the 101, in Agoura. One whole side of the car was smashed in,
two hubcaps were missing, and the hood was up like a tent. We
had our seatbelts on, so we were okay, although my ribs hurt
really badly. We looked at each other, both drenched in vanilla
shakes that had been in the cup holders. Her eyes were bugging
out and I saw that she was about to hyperventilate so I just
hugged her. She was about to cry and I yelled, "**Don't** cry! You
will ruin your makeup!" she listened to me, in all of my wisdom.
I knew she wouldn't want to ruin it because she had it done by a
makeup artist for the 'special event.' There are car accidents,
and then there is ruining a perfect makeup job.*

*Nobody stopped to help us. We mopped the food and drinks off
our cute outfits, trying to pull ourselves together. Being the
Einstein that I was, I got out of the car on the freeway and
checked the tires to see if they were still intact. We decided to
continue in the smashed car, sticky and frazzled, to the show.
The show must go on, people! We thought we were going to the
Academy Awards or something, but when we got there, it was a
nondescript place in the middle of nowhere that was only*

missing a rattlesnake and some tumbleweeds. I half expected some cowboys to come out and have a motherfuckin' shoot-out. I was hoping to meet a rad guy, but when I got there I already knew everybody. Our little clan got there in bits and pieces and eventually formed one big ball of chaos. The couple hundred other onlookers who came there to see the show stood around and watched all of us cause a ruckus. All of the random guys tried to get near Birdie and me. Birdie had her hair professionally done, in big perfect curls. She had on fake eyelashes, red glossy lipstick, a little plaid schoolgirl skirt, and Frederick's of Hollywood spiked platform heels. I had on black velvet platform shoes (they were Birdie's- do you think I can afford shoes?), a tight black vest with no shirt underneath and black and white gingham hot pants. My own friends were hitting on me and girls were snubbing me left and right. All of the random girls tried to get near our guy friends, like Alleycat Scratch, etc. The girls were saying to them, "You **must** be from Hollywood," and they called us sluts because we knew all the guys. It surely didn't look good with all of the guys hugging us and saying hi to us and hanging on us, but I no longer care about such things.

All of the Hollywood people pulled their usual antics, and let me tell you, in an area outside of Hollywood, their antics were completely unacceptable and worthy of being thrown out of the place. First off, Lesli started throwing me up against the wall. I wasn't fazed, but when he started spilling beer on me, that was a different story. Nevertheless, the security guards saw him tossing me around and they jumped him, beat the crap out of him, and threw him out. Then, Michael was thrown out for whipping out his thing and peeing in the lobby, right on the carpet in front of everyone. After that, Robbi (I so desperately want to spell his name with a "Y") was thrown out for drunkenly messing with Faster Pussycat's wires and amps and stuff up front. I saw that one of his front teeth was knocked out; I was told it was from the night before when he tried to jump out of the car on the freeway.

When I returned Birdie's shoes to her at the end of the night, she *noticed that there was a small rip on one of them from the car accident (my feet jetted out in front of me and hit something in her car when we crashed). She told me I owed her new shoes. I was like, bitch, you got us in a **car accident**. If you wouldn't have **crashed**, your fuckin' shoes would still look good. She said that if I wouldn't have **worn** them, they would've been safe at home with no rip. Then I was like, okay, well then my ribs hurt. You need to pay for my medical bills. She dropped it.*

That next weekend my car stalled right in the middle of rush hour traffic by the Hollywood Bowl. My radiator blew up and the car was overheating. Some guys pushed it to the left, into a horrible crack neighborhood, where it sat while I got a ride back home somehow. What was I going to do without a car? Birdie was grounded from her parents' car after crashing it on the freeway, so we were both out of luck. During all of this, I was living at my mother's. As you can imagine, I wasn't exactly doing the chores she assigned me. I was like, *Wait…chores? I just came off speed that I don't remember doing, was raped, and then was dancing with strippers in my underwear. Then I was in a car accident, dodging bullets and trying not to be killed, all while in cute pink outfits.* I don't remember much about my chores, but I do know that I was supposed to take out the trash and I couldn't be bothered, so it was often left there to rot as the garbage men passed our house because the cans were not out front. I also came home at ungodly hours, if at all. Not only that, but I was always banging pots and pans at three in the morning, drunk (I distinctly remember slicing potatoes and making hash browns in a skillet). I had phone calls at all hours of the day and night and I was always rude and hungover. My mother put up with this stuff for only six months or so.

I was fired from the clothing store after missing so many days due to the sprained ankle/hurt foot. Without a job, I couldn't come up with $200 to give my mother for rent that month, and she told me I had to move out. She also cited the fact that I was partying too much as another reason I was being booted. I thought it was totally unfair and didn't see what the problem was.

My sister was majorly on speed by that point and couldn't kick it. She was hooked. I marched straight up to my mother and asked her why my sister could be a drug addict and stay in the house, and I couldn't stay in the house and be a boozer. I really threw my sister under the bus for self-serving purposes. It wasn't like I was worried about her and trying to get her help. It was only to show my mother she wasn't being fair- and to point out that she wasn't paying attention.

My mother confronted my sister and asked her point blank if she was on drugs- she of course said she wasn't. My mom let it go and my sister was back to doing them the very next night. She didn't ask her again, and said nothing about my sister's extreme weight loss and staying up all night. In my house, as long as you weren't making a scene, you could apparently do whatever you wanted. I wouldn't know though, because I was always making a scene.

My mom suggested I go live with my dad. He had been hanging around and was trying to see us; we even went to visit him a few times. I tried to put my hard feelings behind me. I still wanted a dad. Maybe it would work out. Maybe I was just imagining all of that yucky stuff.

When I asked my dad if I could live with him and his girlfriend, Debra, it seemed promising for a whole minute. I was happy to be able to spend some time with him, maybe repair our relationship- after all, it had been three or four years since he lived with us. Maybe he had cleaned up his act a little. He agreed to assist me in paying for school, and I was relieved, until he dumped an entire handful of quarters in my hand for school books. Back then, the cheap little paperback companions were $20.00 maybe, but the rest of the school books ran up to $75.00. I looked at the five dollars in quarters and thought, *Uh oh. This is gonna suck.*

I tried to make myself at home at their apartment in Sherman Oaks, surrounded by dream catchers and Native American paintings. It was a one-bedroom apartment and I was to stay on the living room couch. They slept in the room, which was fine by me, except that the bathroom was off their room. They kept their door shut at night and sometimes I really had to pee. I didn't want to knock on the door in the middle of the night in case they were doing it or something. I would have rather pissed outside in a bowl on the little patio.

The first night I cried myself to sleep. They kept the sliding glass door open for some cat or something, so I was freezing and my nose was running. I felt myself getting sick. The blanket they gave me had blood on it, like from someone's period or something. I was disgusted and longed for my own blankets and crocheted afghans at my mother's place. I stored my one box of belongings under the coffee table. As I lay there on the itchy couch, I thought about what a mistake it was to move there. I didn't realize what misery I would be in. When I woke in the morning, I had spider bites all over me. I went to call Birdie and the phone didn't work. I sat there and stared at the view of a stucco wall- it was the least of my worries, but it depressed me further.

I went to dinner with my dad the next night. He took me to a dark steakhouse where he seemed to know the staff. I told him stories of the latest guys I was dating, and how they were not getting the best of me, how I was in control. I thought he would be impressed, but he told me not to be a ball buster. After a few drinks, he started to tell me things I wished he hadn't. He admitted he had had numerous affairs while married to my mother, some of them with girls only a few years older than I was at the time. He later bragged of a waitress somewhere, who was sixteen and in love with him. Then he told me about lot of gross sexual conquests he had, some of them with people I knew as a child. It was really disturbing and I felt that he had crossed a boundary by telling me such explicit things. I felt horribly and disgustingly violated, but I was frozen. I wrapped my brain in some sort of protective coating and tried to pretend I didn't hear it. *No...no...I am not hearing this.* Strangely, or maybe not, I was sick most of the time I stayed with him. Not only that, but I drank more than I ever had.

A few guys from a popular hair band lived in the same building as my father. He said he was friends with them and told me to go down to the Jacuzzi to meet them. I found it strange, but tried to play it cool and went and said hi. I did have their album after all, and I knew all of their songs. It would be cool to brag about it, I supposed. One night soon thereafter, one of them saw me coming into the lobby from my night out. He wanted to come back to the apartment with me! He was very bold about it and didn't seem to be deterred by the fact that I lived with my father, an acquaintance of his. I turned him down flat. He wouldn't take no for an answer and literally chased me through the halls until I got to my dad's place and shut the door in his face while he tried to invite himself inside (my dad and Debra were out somewhere). As I locked the door, I realized something: my dad had given him the okay to try to screw me. I was really hurt and tremendously disturbed. It tore a bigger hole in my soul. I had come a long way, but still, a part of me always thought, *Is this all I am? Is this my value?* It was so confusing. Afterward I thought, *Well, maybe the guy was just ballsy...maybe my dad **didn't** give him the okay...*

But then, a few days later, I got kind of a weird lecture from Debra. She thought I should go out and try to meet rich men. I knit my eyebrows together and sat down on the stool in the kitchen to listen to her as she boiled some water for tea. *What was up with this lady?* She wanted me to go to the Polo Lounge in Beverly Hills and order a Brandy Alexander at the bar. She said if I sat there and just sipped my drink, I would meet wealthy movie executives and the like. I remember thinking...*Uh...okay. A Brandy Alexander is gonna be the clincher, huh?* She then explained to me that a woman is bought dinner and gifts as compensation for giving her body in the bedroom, and that it was perfectly acceptable. I felt uncomfortable with that statement. It ruined the thought of courtship and romance. Both of those things were very far from my life, but I always imagined that they were at least out there somewhere. Between Debra advising me to trade my body for riches and my mother telling me never to marry and never have children because it wasn't worth it, I was pretty messed up in the head. I never followed Debra's advice because I didn't want rich guys- I liked broke musicians!

My father and Debra were cooking small dinners at first, but then they got on some sort of drug and starting keeping little to no food in the house. I was constantly starving. I longed to be able to go through a fast food drive-thru. I started dropping a lot of weight just because there was nothing to eat. But even worse than that was the fact that they did not buy toothpaste or laundry soap. I am not kidding. I smelled *so* gross. My hygiene embarrassed me at school. I was so ashamed! My dad used baking soda to brush his teeth. I thought, *Okay, fine.* But they used cheap shampoo as laundry soap and it did not get odor or stains out of my clothes. There were no sharp razors in the shower so I had hairy legs and armpits unless I went somewhere else to shower. One day I left school because I smelled so badly. I had no job at this time, so I knew I was in real trouble if I thought my dad would feed me and take care of me properly.

I quickly found out why my father and Debra were eager to have me stay with them. I had a car and they didn't. My car was not running, but that would soon change. They were very secretive and talked amongst themselves for a few days, coming up with some sort of plan. The next thing I knew, my car was towed somewhere, a credit card was "borrowed" and my radiator was fixed on someone else's dime. Once the car was running, I could never use it. They considered it theirs because they had it fixed. I had to take the public bus to school, all the way on the other side of the Valley.

I managed to take my car to school once and found that my dad had left beer cans on the floor and a pot pipe in the ashtray.

There were ashes all over the floor of the car. I was very angry that he didn't think of the trouble I could get into for driving with that shit in my car. Not only that, but he broke my gearshift off and left the car out of gas. Couldn't the guy drive somewhere without having to get fucked up in some way? Couldn't he wait to get home to have beers and smoke pot? I thought, *Whatever, he is going to help me pay for school next semester.* I decided to try to spend as much time away from him as I could.

On the weekends, I took the bus to a place that felt like heaven: Birdie's house. I had to take two buses across town and then walk from a bus stop to her parent's townhouse up a hill somewhere. They lived in a modest place although it was clear that they could have easily been more extravagant.

I would have walked through rain, sleet, and flying monkeys to get to her house because it was there that I could take a luxurious shower. I stood under steaming hot water and lathered up with lemon grapefruit soap from the South of France. I scrubbed myself with almond scrubs and sea sponges, used her coconut-scented shampoo and a vanilla-scented deep conditioner. I was never so grateful as when I was over there showering in the hot water. I got to use her thick, baby blue towels and actual hair products: shine serums, glosses, sprays, mousses, sets of large rollers- a whole salon's worth of supplies. Round brushes, curling irons, barrettes and ribbon. It was divine. I borrowed her Estee Lauder foundations in thick matte glass bottles, powders in deep cobalt blue compacts and lipsticks in heavy gold tubes. It was so much better than using a clothes iron to do my hair and a Sharpie marker for eyeliner. I was using a left-over bottle of Aziza foundation from 1986, I had been so broke. She had a closet of beautiful, expensive, and showy clothing, and shoes stacked in boxes to the ceiling. Her room was a painted a pale, cotton candy pink with white shelves containing stacks of fashion magazines and perfume bottles. Pages of French and Italian *Vogue* were plastered on the walls amongst stuffed animals and a few random childhood trinkets. She was still part child, really. It felt comforting to me. I used to sit in her pink recliner and read her beat-up copies of *Sweet Valley High* while she spent hours on her makeup and hair.

I also loved the feeling of being safe under her parents' roof. I went there as often as I could, listening to her father yell at people in his deep green office, or her mother speaking French or Italian to her friends on the phone. We could *eat* things in the kitchen! Brie and crackers, strawberries, fresh squeezed orange juice, cold chicken, slices of baguettes, chocolate chip cookies with cold milk. I wished so badly that I could move in with her, amongst the comforts of her home and her family and her old, little dog.

We went out every weekend, most of the time wearing coordinated outfits for maximum free stuff. Our favorite outfits were the sheer, short baby doll dresses that the dancers wore in Prince's "Gett Off" video. Birdie had the black with white polka dots and I had the white with black polka dots. We got them at different points in time at Playmates on Hollywood Boulevard. With those dresses, we wore our hair slicked back into high ponytails, big hoop earrings, and false eyelashes. We also did a beach bunny theme: we tanned very dark and wore baby pink lipstick, dark smoky eye makeup, and very tiny half shirts in pale colors, with our hair half up and half down. We had a disco theme with lots of silver glitter eye makeup and our hair in big bouncy, disco curls. Whatever we did, it always caused a lot of commotion. While that was the point, and it was fun, it was also a little embarrassing. I felt sort of childish dressing alike with another girl. It felt very silly- it wasn't me. I also felt it was making a pretty bold statement as to how close we were to each other. Birdie was not well-liked among the girls in Hollywood, and I knew that I would soon have more enemies by pairing up with her in such an extreme way. It didn't deter me though; being around Birdie was too comforting. Her warm home, her girliness, the security of her parents- it was all too delicious for me to give up.

We paid for nothing when we went out. She was exceptionally

beautiful and I had an exceptional figure. Combined, we partied for free every single time we went out. I had already been enjoying that sort of treatment for a few years by then, but it was taken to another level once I paired up with her. People looked at her face and let her talk them into going to the ATM and taking out money to hand over to her. I am not kidding you. A guy handed over his wallet once and she opened it and took out as many bills as she wanted and went and partied with the money. I couldn't believe it. I am sure these people were drunk off their asses, but still. When we walked up to a club, the crowds parted and we were pulled to the front of the lines. We sat down at tables and ordered huge dinners and strangers picked up the tab. Cindy Crawford was the big supermodel of the time and everywhere we went, people thought Birdie looked like a young Cindy Crawford: the hair, the mole, the face, the height.

But there is always something that puts you in your place when you get to that point. In this case, it was the night I realized that there is a little private club above The Roxy. David Faustino, the guy that played Bud Bundy on *Married...with Children* stuck his head out of the door and we laughed about how short he was. He heard us, walked over to us with a bottle of water, and dumped it over both of our heads in front of a huge crowd of people. We were soaked! As we walked away with frizzy hair and smeared make-up, we couldn't even look at each other. People were laughing hysterically and pointing at us, snapping pictures. We were brought down to earth momentarily.

One night we couldn't find anything to do. We went to a party with the dirty Seattle crowd, much to my dismay. Three or four of the black-haired girls went into a dimly lit bathroom at the top of a stairway. They said they were going to do heroin and asked us if we wanted some. I said no. I was too scared. Birdie paused. Then she looked at me and said she wanted to try it. I said, "Are you *crazy*?" But she wanted to experience it. The girls had tried to kick her ass only six months prior and they appeared to be making peace. Maybe that is why she went. Maybe she was trying to prove something. I don't know. But she went in the bathroom with them and did it. I was totally upset by the whole thing, sitting on the stairway, waiting. I felt disturbed, worried for her. This wasn't some worldly dancer. This was a young teenager. I sat there trying to think of how I was going to make sure she never did it again. Would it be too late after the first time? Would she be hooked already? What could I do? What could I say? I knew she really cared about what I thought, so I decided to use that.

On the way home, I told her that I lost a lot of respect for her. I told her I couldn't truly be close with anyone on drugs, especially because of what it had done to my own family. I told her she was becoming a huge loser and I didn't want to be friends with losers. I tried to say anything and everything I could think of. She felt horrible- she started crying.

But she didn't stop doing heroin.

CHAPTER SIXTEEN

Blackmail:

Not So Fun After All

I knew a little of what brought Birdie to Hollywood. Besides her love of adventure and rock music, she had a background story similar to mine: someone in her family had sexually abused her. From what she explained to me, she actually came forward and told on the person, but the whole thing was covered up and swept under a rug because it was a beloved family member. The parents didn't want to make a big scene. From that moment on, her life was never the same. She even had the same violent episodes that I had, trying to attack her parents with knives.

I didn't know the details as far as the lack of protection, but as the victim, I could relate. Feeling like you weren't protected was almost worse than the actual abuse. Abuse may have murdered your soul, but the fact that someone could have helped you, and didn't, really fucked with you. It made you full of rage. It made you ask, *"Why was I not worth saving?"* It made you decide you must be a piece of shit and it made you want to destroy yourself.

Birdie's parents seemed to be nice people. Her mother was a tall, blond Swiss woman and her father a short, dark-haired businessman, a commodities broker formerly from Manhattan. They were cultured and polite and seemed to have it all, except when it came to Birdie. They couldn't control her. She told them what she was going to do and they kind of bowed to her like, *Yes Master*. They always looked worried around her and they never said no to her when I was at her house. They always seemed so guilty, like they were afraid of her telling on them or relapsing into a violent episode. They bought her whatever she wanted, including the very expensive makeup, clothes, and shoes. They appeared to feel badly for not protecting her, even though they were not helping her by giving in to her demands, including driving her down to Hollywood when she couldn't get a ride. Her mother would put on a bathrobe, drive us down there, and drop us off on the street!

My own mother still hadn't acknowledged that she let my father stay in the house with us after she suspected he might be a pedophile. It was as if it never happened. My family was quick to paint me as the dramatic problem child whose word could not be trusted, in case I decided to talk about it. All of my partying did little to fix that image. I was tired and broken down. I was bothered staying with my father and became more involved in partying to cover up my uncomfortable feeling. I became increasingly depressed when I was faced with reality each morning. I was attending college, but was barely making it. My stomach was always growling and I was constantly sick. I felt dirty. I longed for the house I grew up in, before things turned ugly in my life. I longed for the time when I felt protected and secure, back before my dad got into drugs. I longed to be in my lavender bed full of stuffed animals, I longed to be back playing with the kids in the neighborhood, to be back on beach trips, roasting marshmallows at night. I longed to nuzzle my baby bunnies, to eat cinnamon-sprinkled toast while watching cartoons with my sister. I longed to make paper chains during Christmas time, to dye eggs for Easter with my Dudley Shake-An-Egg kit. Adulthood had been downright horrible. I didn't know why anyone would ever want to grow up. It was the biggest bust, the biggest disappointment. I sat on the bus, looking out the windows at the shops passing me by in the Valley. Would it have been better if I had played it straight? Not looked for adventure, not had curiosity for the city that was Hollywood? Not met all of the people I had met? Not been influenced by the girls I befriended? Not seen the things I had seen?

Journal Entry 9/28/1992

I am in school and I'm freaking out because this desk is an asshole. Now I am freaking out because I just wrote that. There is a barrier- well, I guess it's really a table leg- directly to the side of my leg and I don't like it. If it were on the right side, it would be all right. I am about to get up and throw this chair and tip over this desk in front of everyone. I am really restless. I am annoyed, my nose is twitching.

Now I am in a different class, waiting for it to start. I am realizing that my eyes are glossed over and I am tired. I took pep pills in the morning so I could pay attention, but they didn't work. I think I missed most of the lecture because I started daydreaming. There are a lot of things in my life that I can't let myself think about. I have to stay afloat somehow.

Journal Entry 9/29/1992

I accidentally got fucked up; I didn't mean to. I took some Mexican antibiotics that my dad gave me this morning, along with some other pill, and I didn't realize they don't mix very well. I feel numb. I hate myself right now. I just got through with my public relations class and I made two people hate me instead of making two new friends. I wish it were last year. I had new clothes, a new car, and a job. I had an actual manicure and was hanging out with Harmony. Now look at me. I am wearing a T-shirt that smells like B.O., I have to take the bus, I have no job, and I am mingling with the Seattle people. I am a total loser. My dad is supposed to pick me up from school today in that boat of a car he is borrowing from somewhere (my car is broken down again). I guess I don't care if it's embarrassing. This isn't junior high. A big paper was due today in English 101 and I didn't do it because I didn't understand it. I started crying when I was trying to do it on my dad's coffee table. I wish I could think more clearly and just figure it out. I just want to get on to the next class and feel better about it. The teacher sort of intimidates me. She is young, pretty, proper and smart- you can tell she just started teaching because she is all serious about it. She has a huge rock on her finger. She probably has this great life. She has never had to deal with people like me. She has no idea how someone could be distracted, tired, broken, exhausted.

You could say it's nerdy, but I normally like sitting in classrooms (when the temperature is okay) and having bendy, shiny books with highlighted passages and paper clips marking the pages. I like having a big bag and folders full of papers. I normally like to learn. I have to take the bus today and I guess it's alright. There are some things you just have to do.

I have realized a few things about myself in the past few years. First of all, I have felt uncomfortable writing about the real me. I have another side of me that has been buried. It kind of peeked through the dirt the other day. I was watching another old black and white Hitchcock film in Cinema class and I became like, sick with longing to be in the past. I wanted to cry. I actually thought to myself, I am from the past, aren't I? I was someone back then, wasn't I, God? I have to have been. I feel pain sometimes, looking at those old movies. It feels like heartbreak when I see detailed old homes like the one in Meet Me in St. Louis. I feel hurt in my heart hearing that Big Band sort of music- it makes me feel sick because I love it so much. Even the voice inflictions in those old movies- the way the women spoke with those breathy, innocent, questioning voices with slightly British accents- it both comforts me and makes me homesick.

People wouldn't know this about me, but I love literature. I love old books. I like to read Shakespeare and memorize as much of it as I can. When I'm alone I have the urge to do ballet or gymnastics- I like to have balance and form. I also wish that people still had formal manners...sometimes I make guys kiss my hand, no matter how wild they are, and that really is crazy because the guys today will let a door slam in your face (and have, to me). I'm torn on what I would want my future to be. I would love to have a conservative, traditional life where I stay home to raise children with a professional husband. But another part of me questions the rules, criticizes everything and would want to work for my own money and not depend on anyone.

*I don't fix the radio when it starts coming in with static. I often cry when I hear songs by the Beach Boys or Elton John, namely "I Guess That's Why They Call it the Blues," and a few more songs that I either don't know the names of or I do and don't want to see them in writing or I really will cry. I am attracted to abusive people, women or men. And if the person isn't abusive, you can bet I will end up abusing **them**. I always see how far I can get in being mean to somebody. I don't like what I look like. I have sinus problems- my ears plug up all the time. I think it's from the dust in this joint. I used to play hopscotch by myself when I was a kid. I strongly believe in God. I am a very heavy drinker and most of my friends either drink very heavily or do drugs. I have been taken advantage of many times because I was too drunk to stop it. I think about killing myself a lot. I often go nuts thinking of old childhood memories, because it was so nice back then. I love my younger sister Becky more than anything. I don't have nightmares or cavities. I hate to be full and I like to discipline myself. It is hard to sleep at night. I sit and wait for phone calls. I get obsessed with people and can't take a hint sometimes. I settle for less, a lot. I have dancer's feet, the bone structure. I am very scared to die because of what is after death. I always think bugs are crawling on me and my fingers and hands lock up a lot.*

Journal Entry 9/30/92

My mouth tastes like blood again and I am getting the chills. I am sick again. I have been sick since June! I am on Lithium right now so I will calm down and won't kill myself (seriously). It makes you numb. I have never noticed it before. I have been trying to tranquilize myself so I can be knocked out cold, but now I have decided to stay awake. I have been thinking about moving to Colorado. I need to get out of Hollywood before I die. There are less and less people I care about in Hollywood now. I could forget about Lesli. I could forget about Michael and Strange. I could forget Birdie. Maybe I will.

I hate it so much when I am loaded on anything. I hate hearing my heartbeat, feeling blood in my wrists, feeling like scratching people and turning them inside out. I hate moving and I can't stand still. You would think I am a bad person if you heard all of the things I have done throughout my life. I am not really bad inside. I'm just lost. My mom hurts me constantly. My friends indirectly hurt me in various ways. Like when Birdie wanted me to watch her purse, out there on Detroit Street. It is a horrible area of Hollywood, a drug neighborhood. I was sitting by myself, sober for once, under a lamppost. I was sitting on a cement wall for a minute, but jumped off when I saw that snails and worms were crawling out of the cracks. Birdie was down the street with a guy named Stevie. I hate that silver purse.

*I ran into one of the guys I used to know when I was fifteen that night. He said he saw me a couple of weeks ago and I was a real bitch. He said he was saying hello to me and I was really wired and my eyes were really red and I pushed his hand away from me and said "**Fuck** you" when he tried to be friendly. I was secretly pleased to hear that I did that, because he was someone who took advantage of me as a young girl. He pushed his way into my home and into my bedroom, and I didn't have the balls to stop him. My mother and sister were even home when it happened and no one said or did anything. Fuck him.*

I hated that horrible party on Detroit Street. It was a far cry from the fun, colorful, happening parties of a few years ago. This party was a bunch of whores, fat girls, and drug addicts.

Some were a combination of all three. Most of the girls were openly fiending for speed. They sat around rolling joints instead. They are the jealous types- it makes girls look so bad. I overheard their plots to kill Birdie when they discovered that their precious Stevie, one of maybe two people in their whole Seattle crowd who is attractive, was with her. Birdie had on this stretchy red dress and big soft curls in her hair. She pulled a Yankees jersey over her dress and made out with Stevie on the hood of a car. He kissed her like the old movie stars kiss. I always wanted to be kissed like that. I was jealous. Not on display though, naturally. She called me the next day and was mad at me for letting her leave the house in the red dress- she said it made her look fat, and if I were her real friend, I would have told her so.

***

They say to be careful how you treat people on the way up, because you will be seeing them again on the way back down. During my heyday, I had ignored that Seattle crowd, treating them with rude and snobby behavior. They remembered that behavior quite well when I was showing up to their parties with Birdie and were sure to treat me just as bad if not worse than I had treated them. Sometimes they wouldn't even let me in the door, and they almost always called me names.

So needless to say, I was starting to get bored. Don't ask me how it happened, but somehow, I got the great idea that I should be a femme fatale and try some daring shit like Sharon Stone in *Basic Instinct*. I was lying around thinking, *Hmmm...I need to try to put the fear of God into some motherfuckers in this town. I am slipping.* I scanned my mental Rolodex and the first name that popped up was that French piece of shit, Andre. He was Jimmy's good friend and bandmate who I had made out with and who had later called me and said he wasn't even attracted to me and that I was a big ho who seduced him. I didn't like how the conversation ended and it bugged me that he got away with insulting me like that. I had to destroy him.

I decided to call him and try to extort money from him, just for my own entertainment. I had done many things, but I hadn't yet blackmailed someone, and I was itching to do so. I laid in my bed in a hot pink nightgown with bright purple trim and called Andre. When he answered, I told him he had to give me fifty dollars or I would tell Jimmy we hooked up and ruin his fucking life. He thought I was pathetic, because it was such a measly amount. He was like, "*Fifty dollars*? I mean, if you need money *that bad*, I will just let you borrow it or *give* it to you. You are going to *blackmail* me?" I really just wanted to humiliate him for telling me he didn't think I was pretty and I was a huge floozy who seduced him. I was like, *Yes motherfucker, you heard me, fifty dollars. Now pay up.* He said that he was going to call Jimmy himself and explain things. I was like, *Oh yeah? Well that's not going to go over so well you dumb fuck.* We played chicken with each other, both threatening to tell Jimmy. I wasn't prepared to have Andre call my bluff like he did. He must've smelled fear, or been able to tell that I hadn't thought my plan through very well.

I immediately hung up the phone, called Jimmy, and told on myself. I thought it would be better if he heard *my* version than whatever Andre would say. Since I was already toast, I took the Frenchman right down with me. Jimmy went ballistic and told Andre that he had to leave their band, or Jimmy would. Jimmy was the key player in the group; he had founded it and he had the connections. Andre was only the drummer, in the background with no connections, so it was clear what would happen to the rest of the band if Jimmy left. They would fold.

Lo and behold, the band broke up. They had been receiving attention from record labels, were touring with L.A. Guns, and appeared to be on their way to stardom. The other band members were *furious* with me. They had worked very hard and were shocked that Jimmy would let it go because of well, *me*. I guess it was my fault. Oh, okay, fine, it *was* my fault. I didn't have to tell on the guy. I felt bad afterward. I tried telling myself, *Hey, Jimmy cheated on me and betrayed me countless times- why* *should I spare **his** feelings?* But the truth was, I was just being a jerk.

Andre was going down and he didn't want to go down alone. He decided to try to take the attention off himself, by bringing up something that I had admitted to in my drunken stupor at Red Light District: I had been seeing Robbi earlier in the year. Jimmy had recently become close with Robbi because he was painting his drums and doing tattoos for the rest of Alleycat Scratch. I hadn't been connected with Robbi for several months by that time. I remembered Michael warning me that if I told Jimmy about Robbi and me, they would all be very angry with me for screwing everything up. *Yeah, yeah, yeah,* I thought.

The next day I found many nervous answering machine messages from Robbi. The first message said, "This is Robbi. If you talk to Jimmy, DENY EVERYTHING. If you don't, you'll be really sorry and I wouldn't want anything to happen to you." I should have thought, *Bitch please. What are you gonna do? Kill me over some hair band?* But I was all scared, biting my fingernails like a typewriter. Jimmy called me at three in the morning, freshly upset about the Andre scandal. He screamed "ROBBI?!" Then he started yelling at me and calling me a slut. The next day he barged down the door to Alleycat's apartment, started to strangle Robbi, and tried to kill him. I know, I know, it all sounds so foolishly melodramatic.

I knew I had caused the whole chain of events and it could have all been prevented. But at that age, I liked to do crazy things and try out social experiments- I didn't care who got hurt or what trouble it caused. Things weren't shiny and new and exciting anymore. I had conquered the things I wanted to, and I was looking for some other form of excitement, I guess. I had become careless. And I paid for it, socially. That crowd didn't want to deal with me much after that. I was too much of a pain in the ass.

Journal Entry 10/1/92

Well, I can do nothing but continue the horrible saga of my present life. What could possibly happen to me next, I do wonder. I am sitting in a practically empty Cinema class and two other people are talking and deliberately leaving me out of the conversation but I keep adding my two cents, regardless. Well, I know never to blackmail anyone ever again, even though it looks fun and all. So nobody ever speaks to me again. So Jimmy's terribly hurt and extremely angry...maybe he will feel an ounce of what I felt, hearing that he slept with ten different women while dating me. So people will want to kill me. So I won't go out for a while.

Journal Entry 10/2/92

I am sitting here watching a show on the media's influence on beauty and how teenage girls are obsessed with their looks and how unrealistic it is. I guess I am a little obsessed with beauty. But I have to be. It's my bread and butter. It's my way to eat. I can't survive just being the person who loves books and old movies. I have to project something that appeals to people who will help me to like, survive. I can't truly depend on my own family.

*There are lots of little rules and assumptions just being a part of this Hollywood crowd. For instance, if you are walking alone on Sunset in the day, there is no doubt you are wacked on speed. There is absolutely no other reason for you to be out there in the daytime. If you are hanging anywhere near this guy named Anton, you are either on or are buying drugs. If you are anywhere on East Las Palmas you are without a doubt buying drugs- speed, most likely. Same goes for Detroit Street. If you are on Cherokee, you are specifically buying crack. If you are at Ralphs on Sunset, you are a drunk. If you are in Rock n' Roll Denny's on Sunset on any morning, dammit you are on **something** because you're still awake from the night before. Everyone will throw that at you. That, and the wandering*

*around Sunset in the afternoon are two big giveaways. Natalie
goes as far as the Mayfair Market now to avoid being seen at
Ralphs, so people won't think she is a drunk, and Ralphs is right
on her corner. But then again she is paranoid because she is on
speed.*

*Oh, and don't ever eat in public in Hollywood. Christian got
jumped for his hamburger one day. And the Wendy's drive-thru
is not a good idea since Collette got mugged there. It is on the
corner of Detroit Street, no wonder. Yucca is the street on which
to score heroin, if you are a true loser. If you are around
Gazzarri's, the Cathouse or FM Station you're a hesher (not
good). If you're a dancer you want to try to work your way out
of the Seventh Veil or the Star Strip on La Cienega and on to
better places.*

*I had a hellish day at Natalie's apartment yesterday. I must've
heard the word Xanax two billion times. She was on coke last
night and wouldn't shut up. First we went to the Rainbow and
apparently I bumped straight into Axl Rose from Guns N' Roses
by the restroom; I smacked right into his chest and didn't even
realize it or say excuse me. After that, she invited that grody
drug dealer guy Anton over to her place. He was doped up on
heroin, the prick. He wouldn't stop touching me and I had to sit
on the bastard's lap for a good half an hour to LAX in her two-
seater car. I told Natalie he was trying to feel me up and she
didn't believe me! She said he would never do something like
that. Never do something like that? What, is this guy a pillar of
morality? I didn't care if she believed me or not, I scooted back
into her trunk and laid there the whole way home, pouting.*

*Once we were back to her place, he went into the bathroom for
like, a half an hour and when he came out there was blood on
her towels and a Band-Aid wrapper on the floor. His face was so
white and bloodless that it scared me. He came and laid on the
ground and said he wanted to take a nap, just like the typical
heroin addict (Collette, Teddy, Casey). What a junkie bastard,
and a slob to top it off.*

Journal Entry 10/12/92

I took a bus to Birdie's this weekend and we got a ride to Hollywood. She bought speed from some guy for 25 bucks. Before that, we went to the Rainbow and asked if they would let us in because we were bored. I had just finished chewing a hot dog from AM/PM and had a bored look on my face and Birdie slurped away at soft serve ice cream in a cup. We didn't care if we got in or not, but it was worth a try. A man behind us heard and said, "I'll pay her way in" to me. A big man in a suit came up behind him and said, "They need ID, this isn't fun and games," and since Birdie didn't have ID they didn't let us in. Mind you, they used to let me in all the time when I was her age. There must've been a crackdown.

We went and hid on the top of a bank building so Birdie could do her drugs. It was really dark up there except for the lights of the Rainbow's sign. She was trying to bite a straw in half to snort with. These two random hesher guys came up to us and had a six-pack. They gave me a beer. I felt all right around them, they were harmless. No style, no makeup, no done hair. I even told them my real name. Birdie took out her calling card to chop lines and then excused herself to go into a corner and snort speed. The guys asked me if I had older brothers. I said "Why?" they wanted to know how I had learned to party so much. I was drinking a Budweiser for Pete's sake, if they only could've seen me on a regular night!

We went down onto The Strip and Birdie found that guy Stevie from the Seattle crowd and they snorted a bunch more drugs. He seems like a sociopath to me. He has these dead eyes, void of all feeling. Maybe it's the drugs. Anyway, he has this horrible bleached and greasy platinum white hair to his shoulders with really long black roots showing. He has sort of dark skin, full lips, and a round, button nose. He never smiles or talks. I guess he has a cute face, but he just looks like such a serial killer, it gets in the way. By three a.m., we realized everyone was leaving so we squeezed in a car with some of our guy friends and got dropped off at this lady's house. She let everyone in but Birdie and me. She locked the tall, spiked gates and our "friends" left us out there. Birdie started getting dizzy and I took her behind a van, jammed my finger down her throat, and made her vomit, which didn't help whatsoever. As she was laying there all fucked up, she announced that she snorted three LINES of speed with Stevie. According to Natalie, speed is not like coke. You can't do lines of it if you are not used to it- it would be way too much.

I spent quite a while trying to hold her up and she eventually fainted. She fell out of my arms and smacked her head on the sidewalk. It was dark and cold and I didn't even know where we were. Stevie came outside to check on her and we were arguing about who should be taking care of her. She woke up and clung to me and he was mad. He wouldn't go into the house to get me a phone to call for help- he said the lady inside hated Birdie and me, and she would never allow it. I said, "Screw it; I am scaling this fence myself- I will get that fucking phone myself." He didn't think I could do it because of the spikes, but I did. Lesli was walking outside and saw me coming toward the door- he put his arms across it so I wouldn't go in. He said the lady would be really mad if I went in, but I didn't care. I was like, "What is she going to do? There is a girl OD'ing on her fucking sidewalk." He decided to bring a phone out because he knew he couldn't stop me. The phone didn't work! The bitch probably unplugged it. I climbed back over the fence and slit one of my wrists on a spike by accident. Finally, after a bunch of screaming and yelling, Stevie called Birdie's mom for me and she came and got us, completely unaware of anything. I was wrestling with myself, trying to figure out if Birdie needed to go to the hospital or she was going to be okay. When I saw her talking and acting normal, I decided to say nothing.

The next night we went out again. There were eleven or twelve people crowded in a Jeep with no doors and we were driving around partying. People were throwing things at us from the windows of buildings. One of our friends picked up a brick, threw it back at one of the windows, and shattered it. We took off

because a bunch of cop cars pulled up. We raided Natalie's
apartment and partied there while she slept. Then we fell asleep
ourselves and when we woke up, we were still clutching beers.

Although I have done my fair share of partying, I don't like the
road Birdie is starting to go down. She has done heroin with the
Seattle girls and now she is doing speed all the time. It was okay
for other Hollywood girls to do, like dancers and hookers- that
didn't surprise or bother me so much. But Birdie isn't like them.
She is a sweet girl inside. I know she has a lot of pain in her
heart like I do. I don't want her to get into something she won't
be able to get out of.

I met a guy around then that seemed like he would be the answer
to all of my problems. His name was Presley. He had the look,
and wasn't part of my crowd, so rumors couldn't fly. He told me
his hair was naturally dark black because he was Persian. I
thought...*Okay...Persian...nothing wrong with that I guess.* He
had "heard about me" and made a comment that I was breaking
up bands left and right and causing fights on The Strip. I rolled
my eyes but I was secretly intrigued that he thought I had that
much power. I gave him my number.

When he called, he was trying way too hard to be the bad boy
that he thought I would like. I wasn't having it. We yelled at
each other over the phone and I very often slammed it down in
his face. He continuously called back to try to tell me off, but we
just went in circles. Here are the words from an actual
conversation I recorded in my journal:

He said, "Listen to me; do you want to be with me? Why don't
you get your guard down? Do you think I just want to *bang* you?
I could just keep you around and bang you all the time! I am not
a liar. If I say I care about you and I think you're different, then I
mean it! I am so tempted just to get you whipped on me and
DROP you. You are SUCH a HEADACHE."

I said, "Uh, *excuse* me, but you will never get me whipped on you. THAT will never happen. I will not be whipped on anyone."

He started screaming, "DO YOU WANT TO MAKE A BET?! Do you want to BET that I can't get you whipped?"

I said, "Fucking TRY it. You know what? You think you're so fucking great. But guys like you are a DIME a DOZEN. I can find an asshole like you ANYWHERE. You'll get ME whipped? Good luck."

He couldn't talk after that. He got all quiet and said, "Why don't you just let one of those dime a dozen guys talk to you then. This isn't an act, this is my personality, and I'm stuck with it."

I said, "Why do we have to sit here and see who is cooler than who? Why can't you just relax? I can do it, can YOU?"

I realized that day that I had become comfortable taking guys down a peg when it was deserved. I didn't flinch, it rolled off my tongue. It was so hard for me to stand up for myself as a young teenager, so many terrible things happened to me because I couldn't find that strength. But suddenly, in the midst of all of my misery, it was there. It had actually been there for a few years by then. Would I have been able to do it had I not met the girls I met in Hollywood? Probably not. Who knows where I would have been had I not seen women who could stand up for themselves. Sometimes you learn lessons in unlikely places. Another thing I learned from the girls in Hollywood is that I didn't have it as bad as I thought I did. There was always someone who had it worse.

A few nights later, I went to Teddy St. John's. We watched videos in his dad's plush house and got drunk. We fell asleep (nothing happened) and he was tossing, turning, jerking and twitching. I could tell he was having nightmares. I tried waking him up and couldn't, so I slapped him across the face. He woke up and started talking in a completely normal voice, asking me why I slapped him. I told him why and he started remembering his dreams. He said there was cocaine on the ground and he was trying not to touch it, and he wasn't supposed to be hanging out with me, because he was betraying Jimmy. I ditched him in the morning while he slept in his black and white checkered sheets.

Birdie was starting to see more of that junkie, Stevie. They were constantly arguing in parking lots and at parties and I had to sit and wait for her. Two chicks from the Seattle crowd called Birdie around that time and asked her a million personal questions. They recorded her answers and played them all over Hollywood. Birdie was devastated for about one day- until a car promptly hit the girl who was the main culprit. Karma had been an even bigger bitch than she was.

One weekend, while I was at Birdie's, my dad called her house and told me we had moved. I was like....*Wait...we.... **moved**? Doesn't that require some sort of **planning**? Some sort of packing?* He gave me the new address of where we lived. I thought, *What about my stuff? Who packed it?! Where is it!?* My dad said he would come get me, and drive me to the new place.

He pulled up to Birdie's in that big boat of a car, driving very slowly. I don't know whose car it was, but it wasn't his because he didn't have one. He drove me about two miles per hour over to a neighborhood in Woodland Hills, a few blocks from the community college I was attending. I was quite happy to be so close to my school, because I could walk there when the next semester started instead of taking a bus. The new place appeared to be in a relatively nice area, until we pulled up to the house where we were to stay. It was the crappy house on the block. Dead lawn. Old cars outside. Two Rottweilers barking. I thought, *Dude...we are that house? The one white trash house that ruins the rest of the neighborhood? Great.* We entered the place and a bunch of random people were sitting around. My dad started introducing me to them.

"This is Richard, he does construction; and that is Teri," he lowered his voice, "She is a prostitute, but she is a really nice person."

I stiffened. "Those two guys live in the back; this guy lives in the other room... she lives down the hall-"

It was as if we lived in a halfway house. I knew the two young guys in back were dealing drugs, -I forgot how I knew it was so obvious, but I remember being concerned that there would be a raid and I would be stuck in the middle of it. My dad and Debra shared one room, and then there was the clincher: I had to sleep in a makeshift closet! It was big for a closet, but I was pissed.

My dad told me that I could make some extra money if I ran some errands for Teri the hooker. I was hurt that he felt comfortable letting me be around her. I prayed he wasn't trying to get me to be a protégé or something- he treated me like a whore who could be offered up to anyone, as it was. He tried to make it sound like she was a good person; she just did that as a job. She actually did give me twenty bucks to go to the phone company and get her phone line turned on. I probably spent it on Jim Beam. And I recall Richard the construction worker giving me a shot of tequila from the freezer. I felt more and more uncomfortable as my dad partied with all of the people. It didn't feel safe there.

Somehow, my dad and Debra got my car fixed again. I didn't know how they paid for it, because neither of them had jobs, but I was relieved. My dad needed to use it straight away and I let him. When he brought it back, I saw that he left his pot pipe in the ashtray again. I was pissed and said he couldn't use it anymore. I couldn't believe how irresponsible he was as an adult, let alone a father. The deadline for the next semester's enrollment came and I asked him if he had paid it. He said, "Nope. Sorry. Couldn't do it. If you would've let me use your car that one day and just walked to school, I would've had the money to pay for it."

In my journal, I wrote:

*Did I tell you how he was ruining my car? He would insist on
using it. Where was HE when I had to raise the money to buy it?
He wasn't even around! I figured if he'd at least pay for me to
go to school then maybe it would be worth it. I should have
known he couldn't pay for it- how would he get the money
anyway? I thought that maybe he would somehow. But when he
told me he wasn't, I got up and started to leave. I felt like I was
going to break down. School was like, the last thing- the only
thing- that was normal in my life. I was depending on that little
shred of light.*

*He wanted to know when I was coming back, because he needed
to use my car (!). Can you believe that? I went to my grandma's
to cool off, and then I went back. When I first pulled up, he said
he was "real worried" and all this sugary crap. I ignored him.
He said, "What, are you just never going to talk to me again?" I
said I didn't feel like arguing and proceeded to make trips back
and forth, filling my car with my belongings. Debra tried talking
to me throughout the whole thing. I was polite to her. I said to
her that it was all right, I shouldn't be living off anyone
anyways; I shouldn't be waiting for anyone to pay for my school.
I should get up and go do it myself. She gave me a ten dollar bill
that she kept for emergencies. It was evening time, the sun was
setting, and we were out on our white trash driveway in sort of a
golden light.*

*Debra tried to explain in her patient, soft voice how bad my
dad's financial situation had been but I stopped her and said,
"Fine. But he shouldn't have waited until the last minute to tell
me he couldn't pay for my schooling. Now it is past the deadline
to enroll. If he would've given me notice, I could've hustled it
somehow. Now it is too late for that." Then I turned and
mentioned to my dad that it had been light-years since he fed me.
He said, "Oh, why didn't you go 'hustle' money then, since you
were so **star**ving," mimicking me. I felt embarrassed. My blood
was boiling, but I pushed the anger back.*

I told him in an even tone that I was trying to live with it, because it wasn't as important as school. He said, "Well, I expect you to come back."

*"No," I said, looking in his eyes, "You expect my **car** to come back."*

I drove away and never returned.

CHAPTER SEVENTEEN

I Won't Ever Be Normal

I begged my mother to take me back, emphasizing my living with a prostitute and drug dealers. She felt sorry for me, and let me move back in for a few weeks to get myself together.

Journal Entry 11/29/92

I am back at my mom's and soon to be homeless. My dad is back on drugs. But that is no longer my problem. If he wants to remain a druggie, he can go for it. After living with him, I know what it is like to starve and be cold and dirty. It really sucks. I don't want to elaborate on all that.

I am sick and tired of Hollywood. It is such a waste of time being there when you realize that the last real heyday of the place was in 1987 when Guns N' Roses came out. After they made it, no one compared. No one has beaten them yet. All of the other rock bands that came off the Sunset Strip have broken up or been dropped off their record labels. I guess I am trying to say that that big time is over and has been over. There is no one to impress anymore. There is no real 'in crowd' that I am trying to break into. There aren't even any more real great bands to go hear. Why do I even care who hugs and kisses me or who talks behind my back? I don't even matter. Saying that I was part of Hollywood in the early nineties is as good as nothing. The scene is dead. It is dead and gone and I am trying to hang onto it. Right now on the news they are talking about kids graffitti-ing the Hollywood sign. Very telling.

The reason I stay there is because I keep thinking that I won't ever be normal and I should just stick to other troubled people. I think that I will never fit in anywhere because of my troubled past, family problems and the amount of partying I do. How can I go hang around other nineteen-year-old girls, when my friends can drink an entire fifth of Jim Beam to themselves? I don't even know how to have real fun. How do you even make real friends or have a real relationship with a guy? I will never find out if I don't remove myself from Hollywood.

Journal Entry 12/29/92

My dad called here looking for me. I pretended to be my sister, and he believed it. You are going to think I really lost it but I think a ghost is following me around or else God is playing tricks on me because I keep seeing things and things keep happening that I didn't do. Then I get a crazy feeling and think I am going insane. I am trying to smack myself in the head- I must be imagining things. It was God or an angel in the street, in the dark, trying to stop me from driving drunk last night. Anyway, let me tell you what happened.

I went to the Rainbow again (I haven't paid yet) and got completely ripped. Sabrina and Bradley were there in a booth, both blond and beautiful, chatting with Ron Jeremy. I sat with them and had a grand old time. When the night ended, they invited me back to their place, which was up the street from the Whisky. When I was pulling up to their apartment building, I thought that maybe I should just drive home. I was tired and didn't know if I wanted to keep partying, but as I tried pulling away, I saw that white figure in the street, stopping my car, telling me not to drive. It was glowing, tall, kind of iridescent. I parked my car, got out, stumbled to their door, and pressed the intercom.

When I got up to their place, they pulled out a bottle of Jack Daniels, put on some music and the party continued, as it always does in Hollywood. True to form, Sabrina attacked me in the kitchen, tried to pull off my shirt and make out with me. I was just laughing and trying to get away. Her friend from the Tropicana was just standing there and watching. Never a dull moment with Sabrina, she is the same as she was when I was sixteen. Anyway, I drank way too much and the last thing I remember was running to the bathroom to barf.

*When I woke up, I was in their bed! I slowly looked down to see if I was naked and I wasn't- I had my clothes on, although my bra was unhooked. At least my pants and underwear were on! There was a bowl next to me filled with barf. I thought they were sleeping so I was going to try to escape, but then they woke up and started doing it, right next to me! I pretended I was asleep. Dude- how do I even get **into** these situations? Can't I just be some chick who goes to movies and the mall? I swear. Anyway, I "woke up" a little later and Bradley said I not only barfed in their bed, but I barfed all over **him**! I am half embarrassed for throwing up all over another human being, but I am equally mortified about what could have happened if I hadn't! They were obviously trying to get me to do it with them, but I was too wasted- thank goodness. I got out of there as soon as possible, and peeled out back to my mom's. I was trying to hold back my barf the whole way there. When I was a block from her house, I couldn't hold it any longer. I trying to make a left turn and I barfed all over myself in the car. It sprayed the dashboard. It was so disgusting. I pulled into my mother's driveway just as she was coming back from grocery shopping. She didn't even notice I was full of puke and handed me a bag of groceries and kept on walking. She would have to actually **look** at me to notice*

something on me, and she doesn't. I barfed at my new
telemarketing job later on after trying to hold down a bagel.

Six months later, Bradley and Sabrina had a fight. Bradley got
himself real doped up on heroin because he was depressed, and
ended up shooting himself in the head in the bathtub at Teddy's
house. Teddy was out at the store or something when it
happened, so when he came back home and called for Bradley
and didn't hear him answer, he figured that Bradley took off. So
Teddy left the house, unknowingly leaving Bradley's body there.
Days later, Teddy's father came home to a horrid smell. He
found the body in the bathtub, and thought it was his own son. I
don't know how long it took for him to figure out it wasn't
Teddy, or any more of the story, but it was a very dark time. We
were all completely devastated. Sabrina was a widow at twenty-
five. She started dating Bret Michaels of Poison a few years
later.

That December, my social nightmare continued. Jimmy joined
one of the bands I had been friends with, and was instantly part
of my crowd for better or for worse. The fights he had with some
of the main players in Hollywood had been forgiven, and they
all ended up accepting him. His perseverance paid off. I was
painted as the shit-starting tramp, and to a certain extent, it was
true.

I remember walking up to a club with my friends behind me and
looking up to see Jimmy in a full face of make-up and glammy
clothes, with a crowd of converts behind him. It was as if we
were going to have a gunfight at the O.K. Corral. We didn't look
at each other until we were about to pass one another. We locked
eyes and kept walking our separate ways. I felt he was a total
hypocrite for wearing makeup- he had always talked shit on the
glam guys on The Strip. Now he was one of them.

It was sad to ignore someone who I once loved and who had
given me so much love. We were strangers now. We had hurt
each other so much, the damage could never be undone. But as

sad as I was, I was also irritated that he had the nerve to break
into my circle. Who did he think he was? I thought, *I didn't
pound five million liters of Jim Beam in the dirt at Errol Flynn's
for **this** shit.* I had worked hard! But I was the one who bowed
out in the end. Hollywood wasn't what it once was for me. It
meant more to him- he was determined to be in a band, and I
wasn't as determined to stay and fight him.

Journal Entry 12/30/92

*I don't have time to write because I am going to work at my
telemarketing job. I might go out with my co-worker Tammy to
see male strippers afterward. I am sure I will be embarrassed
rather than like it. I am only stopping to write because I have to
tell you about Dusty. He was the one with the condo who was
nice, had a good job, was respectful and housed Razz and
Michael for a summer or so. I thought he had morals and though
he was not my particular type (tall, black hair, dickish), any girl
he ended up with would surely be lucky.*

*But then I got a peek into his life. His seventeen-year-old
girlfriend Michelle, who could pass for twelve at best, was
giggling to me on the phone last night that she was going to look
into stripping. Okay, they all do, at some point. But then she said
that Dusty suggested the Seventh Veil to her. I nearly dropped
the phone. Not only was someone who supposedly loves her
telling her to bend over in guys' faces for cash but he had the
nerve to suggest the absolute scummiest, lowest hellhole in
Hollywood for her to work. It is about one iota better than the
Star Strip on La Cienega, but only by a peroxided hair. I was
pissed that Dusty would pimp her out like that and I am
convinced she doesn't know better. She is very young and not
even from here! She is from Utah! He was the only nice guy left.
Now he is going to have his seventeen-year-old girlfriend bring
home the bacon? Maybe he was like that all along and I just
didn't know. Anyway, she said Shandy Becker was going to show
her some moves. I nearly spit out my cranberry juice. Shandy
Becker, the drug dealer? She looked like an old oak tree, all*

*knobby and gnarly. When was **she** a dancer? In the Roaring*
*Twenties? She is like, **old**. She has to be in her thirties already,*
unless those drugs have aged her that bad. And where did she
dance? An old folks' home? Michelle was naively giggling about
how much money she could make and that she didn't mind
nudity and she just wanted money. She wanted me to go with her
and I told her it wasn't my thing- I wanted money too, but not
that bad. I wished her my sincere luck.

Little naïve Michelle went on to become a stripper at the
Seventh Veil. Not only that, but she dumped Dusty and moved
in with the guy who owned the club. Over the years, she
completely transformed from the fresh-faced, coltish brunette
wearing a Venice Beach T-shirt with beaded fringe. I saw her
about six or seven years later. Her dark long hair was bleached
platinum blond, she had breast implants and she was done up
with a lot of thick stage makeup. She was very beautiful but no
longer smiling. I could hardly recognize her. She was with a
much older man and two young children. We looked each other
right in the eyes and knew who each other were, but neither of
us said anything.

I continued to work at my telemarketing job. The job started at 4
p.m. and ended at 8 p.m. We all sat in a room staring at a wall. It
was so dull. I remember driving over there in the rain, listening
to The Cure and daydreaming. I had to call people and ask them
if they would take a survey, which was really a disguise to make
them listen to my pitch. I asked them what they hated most about
going to the supermarket. *The lines? The prices? The one cart*
with the messed up wheel? (That was my favorite one to say).
After they answered, I said, *What if you didn't have to go to the*
supermarket anymore? I explained to them that if they ordered
their meat from our company, it would be delivered to them,
fresh and vacuum packed. I had a sheet to tell me what to say to
any of their objections, including if they said they were
vegetarian. I think we had some fresh vegetables that we would
also deliver. If they had no room, that was no problem: We sold
a freezer. We would deliver that bitch and put it straight into

their dirty garage. They could fill it with beer if they didn't want to keep buying meat.

I got a few leads at first. When you got a lead, you had to pass it to the boss, Kenneth, in the other room. He was watching us through a glass partition. He was a young guy, real salesman-ish. He had a huge shnozz and dark, feathered hair- pretty unfortunate looking, but he had personality. One day Kenneth gave us each a garbage bag of frozen meat, and I was shocked to find after cooking it that it was really very good. My sister used to beg me to make a sandwich with one of the chicken breasts.

I don't remember many of the people from the job except for Tammy. She was a petite 27- or 28-year-old whose father owned a bunch of adult bookstores and porn shops on Van Nuys Boulevard. She confided in me that she found Kenneth hot, and started dating him shortly thereafter. She often came to pick me up in her aqua blue Corvette. I went to her huge house in Studio City where she still lived with her father, and we laid out by her pool. Tammy talked about wanting to be a stripper as we laid there on the Hawaiian print beach towels. Shit, who was I to stop her? I went with her to a bikini bar in Tarzana and watched her do amateur night. I was there for support but I soon felt embarrassed for her because she was *so* not sexy. She had long, brown, permed hair, which was really out of fashion by then. She also had big caterpillar eyebrows and didn't know how to apply makeup properly. But none of that mattered in the dark under a neon light when Mötley Crüe's "Girls, Girls, Girls" was blasting. She ended up winning the contest and was hired. I was not surprised after I watched the next featured dancer. She was wearing glasses and rolling around the floor to Def Leppard.

***

Birdie and I were out one night feeling all pretty and popular and having a good time. Things immediately skidded to a halt when we saw Ashley Allesandro. Everything turned slow motion: She was in a fluffy, white fur coat, with her long blond hair and round angel face, getting out of Kit Ashley's white Jaguar in front of the crowds of people at the Rainbow. Both of our jaws dropped, because we had both dated him. The slow motion continued as Birdie scoffed and my eyes narrowed. Birdie tried stepping forward and I put my hand on her arm to warn her not to act like she cared. Her curls bounced as she teetered on her Frederick's of Hollywood heels. We were on our way out.

We heard through the grapevine shortly thereafter that Sabrina had gotten her hands on Ashley. I thought to myself, *Isn't that, like, child abuse*? But before I could think too much about anything, a smear campaign was started on Birdie and me. Rumors started going around that we were lesbians. I didn't think lesbians were such a horrible thing to be, but I didn't want to be labeled a man-hater. That was so un-sexy and I was all about being sexy. I thought about dumping Birdie as a friend to quell the rumors but then I thought, *Wait, she is a pretty good friend.* That, and she had too much on me. Had Ashley started the rumor? Nah, she had just slept with Sabrina. Was it Jimmy? The Seattle clique? It could've been anyone. Nonetheless, it was going to ruin the remainder of my image if I didn't fix it immediately.

With our popularity on shaky ground, Birdie and I started to turn our efforts to the L.A. celebrity crowd at Bar One; a place where we were considered new and fresh. We pushed our way through the crowds standing outside of the red velvet ropes and waited an entire second for the bouncer to check our names off the guest list. I loudly sighed and said, "I can't be *bothered* with this." We then glided through the door like princesses, to the crowd's dismay. We sat with Rich Ross and he said we could order whatever we wanted. I should have ordered some filet mignon and lobster or some foie gras and Dom Perignon, but I was a girl of simple taste and ordered up the classiest of drinks for us: Midori Sours. They were the Cosmopolitans of the early nineties.

Rich Ross said he wanted to set us up with two twin models, but I said I needed to see them first and he was offended that I didn't trust his judgment. The man wore running shorts every night of the year. How could I trust his judgment? Anyway, Birdie ended up in the men's room, snorting a bunch of coke with a businessman in a suit. I ran into a few blonds from my high school, who used to snub me back then. They were on *my* turf now. I relished the attention and the paying of homage.

That New Year's Eve, we were supposed to go to a party hosted by that crazy magician, Fig. He always had a huge rager up in the hills, with ice sculptures, dancing, and a huge lit up pool overlooking Hollywood. I recall seeing some plastic dog poo at one of his parties- it was so random. Anyway, the town's other New Year's Eve option was a rich girl throwing a party at her parent's mansion in Pasadena, but there was no way I could go because of the Seattle crowd of girls she hung with. Again, they didn't care for me and they cared even less for Birdie. They were still very territorial over Stevie, whom Birdie was still dating on and off. They also loved Lesli, but they knew better than to try to fight *me*; I would tear a bitch up.

We ended up going to Shandy Becker's, as a last resort. Of course some drug addicts would have us. Michelle and Dusty were there; Razz, Missy (she was back), Razz's friend Jay Jay, Teddy, and of course The Becker. We were all supposed to pile into a limo and go to a party at KNAC DJ Tawn Mastery's house. At the last minute, Teddy wouldn't come out of the room because he was too strung out. Shandy shut herself in her room with him and they both stayed home on New Year's Eve. Whatever, none of my business.

Here is what I wrote about the night:

I missed Missy so much. We hugged to death when I saw her and caught up on gossip. I introduced her to Birdie, who fell in love with her too. Missy looked like a model in a black sparkly dress and her long hair back to blond. Her baby face looked especially pretty with pale pink lips and black, fringed eyelashes. She was telling us how she hitchhiked across the United States with a

bunch of her friends when she was fifteen. Her parents were
trying to tear her between them and she said, 'Fuck this.' She
imitated her teenaged self, leaning back with her pelvic bone out
toward us, sticking her thumb far out in front of her with a sneer
on her face.

Everyone snorted a bunch of coke except for Michelle and me.
We all piled into a cab and went to the Rainbow, which was jam-
packed, and squeezed into a shiny red booth. Jay Jay bought
everyone a bunch of drinks and food. When it turned 1993, he
popped a bottle of champagne high in the air. It started
overflowing and everyone put their glasses under it and caught
it. We all kissed and hugged one another in our gold and silver
sparkly outfits, laughing and feeling jovial. It was all fine and
dandy until Jay Jay left with some chick and left us with the
check, which no one had the money to pay.

I was held there until someone coughed up money. Birdie, in a
metallic bronze dress and long ponytail, opened her big mouth
to tell the waitress that working while intoxicated was against
the law. The manager came over and cussed Birdie out in the
worst way- she had tears in her eyes when he was through with
her. Anyway, we all went directly back to Jay Jay's afterwards
to yell at him for ditching us with the bill. When we got there, we
saw that he had brought home some tweaked-out chick in a
purple sequined dress. I took one look at her Adam's apple,
grabbed Jay Jay, and dragged him to the kitchen immediately to
tell him he had brought home a transsexual. It was a guy. Maybe
it was my experience in the beauty supply store dealing with
many transgendered "ladies," or maybe it was because I was
the only one not on drugs, but I knew Lisa was a man.

Jay Jay freaked out. Poor Lisa was indeed a man in drag, with
tits and makeup. I got drunker and was being mean to her, as
per Razz, who was thrilled someone was being mean. He said I
took after him ("She takes after me! I am her uncle!") Then Lisa
proceeded to read Birdie's palm. She told her future, and said
she would die young.

*To change the subject for a minute, I drove past my old
neighborhood the other day, after visiting my friend Amelia,
who I am supposed to move out with. It was so weird. I looked at
each house and remembered who used to live in them when I
was a kid. Some of them are still there. It felt so weird to see my
old house, and the windows that I used to climb through. I drove
by Jeff Hunter's. That was a sacred place to me for years, before
I reintroduced myself to him. I drove by all the spots on the
sidewalk that were uprooted by tree trunks, pushed up into
bumps that we used to "pop wheelies" on with our bikes. I drove
slowly by the front of my high school. I was going "boom!" in
my head to each spot that changed my life. I saw the spot where
scummy Casey stopped his truck and rolled down the window to
talk to me. Boom! Just like that, my whole life changed. I never
turned back from that day, when I was in my concert T-shirt and
bare feet right on the sidewalk. I was instantly in deep trouble. I
can't believe he was cruising the high school looking for young
girls, and that I was the one who was troubled enough to take
his bait.*

*I saw all the spots where I sat and cried and all of the places I
walked with Abby when we were ditching classes. I saw The
Wall, where all of the stoners sat in the morning smoking
Marlboros and Camels. I was short of breath thinking of all of
the memories I had there. It is really amazing to me that I didn't
know how big the world was. It only consisted of that little
neighborhood for so many years, just me and my sister and our
parents. I had that school counselor who tried to help me. Now
there is no one to take care of me. I have to do things for myself
now. I have absolutely no idea where I am going in life.*

Sadly, my sister was completely strung out on drugs by that
time. She wasn't just doing it here and there; she had a serious
problem. No one tried getting her help, including me. She was
dating a guy named Jared, who was a drug addict and came from
a family of dealers. He got her hooked even worse. She looked
like a skeleton. Her beautiful, shiny hair was broken, brittle, and
orange; her caramel skin was pale and ghostly. Her bones were

showing and her eyes were sunken. She was really moody and often flew into a rage over nothing. But I was used to that- it was the way I operated myself. Everyone around me was on drugs as well, so nothing stood out to me. I just felt it was a shame she was hooked, too. First dad, and then her. Was I next?

Journal Entry 1/24/93

*Presley just called here and asked me if I had been on any dates lately. I figured that since I don't really see him out that maybe he wouldn't know who I was talking about if I named someone. So I admitted to a date with Kit Ashley on Wednesday night. He knew exactly who he was, and was pissed. He said, "Did you kiss him? Did you fuck him? Do you like him better than you like me?" I said no to all of it although some of it was a lie. Then he got angry and started calling me a hussy and saying that bands all over the place were scrapping because of me. The conversation wasn't going too well at that point. He tried telling me I was whipped on him, again. I literally didn't even know who he **was** when he first called. He was telling me that if he snapped his fingers, I would sleep with him. I said, "You have already snapped them a few times and it hasn't worked." He was livid. He needs to lose that double chin before he starts talking like that.*

Anyway, I went out with Natalie again last night and we went to The Roxy and the Rainbow. I saw Lesli in the Rainbow and decided I would be rude. He had some girl on him but was still yelling for me to come to his table. I passed by him, raised my eyebrows in a rude Valley Girl sort of way, and just looked away. He kept yelling and yelling above the crowds. I never came back. He has been hanging out with Kim Fowley a lot, and I don't know what that is about. Kim asks a lot of questions about what kind of music we are into- he is interested in what the kids like these days. I think he used to be the manager for The Runaways. He looks like he is wearing powder on his face, even though he is an old man with a cane.

After that, we went to Ten Masa and then to some underground club on Cahuenga at 3:30 in the morning. I was very uncomfortable there. Natalie's drug dealer, Anton, was there with sores all over his face and a huge bandage on his nose. He was so gross. He had a bottle of beer spiked with this new drug they call liquid Ecstasy [later called GHB]. *He was so repulsive and so on heroin. He tried to kiss my hand. Oh, the irony. I didn't fit in at the club because I wasn't dressed in black, I was too young and I wasn't tweaking on drugs. Something exploded in there and a bunch of white smoke filled the room- I was choking so badly. I wanted to get the hell out of there, but I had to wait for Natalie to score her drugs. People and their drugs...man...they will withstand anything to get those drugs.*

CHAPTER EIGHTEEN

How it All Died

Journal Entry 1/26/93

*Went to the No Bozo Jam at the Whisky with Birdie. Some guy bought our way in and bought us drinks. He said, "You gotta **buy** friends in Hollywood." I didn't argue with that. There was a long line for the women's restrooms and no line at all for the men's restrooms, of course. We barged into the men's room and went into a stall. Birdie got out her compact and put a bunch of speed on the mirror. I noticed there were chunks of brown stuff in it. I was like, "Birdie…. there is heroin in there." She didn't care and went ahead and snorted all of it. The drugs made her sit in a corner with her eyes bugged out all night. A bunch of our friends "jammed" on stage. True to form, Lesli tried to do something cool and it backfired. The idiot tried to do a stage dive and everyone moved out of the way instead of catching him. He hit the ground so hard he shattered his hip. He had to be carried out and put into an ambulance.*

I went to visit Lesli in the hospital, where he was in traction- his legs were strapped into bars that were hanging from above him. He couldn't move. I don't know exactly how it happened, but I started to fall for him. I thought maybe I could really be with him and actually started to open my heart up to him a little bit. I thought that maybe I had been wrong about him. Maybe he was the one, the one I had been ignoring. He started telling me he loved me and that we should be in a relationship. I finally agreed.

I was walking into a party one night soon thereafter and looked up to see him walking across the street with a young, pretty girl. I had a bottle of Jim Beam with me and I went over to him and tried to break the bottle over his head, but he caught my arm in mid-swing and held it. I felt like such an idiot. I had been played- not a good feeling.

Journal Entry 1/27/93

Razz's dream has finally come true after all of this time: he is now in a relationship with Missy and is living with her. The other night, she and I went out because he had to work for Prince's club, Glam Slam, driving someone somewhere in a Rolls Royce. When we were leaving, she wanted to stop by a liquor store but it was closed. She knocked on the window and they got a look at her and opened up the store for her. We drank beers in the car on the way to Hollywood, then we stopped in a parking lot behind a restaurant on Santa Monica Boulevard and made these gnarly drinks out of Seagram's and Diet Pepsi. Once we were sufficiently drunk, we walked down the street to the Troubadour and finagled in for free. Then we went to the Rainbow with a bunch of drink tickets she stole from Razz's pocket. My kinda girl. We got even more wasted and went to Del Taco afterward. There was a huge line of people, so we tried cutting in front of as many people who would agree to it. When we got to this sassy queen wearing no shirt, we were stopped. He wouldn't let us cut, but we started disco dancing with him right there in Del Taco. He stuck his tongue in Missy's ear and then licked his finger and removed some flakes of boogers out of my nostrils! He said, "No one else will do this for you, but I will." It was out of control. When it was finally my turn to order, I couldn't even speak English and they took full advantage of it because when I got my tray, there appeared to be one of everything on the menu, things I didn't even order. Then I went and put my mouth under the ice machine while Missy pushed the button. This one guy tasted his soda and didn't like it, so he chucked it all the way across the restaurant and it exploded like a bomb on his friend. I took my tray of food outside and gave a burrito to a bum, who said, "God bless you" and then I gave some tacos to some of my friends who were outside.

Saturday night I went to a party that I barely remember; I just remember Jimmy's hands around Michael's neck and having Michael jump into my car. Jimmy threw a beer at him, and it splattered all over my car.

That night was the beginning of my ritual of going to Del Taco after drinking all night. Eating fast food all the time started to ruin my figure very quickly. And that was really what I was riding on, in that town.

I was officially a has-been, washed up at nineteen years old.

I started hanging around bubbly Missy every weekend. I still idolized her and I always had the best time with her. I also felt safe with her, which was a quality that made me cling to certain girls. I started to hang out with her so much that she told me she was going to kick Razz out of her place so I could move in. At first I thought, *Cool! I would love to move in!* Then I thought, *Oh...Razz would be crushed! He has been chasing her for years! He finally got to move in with her and she is going to throw him out for me? He will be so pissed!* And that is when it hit me:

Screw *him!*

In March of 1993, I told Missy I would move in. She booted Razz out on his ass. He was so mad at me; he couldn't believe I moved in. He asked me how could I do such a thing.

I said, "Easy. The same way you became friends with MY ex-boyfriend and betrayed ME."

He asked, "Is that what this is about?! Jimmy?"

I said, "Why the hell should I be loyal to you?"

He couldn't believe I was as cold as ice about it.

Missy was really comforting to me. I felt at home in her house because it was messy and lived-in. And not only that, but she was truly generous with me. Everything that was hers was also mine. Clothes, shoes, food, anything. She really did take care of me. She was like a mother and a big sister. I really looked up to her.

Missy's little duplex was well shaded and cool, because it was blocked on one side by a huge bank building and the other side was full of trees. There was a little courtyard between the cottages, with tons of potted plants and lots of house cats lounging around. It was fun living with her. I loved it. I didn't bring much with me, so I only had one shelf in the linen closet for my things. She had posters of Perry Farrell from Jane's Addiction in her bedroom and a Missing Persons album cover tacked up next to the toilet in the bathroom. The bathroom walls were a huge collage of models from *Vogue* in different fashions, mostly Calvin Klein and Versace. She also had a lot of Georges Marciano Guess? advertisements on the walls. There were tons of hair extensions lying around the place and bras hanging on the doorknobs. The floors were wooden and the place echoed.

We had barbecues with all of her dancer friends, where we filled the bathtub with ice and then bottles of booze. We played disco songs and danced on the couches and tables. Her co-worker and friend, Lisel, ended up moving in next door at some point. She started to go out with us a lot. She was always really fun and wild when she drank, but was a mother figure in the day, telling us to wear sun block and be safe. We all went to Raging Waters that year, hopping on inner tubes in the big wave pool and crashing into people all day. We had such a great time in our unlined Ziganne's stage bikinis that weren't made to get wet, eating "Dippin' Dots" and taking pictures in the photo booth.

One night, Missy and I were leaving Canter's Deli on Fairfax with some of our friends. It was about two in the morning. Some guys said something rude to Missy, and the guys we were with started fighting with them. We all finally jumped into our friend Dave's car and left, but the other guys jumped in their car and started following us down Fairfax. They were driving really fast on our tail and we couldn't shake them. Dave said, "Everybody hold on!" and slammed on his brakes. The guys behind us smashed straight into us, totaling their clunker car. We were in a Nissan Pathfinder, so all that happened to us is that we got whiplash. Their hood was up like a tent and steam was coming out of it. Dave yelled, "Everybody out!" and the guys in our car each grabbed something to fight with and jumped out into the street. I had been in that sort of situation before, so I stayed put. But not Missy. She grabbed a skateboard, jumped out of the car, and started smashing the rude guy's windshield. It was so late that barely any cars were coming by. The ones that did drive by just went around us. The guys jumped out of their totaled car and everyone proceeded to brawl in the middle of the street. Missy was fighting with a guy and he ripped some of her hair extensions out. I got out of the car and was collecting her hair off the ground! Once the guys were laying there with X's over their eyes and little chirping birds flying in a circle around their heads, we all took off to get Slurpees from 7-11. I will never forget looking at Missy with blood on her shirt and a Slurpee straw in her mouth.

I wrote:

We have this philosophy- don't stress about anything. We wait until the last possible minute to cough up money for bills. That

*way we have two months of relaxing and then two weeks of
stressing over the stuff being shut off. It is not a very good
philosophy, I will admit. Everything is cool, except for the phone
company is shutting off our phone on Monday if we don't pay
the bill and we don't have the money. The electricity is going to
be shut off on Tuesday, same situation.*

*I am in the living room at Missy's. The aquarium is making a
relaxing sort of bubbling sound. We have one fish, Dre, and he is
floating around by himself. It is 12:30 a.m. and I am watching a
talk show about embarrassing spouses. The coffee table has my
three-pound weights, a couple of bowls with soup still in them
and a Michelob beer bottle. There are a bunch of nail polishes,
old bills, and full ashtrays. The VCR is sitting in the middle of
the floor because it is broken and Missy threw it across the
room. I am eating a sour pomegranate. Missy and I are very
much alike. I think the reason we don't fight is because we never
get too deep. We don't talk about anything serious. We keep
everything on a cool level that I like and that doesn't stress me
out.*

It was the first time I had actually contributed to a roommate
situation. I didn't have a lot to give, and I was always late with
the money, but I actually started pitching in for bills and rent. I
didn't want to use her or screw her over. We handled all of the
bills in a totally irresponsible manner, but she taught me about
living on your own; about the process of bills, how often they
came, what the minimum payments were, how much you could
get away with, what wasn't acceptable. I went with Missy to the
grocery store and saw how much food cost. I went with her to
pay the rent to the landlord. I was learning a little bit more about
how to be a grown-up.

Every weekend I drove to Hollywood to pick Missy up from
work. We drove straight to the 7-11 across from the Whisky and
got two partially filled Big Gulps of Coke. We would then bring
the huge cups back to my car in the Tower Video parking lot and
fill the rest with Jim Beam from the liquor store. We sat in the

dark, listening to Dr. Dre's new album, *The Chronic*, which featured a new rapper called Snoop Doggy Dogg. We drank, laughed, and re-applied our makeup. After about a half an hour, we got out of the car and trotted down to the Rainbow and got even more trashed. There were many rock star memories that I only slightly remember because of the drunken haze in which we lived. I couldn't do as much writing that year because I didn't have anywhere to hide my journals. I do remember that Missy traded shirts with Slash from Guns N' Roses one night, but the rest is a blur. Sometimes we got there so late that the Rainbow was closing and people were leaving. We would just go mingle in the crowd in the parking lot next to The Roxy. We looked for our friends and found other places to party.

But the Sunset crowds weren't what they used to be. The new scene was called "Grunge" and I am sure VH1 could do a better job explaining that shit than I could. Even the name sounded dirty and grimy. There was no glitter and most definitely no cool colors. Even their style of partying was different. There was no silly string, confetti, or champagne being poured on your head. There were no balloons or beach balls. The Grunge guy's idea of a party was stomping into a dirty brown room wearing a dirty flannel shirt from a thrift store with some dirty-ass combat boots. He would have a beanie over his brown curly hair and a goatee on his face. After growling a throaty yell into the sky, he would then shoot some heroin. He would scream another powerful yell in the desert and then go and kill himself afterward. It was depressing, to say the very least.

Although Missy and I were leaning toward rap over Grunge, we started wearing little tied-up flannels, combat boots, and men's Calvin Klein underwear peeking out from baggy jeans. We plucked our eyebrows within an inch of their lives, to try to emulate the model of the moment, Kate Moss.

The leaders of the Grunge movement were the Seattle bands: Nirvana, Pearl Jam, Soundgarden, Alice in Chains and many more obscure ones that someone cooler than me could surely tell you about. All of the bands had albums out the year or so prior, but they started getting more popular in 1993. I started seeing Pearl Jam at more parties, and guys from Soundgarden at the Rainbow. My sister had the Nirvana CD, because they had filmed their video for "Smells Like Teen Spirit" using many of the kids from her high school. Her friends were moshing in the depressing video. I listened to the CD to see what it was all about. It did strike me music-wise but I didn't tell anyone. It made me realize all of the sadness I held in my body and it made me want to scream along with it. That was one of two or three CDs in our house, because we still had mostly cassette tapes at the time.

So what happened to The Strip? Half of the people we normally partied with left Hollywood. They realized that their glam bands were being overlooked by the record companies for the new sound of Grunge. They returned to the states from which they came, with no record contract in hand. Others stayed in town and tried to adapt, landing jobs in the film or television industries. They took off the tight pants, cut their hair a little and took off their makeup. It was weird to see the guys that had been in makeup and pink suddenly wearing lumberjack flannels and Doc Martens. There were a few people that stuck to their guns and wouldn't change their look or their musical aspirations, but they only looked outdated. With the exception of a few bands who made it in Japan, there was no place for them.

No matter what look they chose, the people who stayed seemed to be hitting the drugs. Many of them chose heroin. I blamed the Seattle clique for that. Some of the party crowd committed suicide. Some went to rehab. Some of the girls in our crowd started working for a Hollywood Madam named Heidi Fleiss and others disappeared. And surely many of them just went elsewhere and got new crowds.

The Glam Rock, "hair band" scene was over. And just like the rest of them, I was left standing at a crossroad. Would I continue on with these people? Follow them wherever they ended up?

What would become of me? I didn't think I could ever live a normal life after all that I had been through. I was afraid of regular people; I only felt comfortable around people who were wild. I didn't know what to do. I wasn't sure who would have me. I closed my eyes and prayed to God to do whatever he wanted with my life. I figured he would know much better than I would.

The first thing that happened was that some guy at my telemarketing job told me he knew someone at a nice restaurant in Encino, and that I should apply there. He said he would hook me up with a job. I went into the restaurant the next day. I took an escalator past potted palm fronds up onto a beautiful brick patio. Gorgeous people of both sexes were walking around with handled shopping bags. Everyone looked so...*manicured*. I saw hair that was highlighted, skin that was dewy and taken care of. I saw tasteful nails in hues of barely-there pink. I saw soft leather handbags. I saw white teeth and delicate tank watches. Men wore starched shirts and had shiny leather shoes. I walked through two huge, glass doors and was immediately blinded by the sunlight pouring through the place. Half of the walls were also glass, so they let in natural light. The other walls were mirrored. It was tidy and crisp-looking, with glass tabletops over bleached white tablecloths. The servers were wearing burgundy aprons over white polo shirts and white pants. They all looked freshly showered and scrubbed. The place was the exact opposite of where I had spent the last three years of my life.

The next thing I knew, everything turned slow motion. This beautiful creature behind the counter looked up at me and we locked eyes. I saw thick, dark eyebrows, smoldering honey-colored eyes, and short, dark hair. He looked rather preppy, like a fraternity guy who played lacrosse or something. I asked him for an application, and he looked right into my pupils while talking to me. I felt sick to my stomach. I hadn't been nervous over a guy in years. But this guy was so striking and so different from the guys I was accustomed to, that it took me aback. I was very surprised at myself for the reaction I had.

My life changed in that moment. I had been waiting for something to make me lose interest in the people I was keeping company with, but nothing was as interesting, so I kept going back. But now…now there was this new possibility. I actually found a normal looking guy attractive! I would simply start dating him, then-

tire screeching sound

It suddenly dawned on me. My shoulders dropped a little as I stood with the application in my hand and he went back to packing a 'to go' order into paper bags. He wanted nothing to do with me. I looked at myself in the mirror next to us. My makeup suddenly appeared very heavy. My hair looked dull and brittle. I had gained weight from all of the late nights at Del Taco. I looked dirty and bloated. I did not know how to groom myself properly. I was no longer "fresh" or beautiful. I had become a sloppy drunk during my nights out with Missy. On any given night, I was slurring, foul-mouthed, and ill-mannered, with a complete lack of morality. I did whatever I wanted, indulged in any behavior I felt like. I gave in to any impulse I had. There were times when that was awesome. If someone was an asshole, I said, "You're an asshole" to their face, or slapped them. If someone did me wrong, I punched them in the nose. And hell, it was always great going to the store in my bright blue mud mask and pajamas. But I had no pride in myself. I was violent and abrasive, cursing and yelling at people, throwing food or bottles when I became angry. I fell over tables, out of car doors, danced on bars and then came crashing down. I was an embarrassment. A total mess.

As I was leaving, I knew I had to change it up. I wondered, *Where will I go from here? What is next for me?* Would I play it straight, become 'normal'? Or would I get into even *more* trouble?

WHAT BECOMES OF ME?

IT WILL SHOCK YOU!

GET THE SEQUEL

CONFETTI COVERED
QUICKSAND

AND READ
EVEN CRAZIER STORIES!

AND DON'T FORGET TO PICK UP
THE SUNSET STRIP DIARIES
PREQUEL:

VALLEY GIRL:
CHILDHOOD IN THE 80'S

WANT TO KNOW WHAT I LOOKED LIKE IN MY
SUNSET STRIP DAYS?
CHECK OUT MY AMY ASBURY FACEBOOK PAGE

FOLLOW ME ON TWITTER
(ALTHOUGH I HAVE NOTHING INTERESTING TO SAY WHATSOEVER)
@AUTHORAMYASBURY

Amy Asbury still has a few band flyers, continues to love old films and still misses her bunny rabbit. She is the author of three books, and co-wrote a fourth with her sister, Becky. She lives in Los Angeles with her husband and son.

IT WASN'T JUST AMY WHO HAD A WILD
LIFE. CHECK OUT HER SISTER'S BOOK,

SMELLS LIKE:
MUSIC, DRUGS, AND LIFE IN THE 90'S
BY BECKY ASBURY

Mosh pits, Venice Beach, raves, mind-blowing concerts, snowboarding, hipster record stores...This was the 90's for Becky Asbury. She was part of Generation X, the MTV generation. They were the first generation to be heavily affected by divorce and broken homes. They were the generation whose mothers went back to work in droves. The generation of many latch-key kids, raised in after-school programs. They grew up searching for their identity. They were numb, they were bored, they were angry, cynical, and alienated. They were called unfocused, uncommitted, apathetic slackers. But the truth was, they were *lost*.

SMELLS LIKE is a true story about a girl who came from a typical eighties middle-class family and what happened after her home life was shattered. Some kids ran off and caused chaos, but Becky Asbury turned quietly to drugs, namely Crystal Meth.

How did she get drugs? What did it feel like to do them? What did it do to her physically and mentally? Read true diary entries from the life of a girl in 1990's Los Angeles trying to figure out who she was; working in record stores, listening to Grunge, and all the while wishing she could get it together and become a ballet dancer.

Grab your flannel shirt and put in your nose ring, it's time to dive back into the decade that reminded us that sometimes you have to lose yourself in order to find yourself.

ESTEP & FITZGERALD
BOOKS

ISBN 978-0-615-43987-7

52000>

9 780615 439877